HARVEST:

Memoir of a Mormon Missionary

ISBN 978-0-615-38599-0

Printed in the United States of America
10 9 8 7 6 5 4 3 2 1

AUTHOR'S NOTE: In an effort to preserve privacy, names of persons portrayed in this book, including that of the author, have been changed. This is a work of memoir and subject to the imperfections of memory, but I have been faithful to what I remember and to what is in my diary and other records. The dialogue is, of course, a reconstruction, and a few minor characters are composites.

ACKNOWLEDGMENTS

Many thanks to my editor and best friend for her invaluable contributions to this book. Her example was encouraging, her encouragement timely, her time generous, her generosity honest, her honesty critical, her criticism incisive, and her incisions smart editing. Had this book been without her, it would have been wanting.

Words fail to express my gratitude to my family for always giving me their bighearted love and acceptance, even in times when I have not made it easy for them to do so.

HARVEST –

A Time to Pluck Up that which is Planted:
Memoir of a Mormon Missionary

1

Like Clockwork?

To every thing there is a season, and a time for every purpose under the heaven.
Ecclesiastes 3:1.

I lay in bed and listened for the click. A distant clocklike click, a cog-like click. The Pavlovian click of emancipated exhalation and unbended mind. The click of the lock on the bathroom door as my companion, Elder Quamme, began his morning shower.

That click meant precious privacy, a guaranteed five minutes of unobserved freedom, the only time of the day that ever belonged solely to me, my time, a time filled with fantastic possibilities, a time to love, a time to hate. Most days I would simply continue to lie on my mattress, look up from my study of Russian grammar, stare at the cottage cheese ceiling, and let my thoughts roam, sometimes all the way back to the streams and mountains of Idaho. Some days I would get up and walk out of our small bedroom, past the occupied bathroom, and into the kitchen, where I would peer out from the lone window of our fifth-floor apartment at the elephantine block of concrete apartment buildings squatting stolidly across the courtyard. I'd sigh at the muddy grey slush of the courtyard and wonder how a thaw could be so cold. I'd stand there in reverie until the patter of falling water from the bathroom dried up and then I'd climb back on the mattress in the corner of the bedroom and bury my face again in *Modern Russian: An Advanced Grammar Course.*

HARVEST

Today, however, was the day that I would finally allow myself to act upon the thought that had been sustaining me for the past week. And not just sustaining. Tantalizing.

Click.

My pulse raced and my palms started to sweat. Queasy and euphoric with anticipation, I fought back the urge to act until I heard the sound of Quamme's shower water. Then I eased myself off the mattress and tiptoed over to the sofa, an ugly horsey thing with no cushions – just a hard wooden bench with a tall slab for a back and two thick side slabs for armrests, all of it covered by a wiry orange upholstery, stained and frayed. The sofa stood next to what I thought of as the forest wall – a smudgy, smoky verticality crusted by a peeling and yellowing wallpaper that depicted a lonely stand of poplars in a bleak and anonymous autumn.

Quietly as I could, I pulled the sofa away from the poplars to reveal an egg-sized chunk of raw pig meat lying in the dust on the cracked brown paint of the floor. My heart surged hard against my breast, spurred on by an intense excitement, dizzying and oddly sexual, as I picked up the raw meat and held it in my hand. I brushed the dirt off as best I could, carefully picked off a few pubic-like hairs and flecks of lint, and looked at what I hoped would be my salvation, brown-pink after sitting behind the sofa for three days.

I knew nothing about trichinosis other than how to spell it, that one got it from eating undercooked pork, and that it made one sick. How sick I did not know. Sick enough to get me sent home and not sick enough to cause serious damage, I hoped. The name sounded promising, like tuberculosis, which was an excellent example of the kind of disease I was looking for.

In fact, I had tried and failed to contract tuberculosis. For a few weeks now Quamme and I had been drinking unpasteurized milk that we bought in one-liter Sprite bottles from a babushka at the market near our apartment. Quamme drank the milk because he had grown up near the dairies and farms of Idaho, loved the taste of fresh milk, and hated the sterile and burnt hospital taste of the boxed milk sold in Russian stores. I, too, hated the boxed milk and had even grown up *on* one of those Idaho farms, but, unlike Quamme, who only had four months left before his two years were up and preferred not to contract tuberculosis, I nursed the secret hope that I would get sick from the babushka's milk and get sent home, back to Idaho, the land of privacy and flyfishing where I spoke the language and where people loved and cared about me, back to a normal life without rules forbidding human touch, girls, books, and newspapers, back to living unobtrusively, to removing the suit and tie and flowing smoothly along, never to waylay passersby with my message about God's one true Church ever again. But after a few weeks of relative missionary health, I had decided that the babushka's cow must be clean and that I must be more proactive if I was going to get sick. Hence the trichinosis idea.

The idea was first hatched when Quamme and I bought a piece of a pig at the big open air market in Novokuibyshevsk. The pig was hanging stiffly from meat hooks – face, skin, hooves, tongue, and curly tail intact. Only its eyes were missing, having been removed to help drain the blood. People were bidding for bits and parts for the butcher to hack off, weigh out, and wrap up in brown butcher paper. Black flies swarmed the carcass and a dark hunger swirled my stomach pit. I was sucked in. Tempted. The swine seemed to me to be so corrupt and degenerate, so scrofulous, so morbid and naked and carnal. Sin was somehow lurking in those empty eye sockets.

Quamme was drawn in as well, most likely by his ongoing attempts to experience Russia like a local, something that I really liked about him. Strict mission rules generally frustrated our efforts to not only be in Russia but to do as the Russians, but our choice of sustenance was an area of exception. Governed only by a rule preventing mushrooms and fish, we spent lots of time expressing our free will and creativity through our choice of food. We dreamed of food on the street or between doors while proselytizing and we wrote letters home in which the only departure from the quotidian reportage of miniscule missionary successes was a breathless description of our latest culinary exploit of goat tripe or fatty meat jelly.

So we went and pointed to our own part of the pig to take home, where I would later run my finger across the rough skin and shudder at the coarse black hairs piercing through the skin from their bed in the thick white fat of the pig.

Quamme and I used most of the greasy pig slab by frying rice in strips of its fat and cooking the meat to make a passable plov. From market to mouth, though, this whole pig episode, from first seeing it hanging from meathooks with the scraped-out eye sockets and the dried blood in the corner of its mouth, to the sweaty smell of the rice frying in the pig's white fat, to the revolting thought of those impossibly thick black hairs, just felt so filthy and debauched to me that it spawned the idea of cutting off a piece of the remaining pig and eating it raw in the hope of contracting trichinosis. The added touch of putting the meat to rot behind the couch for three days came from my ignorance about how pig meat becomes infected with trichinosis and my general belief that leaving meat to rot behind hideous orange couches could not be healthy for it. I didn't know that trichinosis is spread only when a mammal eats another mammal infected with the encysted larval stages of the *Trichinella* roundworm, and that it was therefore impossible for the meat to become infected sitting in the dust behind the couch. But no matter. Even had I known, I would have still put the meat there in the hope of attracting some kind of seedy parasite or slummy germ.

So there I stood, meat in hand, ready to pop it into my mouth and cast my fate to the vagaries of the *Trichinella* roundworm. No, I knew that wasn't right. God controlled the trichina worms as surely as He had created them – I was putting my fate into His hands. No, that wasn't right, either. Some things were predestined in God's plan, some things probably weren't – surely God had not deigned to micromanage the lowly presence of trichina worms in this pathetic scrap of meat. Or, maybe He had and their presence *was* predestined, but my choice of whether to eat the meat *wasn't,* so the exercise of my free agency put my fate back into my hands. But God was omniscient, so He knew whether I would eat the meat or not, and He was omnipotent, so He could have planted the worms there or not, so my fate was still in God's hands. Right? Or not? I'd been going roundabout this tiresome circle of thoughts for some time now. Now was the time for action, for mastication.

I placed the lukewarm piece of meat onto my tongue and began to slowly chew – my only thought being a fleeting concern about the potential taste. The meat was tender and readily released its bloody juices. They trickled into my throat, tickling me into swallowing. Salty, sweet, tomatoey, and fleshy, it wasn't bad and I savored the mellow mix of flavors. My heart slowed down, and I stopped trembling. I chewed contemplatively until I had finished and then I sat down on the hard bench of the sofa, leaned my head back, and closed my eyes.

I turned my thoughts inward, deeply inward, past the coppery aftertaste in my mouth, past the wet itch in my throat, and into the dark place where I knew the pig was being transubstantiated into proteins and possibly even into pathogens. What was happening in there? I focused all my concentrative power there, analyzing every slight sensation, real or imagined, every little churn and grinding, every little absorption and secretion, every little deployment of acids, enzymes, and bile. Nothing. This was the body, *my* body, this was the physical realm, *my* realm, but I was clueless as to what was happening and helpless to control it.

I was ashamed to turn to the spiritual realm and face God in prayer after what I had just done, so I simply relinquished control of my thoughts and was left with an open focus, ready to listen to any still small voice from above or autonomous thought from within. Nothing but heartbeats and worry. The same incessant ticking as before. The same strain, like something fundamental within me was being pulled in opposite directions. Finally, my focus settled on my breathing, the one life process I could control. I began to breathe more and more deeply, consciously willing myself to take each new breath, waiting longer and longer each time, delighting anew every time the delicious air rushed in cool and fresh. Now deeply relaxed, I began to feel something. Vague and diffusive, I was unaware of where it had come from, why it had come, or what it portended. I knew only that I felt better than I had since coming to Russia two months earlier. I had the sense that even if I had failed to ingest my little worm-ticket home, things would be okay, that I would be able to cope with the challenges of being perfectly obedient to mission rules, of approaching strangers and meeting new people, of learning the language, and of teaching with the Spirit.

More than anything, though, as I continued to deliberately breathe while sitting on the hard orange bench, I somehow felt more in control, more aware at that gut level where the cool air became sentient life that, although my path might be predetermined, it was at least up to me to discover where it would lead. I was far from happy, but I was no longer dangerously unhappy.

2

Worlds Apart

The unhappiness had surfaced gradually, revealed only once the excitement of novelty had receded.

The initial excitement had begun building upon my discharge from the compounds of the Missionary Training Center (MTC) in Provo, Utah. I had spent ten incredibly focused weeks behind those sandy brick walls, and had thrown myself heart, mind, and soul into the strictly scheduled regimen of instruction in methods of successful proselytizing and the basics of the Russian language. Motivation and inspiration were in the air there, and I had sucked them in with great gulps, riding an all-time high, filled with purpose, ambition – I was on a mission. I had been pumped up by weekly devotionals where Apostles of the Lord praised, flattered, and blessed us, the very elect, the chosen ones, the great generation, the Lord's humble servants, His representatives, doing His awesome work, there was nothing we couldn't do – if we were worthy to have the Spirit. I had been brought to tears by the gushing outpourings of the Spirit during the spontaneous gatherings of missionaries in the dorm stairwells as we prayed and sang hymns together. I had been solemnized and awed by the weekly trips across the street to the temple, the House of the Lord, the place where people actually communed with God, the place where the secrets of the universe were revealed, the most sacred site on Earth. And I had been fired up by the thousands of ardent adolescent voices roaring out that great battle hymn of Mormon missionaries –

"Called to serve Him heav'nly King of glory; chosen e'er to witness in His name, far and wide we'll tell the Father's story, far and wide His love proclaim" – first in English, then in rounds with dozens of different languages reverberating in passionate harmony.

Heeding the constant reminders from our leaders not to waste the Lord's time, I had spent the few scraps of free time we were allotted in the MTC memorizing "discussions" about the Gospel, anxiously trying to build my relationship with God through Gospel study and prayer, and writing upbeat letters to friends and family about the wonderful spirit there. Towards the end, however, truth be told, I had taken some time off in the evenings to mess around with the other Elders in the relative privacy of our Spartan dorms – walking on our hands down the hallway to see who could go the furthest, facing off in breath holding tournaments, divining the maximum number of smuggled cafeteria grapes that could be thrown off the ceiling and caught in our mouths before we had to chew, and playing chess with boards sketched on sheets of notebook paper and figures drawn on folded Post-it-notes. The guilt for wasting the Lord's time and the rebuke from our sanctimonious peer leaders upon their discovery of our surreptitious slacking were well worth being able to stave off the creeping claustrophobia.

After ten weeks of being literally and figuratively walled off from contact with the outside world with my identically dressed and conversion obsessed associates, the van ride with eight other missionaries from the MTC to the airport in Salt Lake City was exhilarating – goose-bumpy lightheaded stuff. Adolescent freedom. First time behind the wheel without adult supervision kind of thing. Each gussied billboard along I-15 leered out at me, singing me its slick Siren song, simultaneously repulsive and seductive in its appeal to consume, its promise of happiness, and its subtle call to conform. I had forgotten what the "real world" was like, with all its superficiality, commerciality, vulgarity, and intoxicating vibrancy. Babylon. I pitied it for its ignorance of what really mattered, and I tried to drown out with a blustery confidence the nagging thought that I should admit to myself that I also feared its potency.

I was more excited about seeing my family at the airport than I as Elder-Young-fresh-from-the-MTC-and-the-otherworldly-realm wanted to admit to myself, but my excitement during that van ride was not due solely to such earthly considerations as freedom and familial sentimentality. I leaned my head back on the headrest, shut my eyes to the lure of the world's billboards, and imagined that I was sitting comfortably in the living rooms of Russian investigators. While outside the wind whined and the snow whirled against the night-black icy windows, we sat in overstuffed leather chairs next to the fireplace. I looked into the eager, shining eyes of these lost souls hungry for the truth, and I taught them about the restoration of the Gospel with the power of the Spirit so strong that it electrified the pregnant air with a crackling intensity. Our bosoms burned and our eyes welled from the surging waves of emotional fullness raging through our bodies, from our twittering toes to our tingling scalps. I pictured the expressions of childlike joy on the glowing faces of humble, grateful Russians as I lowered them gently into the warm waters of baptism. I imagined the serene gratification I would feel upon witnessing the post-baptismal change in their countenance as they continued to live righteously according to the principles of the Gospel. How the light of Christ would shine in their honest faces! How they would radiate peace and love and meekness!

My florid daydreaming was cut short as the van stopped at the curb in front of the terminal. My family and a few friends were inside. After quick tight hugs with family and warm handshakes with friends, it was down to business. Get the check-in and security out of the way, then we could all talk without the feeling that there was work left to be done hanging over our heads.

I was a little dazed and bedazzled by my reentrance into the normal world. The shallow showy splendor. All the flashy, sex-dripping advertising for perfumes and liquors, all the glossy magazine covers. The shelves of brightly packaged candies and snowy globes of miniaturized Temple Squares. But it wasn't just the world's trappings that seemed so different. It was the people, too. They were dressed so colorfully, so garishly, and with such variety - some were immodest and I had to avert my eyes. And their laughter and discourse seemed harsh and loud and entirely too raucous after the muffled giggles and reverent hushed tones of the MTC.

It was 1999 and my friends and family passed through security with me and we walked happily and silently to the departure gate where the silver plane that would begin to take me halfway around the world perched outside the window. We sat facing each other and smiled. Conversation on my part was a little awkward. For ten weeks my thoughts had been so fanatically and rather frantically focused on the Russian language and the Gospel that I found it difficult to relate to people whose thoughts were not similarly fixated.

My parents sat watching me closely, their faces lustered with an anxious pride as they soaked in every detail of the elder son they were sending off to Russia for two years. This was the moment. It was finally happening. After years of family home evenings, bedtime stories from Church books, early mornings of bleary-eyed family Scripture study before school, family prayers with the six of us kneeling in a circle, Church films with popcorn and root beer floats, hymns sung around the family piano, and Sunday dinner conversations over pot roast and potatoes, it was time. I was wearing the suit, white shirt, tie, and nametag. I had the missionary haircut and we were at the airport. The plane was gleaming through the window. Other missionaries sat nearby with their families, their youthful exuberance periodically poking through the conscientiously applied mask of solemn spiritual maturity. Mothers' eyes were wet with pride as they adjusted the ties of their sons, their missionaries, their Elders. Young kids unburdened by the obligation of quiet dignity were bouncing around with excitement, thrilled to see their big brother again. A few gates down more large Mormon families were waiting with banners, balloons, flowers, and cameras to greet those missionaries returning home with honor from their labors throughout the world.

I had been afraid that no one would recognize the difference in me. That Elder Young would be the same as Jacob Young. That the increased spirituality, maturity, and light of Christ which I felt sure that I had developed at the MTC would not manifest itself in my face and demeanor. My mom had put that fear to rest, however, as soon as she had met me and told me how peaceful and happy I looked. I felt her warm blue eyes on me now. I would miss her more than I would have thought possible.

"I bet you'll miss all those ice cream sandwiches over in Russia," She began with a smile. "Or maybe they have them over there, what do you think? It's too bad I can't send some over. Or you might not even want them over there, with how cold it is, who knows." Ice cream sandwiches had quite possibly been the favorite topic of my letters home from the MTC, as I had repeatedly raved about the Mississippi Mud ice cream sandwiches in the cafeteria. They had been kept in an unlocked and unsupervised freezer, and the unrestricted access had led me to engage in what could politely be called overindulgence.

It felt as if no one knew quite what to say. We hadn't seen or talked to each other for ten weeks, and we would not see each other again for two years. Small talk and light banter just didn't seem to fit the portentousness of the occasion, and we would leave the weighty stuff to significant looks, jerky movements, strained voices, and extra-hard squeezes during a hug.

My dad turned to practical matters, speaking in his quiet, gentle voice. "I activated this credit card for you," he told me as he handed me a Visa card. "They've gotta have some ATMs over there, so if you need money for whatever reason you should be able to get it." His voice had cracked just a little – enough to let me know how close to tears he was. I was getting there, too.

"Thanks Dad," I said as I stuck the card in my wallet.

Over the past few years I had worked moving pipe and stacking sod to save up a few thousand dollars for my mission – not nearly enough to cover the whole cost, but a good start. Before I left, however, my dad had told me to put the money in a two-year CD so that I'd have some cash for school when I got back. He would pay for everything.

After a half an hour or so of small talk and posing for photographs it was time to part.

I first hugged my little sister. Fourteen years old. Beautiful, blonde, and athletic. Fun and thoughtful, curious and adventurous, lover of quirky and endearing nicknames. I had constantly teased her growing up, but I loved her and was proud that she was my sister. I saw that her eyes were red and I ached inside.

Next I hugged my younger brother, my best friend growing up. We had spent so much time together. Playing Nintendo in the basement, bouncing on our three-wheeler in the early dawn through frosty fields on our way to move pipe, challenging any takers to two-on-two basketball in driveway courts around our small town. Although two years younger than I, he was an inch taller at six feet four, with broad shoulders and hands large enough to easily palm a basketball. He squeezed me and his body shook with sobs as he told me through tears how much he loved me and looked up to me. I squeezed back tightly and began to cry.

My veneer of adult self-assurance and composed spirituality had cracked now. As I look back at the photographs of that day I'm struck by how boyishly vulnerable I looked. I cried and hugged tight my older sister, my compassionate, considerate older sister who'd taught me about fairness and sharing and kindness and caring.

Finally, I cried and hugged my parents while they cried and assured me of their pride in me, of their love for me, and of their faith in the fact that I was doing the right thing.

I had just turned nineteen and I was eager to serve the Lord and to prove to myself my independence. I didn't grasp the finality of that parting. I didn't anticipate the aching loneliness that would follow in my isolation from everyone I loved. Sure, the Church would allow me to make biannual phone calls on Christmas and Mother's Day, and to write weekly letters that would arrive weeks after they were written. But I would no longer be in their world, nor they in mine, in any meaningful sense.

3

First Bumbling Sickle Thrusts

As I walked down the jetway to board the plane, never turning back to wave goodbye, the doughy heaviness of the parting morphed into an airy, premature nostalgia and the heady excitement began to return. I looked down at my nametag:

> **Стариейшина Янг**
> **Церковь**
> **Иисуса Христа**
> **Святых Последных Дней**

I was Elder Young of the Church of Jesus Christ of Latter-day Saints, and I was about to fly out of the country and into Russia, a foreign land, the lair of communists and bears, the great unknown, and I was flying into this great unknown to offer to the people who used these strange letters what might be their only chance at eternal life with God, their only shot at eternal happiness. It was hard to comprehend that I was a part of something so important, so grand, but I was. I knew it. The nametag proved it.

I hoped for a window seat, preferably one next to a non-Mormon, any non-Mormon would do, so that I could strike up a conversation and steer it subtly towards the Gospel – not yet having internalized the reality that there was neither need nor room for subtlety when serving in God's army of clean-shaven recruits all dressed in dark suits, white shirts, and conservative ties, all carrying identical Church-approved handbags, all sporting short neatly-parted haircuts, and, of course, all prominently displaying nametags.

I had already had some experience in proselytizing, in apprehensively making that initial approach, in sharing my most precious beliefs, in baring my naked feelings, in withdrawing in shame and embarrassment upon being spurned.

I was ten years old and had a newspaper delivery route around my tiny hometown. At the end of each month I had to go knocking doors to collect the subscription fees – the worst part of the job for me since I hated to ask for money and some people were nearly impossible to catch at home. But I actually looked forward to collecting from one old man who lived alone in a trailer on the edge of town. He was always at home, and there were always empty cans of Hamm's beer lying around the trailer. Though few other people ever tipped me, this old man always gave me fifty cents and told me to go buy myself a pop. I would then go to the only store in town, buy a Strawberry Sunkist, and stand on the street and guzzle it greedily.

I felt a tender pity for this kind old man who lacked the joy of the Gospel, and I told my mom about it. Together we came up with a plan to deliver a Book of Mormon to him the next time I went to collect.

I usually delivered newspapers on my bicycle, but for this occasion my mom drove me around in our old Chevy pickup. When we drove up to the old man's trailer, I carefully wrapped the new blue Book of Mormon with shiny gold lettering into the newspaper to conceal it for as long as possible. I knocked and heard his voice inviting me to come on in. The old man was sitting at his card table when I entered.

"Looking to take my money again, huh?" He smiled and shook his head as he started to stand up.

I swallowed hard, uncovered the book, and shakily delivered my speech, delirious with pride that I, a ten-year old boy, was doing God's work: "I want to give you something that has brought a lot of joy into my life. I know that it will do the same for you, and that if you read it and pray about it, God will tell you of its truthfulness." My arm snapped stiffly out, presenting him with the book.

"I'm sorry, I can't accept that," the old man responded sadly as he sat back down.

I hadn't expected this. I felt my face burn, and I managed only a quick "that's okay" before rushing back to the truck without collecting my money.

"What happened?" my mom asked when I opened the door to the truck with the Book of Mormon still in my hands.

I felt the humiliating pang of rejection. I could only answer: "He didn't want it."

The next day I returned to collect. I avoided eye contact with the man. He still gave me a fifty cents tip, but he no longer cheerfully told me to go and buy a pop with it. The little routine had lost its magic. I soon broke my leg and found someone to take over my newspaper route, and I only saw the man again from afar when he came to watch high school basketball games.

There had been many other proselytizing experiences, of course. Most had been just small things, little stitches in the fabric of a daily life embroidered by the mantra "every member a missionary," minor adjustments to how I otherwise might have lived my life. Like the time in high school when I met a great but non-Mormon girl at a statewide leadership conference. There had been an immediate mutual interest and attraction and we were gravitating toward each other and getting closer until I pulled away during what otherwise might have been our first kiss. Although I had kissed Mormon girls before, I hadn't even met many non-Mormon girls, let alone gotten that close to any of them, and so I was in proselytizing mode, conscientiously endeavoring to set the example of a perfect young Mormon lad so that she might later be impressed with my virtuous forbearance and devotion to my religion.

But the chance to proselytize on this plane – this was something new and different and incredibly exciting. I had now been specially called and ordained as a missionary by those with the authority to do so. God Himself in His infinite wisdom had chosen me to be His representative, His mouthpiece. He had chosen the place where I would serve, a place where I was needed, a place where I would make unique contributions. In the words of the revelation in Section Four of the Doctrine & Covenants which I had carefully memorized as my patriarchal blessing and leaders had counseled me to do, I was about to "embark in the service of God" in the "marvelous work . . . about to come forth among the children of men." I was about to stride boldly with my sickle into the missionary field, "for behold, the field is white already to harvest; and lo, he that thrusteth in his sickle with his might, the same layeth up in store that he perisheth not, but bringeth salvation unto his soul." I was not at all discomfited by the graphic, rather grim, characterization of the service I was about to embark on as the reaping of ripe souls with a sharp scythe to store for my own future benefit. The image of idyllic white fields waiting to be harvested was tremendously romantic to me.

I couldn't thrust in my sickle right away, though, because I was assigned a window seat next to a fellow missionary. So I read the touching notes of encouragement and love which my family had given me at the airport and ate the candy which my mom had slipped into my bag as an early Easter present. I felt a tug of sadness when I found out from my older sister's note that she'd gotten engaged to be married, and that I, of course, would miss her wedding. That sadness was quickly subsumed, however, by a feeling of immense gratification that I was already sacrificing for the Lord.

When our group of eight missionaries got off the plane in Chicago, we eagerly compared notes to see if anyone had placed a Book of Mormon or secured an address. But no one had anything to report since most missionaries had either sat next to a fellow missionary, a member, or a nonmember who was all too familiar with the Church, the flight being out of Salt Lake City.

The Chicago terminal, however, was teeming with nonmembers who had probably never heard of the Church. I looked into the eyes of as many as I could as they streamed past me. I wished so badly that I could somehow alert them, telepathically perhaps, through the force of my intense desire, to the importance of the message I was dying to share with them. Elder Young was getting more looks of curiosity than Jacob Young ever had in nineteen years, and I remembered to smile before people quickly looked away – MTC training at work. I felt like I should be doing more – all these people lacked the truth, and I might be the only chance they ever got to hear it. I was there for a reason. They were there for a reason. They were meant to see me and my nametag. This could be it, the moment they would remember millions of years from now, the moment they were introduced to the truth by an inspired Elder Young. Or maybe I would just plant a seed. I wondered if I should start approaching people, start stopping them with a Book of Mormon in my outstretched hand and an urgent look in my eyes, but no one else was doing this and I was too timid and unsure to lead, and so I simply decided to wait until the Spirit directed me to do so, hoping that I would be able to recognize the Spirit's promptings once someone who had been primed to receive the truth met my eyes.

Meanwhile, we were walking to the gate for our flight to Moscow that departed in a few hours when we passed a lifelike cutout of Michael Jordan forming half the back of a nearby bench, tongue a dangling. One of the Elders took out his camera, handed it to his companion, sat on the bench, put his arm around Mike, and posed while his companion took the picture. The rest of the missionaries stood by self-righteously, letting their disapproval of this light-mindedness be known with sighs of impatience and looks of nervousness as they scanned the vicinity for possible witnesses to the scandal of God's servants acting like tourists. I was torn. I liked Mike, and this looked like a great photo-op, and who knew if I would ever be back in Chicago. I took out my camera and handed it to my companion, the serious Elder Viska. He frowned and told me to hurry.

Click.

Then came the guilt. Not only were the lost sheep passing me by while I did nothing to bring them back to the fold, but I was out lolling in the lap of leisure with Mike while wearing the nametag. I felt like I was already letting the Lord and myself down.

The ten weeks of pent-up preparation and psychic motivation had us all on edge, bursting with anxiousness to begin this mighty work. The buzz began to build to a fever pitch when we reached the gate. The gate area was full of Russians. And not just Oleg and Olga, the young married couple humbly seeking the truth, as role-played by our MTC teachers. Actual Russians. Some were richly dressed in full-length mink coats and carrying immaculate sable shapkas in their manicured hands. Some were lugging shabby and frayed nylon tote bags as if they were walking back from their neighborhood market rather than about to fly halfway across the world. We began by hovering near groups of them, eavesdropping on their conversations to see what we could understand. We looked hesitantly at each other, trying to decide how to proceed: "Should we proselytize? Try to give a first discussion? But how do we start? What if we don't understand them? Who should go first?"

Finally, the handsome and charismatic Elder Olsen, the tacit mutual pick for most likely to succeed, summoned up his boldness, that sine qua non of missionary work. With his companion a step back and the rest of us in stealthy pursuit, he approached a nearby man standing alone, one of the well-dressed ones, and, after the standard introduction – "Hello, my name is Elder Olsen, I'm a representative of The Church of Jesus Christ of Latter-day Saints" – he began asking him the few non-religious questions he knew how to form: "How are you? Where do you live? Do you have a family? How old are you?" Viska and I leaned in and strained hard to understand the man's responses, but they were too fast and mumbled. The man was polite but clearly looking for an escape. Elder Olsen nodded his head as if he had understood, but the conversation died out quickly once he'd exhausted his getting-to-know-you questions and turned religious.

"What are your beliefs about God?"

"No, no." I understood that part. "No. That's not for me. Excuse me." And with a wave of his hand, slight bow of his head, and a bemused smile, the Russian turned away.

Feeling Olson's rejection as my own, I wished that I could ignore the fact that there were at least a hundred more Russians to approach. Fortunately, someone got out their discussions and started studying, and we all jumped right to our books, relieved to find an endeavor just as important as proselytizing – preparing for proselytizing – to occupy our time, the Lord's time, until we boarded.

We were flying Aeroflot to Moscow, and once on the plane I listened attentively to the announcements in Russian to see what I could make out. Which wasn't much – something about an airplane. I looked at the flight attendants, all women, dressed in tight plum-blue uniforms with short skirts that revealed their nylon-tan legs. They wore heavy makeup with thick red lipstick and displayed an affinity for dyed hair – watercolor black, rhubarb red, and icy-white blond. My future inductors into the brave new world of Russian repartee. For the first time in my life I was about to engage in a real conversation, in the real world, with a real person, for a real purpose, in another language. Using words I'd never used before, using grammar I'd had to learn like trigonometry. These words still meant nothing to me, really. Incantations. Abracadabra, hocus pocus, amatsu tsumi. Would these words, these sounds, really work? Would these red-lipped icy-haired women in tight plum skirts have any clue as to what I was saying?

They were coming down the aisle with the drink cart, so here was my chance to find out. The flight attendant, an icy blond, was taking orders in both Russian and English. I had to prove my language ability so that she'd speak to me in Russian, so ordering a Coke obviously wouldn't do. Orange juice was hard to say, I wasn't even sure if I knew how. That should impress her. So when Ms. Icy unsmilingly asked me in heavily accented English for my drink order, I let loose with my best "Apelsinovi sok, puzhalsta." Partial success. She had understood, but continued in English to ask if I wanted ice. I made one last effort to engage her in Russian, and replied: "Да, с льедом (Yes, with icy)." She smiled and I felt like a success. I then replayed this exchange over and over, agonizing over whether I had said everything properly. Later, while studying Lesson Three of my grammar book, I learned that ice is one of those masculine nouns that has a mobile vowel which disappears when it is declined into other cases, and that I had flubbed my first exchange. First flub in a flood of flubs that never dried up until I left Russia.

I was too excited to sleep. I took out my other, non-Elder-Viska, constant companion of the last ten weeks – a spirally bound book with a picture of Christ on the cover which contained all six missionary discussions in Russian. All the words were accented so that a missionary could properly pronounce the word without looking it up in the dictionary and learning its meaning. I had done very well at memorization in the MTC, and had the first two discussions memorized word for word. I could deliver them fluidly and rapidly and could even understand most of what I was parroting. I had carried this book with me everywhere, and in every spare moment, whether standing in the cafeteria line or sitting in the hall during the ten minute break between classes, I had worked on memorizing. I now brought the book out to start on the third discussion, intending to take advantage of the long flight to memorize at least two principles. But I was too wired to concentrate, and I began instead to look around the plane.

On my left was Viska: asleep, head back and mouth agape. I peered over the seats in front of me, trying to locate the other missionaries. Elder Olsen was up there talking to an old man still wearing his ragged shapka. I then looked across the aisle and immediately snapped my head back. To my right an attractive blonde girl was bending down to pick something up from the floor, exposing the top of her large breasts. Immediately the guilt hit me hard, even though my look had been entirely unintended. But I felt guilty because the natural man, the enemy to God, was alive and well within me, and he had liked the look – he wanted to look over there again and see her face. To smile at her. To talk to her. About something other than the Book of Mormon. I made a conscious effort to put off the natural man and rid this image from my mind, and I ultimately succeeded.

But what I could not get rid of – no matter how desperately I tried to focus on memorizing my discussions – were the smoldering embers from that brief euphoric hormonal rush which had passed through my body like a forest fire, leaving me empty and charred. I had not felt this feeling this potently since entering the MTC. I had only had wistful reminders of it some nights lying in bed on my stomach before I would dutifully roll over onto my back. For ten weeks I had kept my mind hermetically clean, a feat which I had attributed to my increased spirituality while at the MTC. But now I feared that my clean mind had been largely the product of an environment devoid of temptation.

As the cabin grew dark high over the icecap of Greenland, I wrapped myself in the airline's thin navy-blue blanket and then pulled it over my head to wall myself in again. I tried to recite the first discussion in my head, but I couldn't concentrate. I then tried to daydream again about what it would be like once I got to Russia, but all that came to mind were fragments of romantic images from church movies like *Called to Serve*, where gallant missionaries from around the world strode briskly two-by-two into the sunset as the stirring chorus of the Mormon Tabernacle Choir swelled to a fervent crescendo.

Sometime during the flight's groggy night, when I had lost all sense of time and space and was unsure if the oblique glow on the horizon was Russian dawn or American dusk, word percolated back to me that Elder Olsen had engaged a Russian passenger in conversation and had given him a Book of Mormon! The news of this success bolstered my optimism, although I also felt twinges of guilt, panic, and jealousy. It must have been the old man in the ragged shapka, I thought. Why had I not been doing the same instead of looking at girls? What kind of seeds might I had planted if I had been as responsive to the promptings of the Spirit as I had been to the urges of the natural man? Would I ever be worthy enough to be responsive to the promptings of the Spirit? Would I ever be able to throw off the natural man and thrust in my spiritual sickle? Or would I fail as a missionary?

4

In which the Truth of God Goes Forth Boldly and Nobly to Sound in Every Ear

I didn't have to wait long after arriving to Russia to start planting some seeds and testing my missionary mettle.

Upon arriving to Samara, we were whisked to the initial orientation at the mission home, where we met the president of the mission, President Hatcher, a kind man with a full head of grayish silver hair. Orientation was a haze of blue office carpet, crash course in all things mission, peak performance pep talk, motivational extravaganza, and the cilial soup of exhausted eyelids. I was jetlagged and just wanted to get my city and companion assignment and then go to sleep. All I later remembered from all the can-do, win-win talk was that President Hatcher emphasized several times that we should not be afraid to open our mouths and that he wanted the missionaries to write in BIG LETTERS in their weekly letters to him.

"I don't care if you only write only one sentence to me, as long as it is in BIG LETTERS," he'd seemed pleased with himself as he told us this. "And why should you write in big letters?" he'd asked rhetorically.

"I'm glad you asked," he'd continued. "Big letters demonstrate confidence, and a missionary can't baptize without confidence."

At some point President Hatcher must have also given me my assignment to a city and a companion, because the next day, at exactly ten o'clock in the morning, I stood with Elder Quamme at the threshold of a small apartment in Novokuibyshevsk, a compact city of about 100,000 people. We were heading out to go contacting. But not before pausing at the threshold in our suits and trench coats to offer up a companionship prayer. I pleaded earnestly in broken Russian for the Lord to direct us to those souls who were seeking the truth, and we were out the door and into the cold to contact.

Contacting was where it all began, the core of proselytizing, the legwork, the lay work, the grunt work, the groundwork. The plowing, the sowing, the tilling, the drilling. The praying that someday some seed, some tuber, some bulb, some shoot would yield sweet white harvestable fruit. The fishing for men, the baiting, the watching, the waiting. The trawling, the dredging, the casting, the reeling. The hook, the line, and the line, the line, and the line: "Hello, my name is Elder Young. I am a representative of The Church of Jesus Christ of Latter-day Saints. Can I share with you a message about God?"

In general, we employed two basic contacting methods: (1) "street contacting" in which we would station ourselves at nodes known for their high pedestrian traffic and approach the people streaming by in the hope of getting them to stop so that we could give them the first "discussion"; or (2) "knocking" in which we would go door-to-door in the hope of being invited into people's apartments so that we could give them the first discussion.

President Hatcher required us to teach thirty discussions a week, an extraordinarily high number compared to most other missions. The discussions, or Ds as we called them, had to be given in their entirety, word for divinely inspired word, in order to count as one of the thirty. This high volume approach apparently worked well, for the Russia Samara mission was the highest baptizing mission in all of Europe during the time I was there.

So we left our apartment that morning of my first day to pursue our 30 Ds. Quamme was carrying a small table and a packet of pictures. I was carrying a giant piece of plywood covered in purple wallpaper and adorned with big pictures accompanied by explanatory exclamations: "Families can be Together Forever!" below the picture of the Salt Lake City temple; "A Modern-Day Prophet!" below Joseph Smith's picture. Bold black letters at the top spelled out "The Church of Jesus Christ of Latter-day Saints," and bigger and bolder letters at the bottom proclaimed "Free Pictures!!". Quamme called it a signboard.

We walked for about twenty minutes into the heart of the city, and I tried to deal with all the stares by carrying the signboard as proudly and confidently as I could to mask my embarrassment. We stopped at a downtown street corner adjacent to a busy bus stop and set up the table next to the wall of a building. We placed the signboard upright on top of the table and leaned it against the building, and then spread out a bunch of pictures in front of it. The pictures formed a patchwork quilt of mythos and Americana: white-haired God and Jesus Christ appearing to Joseph Smith in pillars of light, Adam and Eve hiding their nakedness in the Garden of Eden, Moses trembling before the flaming bush, the angel Moroni floating above Joseph Smith in his log cabin bedroom, picture-perfect Mormon families kneeling in family prayer, shining LDS temples set high in the foothills of the Rocky Mountains.

"Russians love free pictures," Quamme told me as he arranged the last of the pictures on the table.

Throngs of people were walking past the signboard. Most were probably walking along their usual route to work or to the market and must have had seen missionaries standing here hundreds of times before with the signboard. They kept their heads down, carefully avoided eye contact, and rushed on by. The rest had either never seen the missionaries before or, if they had, were still curious about the signboard and the spread of pictures. Most of these slowed slightly, cast a sidelong glance, and then quickly moved on. A few, however, were drawn in, at least temporarily.

An old, weathered man in a dirty coat approached the board. It was happening. I was wading into the white field. Truth was about to be taught. Quamme sidled over to the man and began asking a few simple questions which the old man simply ignored. As Quamme launched into a recitation of the first D, I listened in attentively, watching the man sift through pictures with fingers stained tobacco brown-yellow from decades of smoking unfiltered cigarettes to nubs. I assumed that Quamme would bring me in to recite the second principle in the D once he got to that point.

Quamme was speaking animatedly and gesturing expansively with his large hands, which stuck out rather conspicuously from the too-short sleeves of his thin and faded black trench coat. The bottoms of his suit pants were wet and dirty from the slush, and stiff and stained to the knee with a winter's worth of salt, his shoes well-worn and unpolished. His tall bony frame was hunched at the shoulders, and his bare head balanced on a long neck, his hair towheaded and closely cropped. His facial features were clean and fine, the overall effect being one of intelligence and pleasantness.

Quamme's look of intelligence and pleasantness was lost on the old man, however. Despite Quamme's enthusiastic presentation, the old man never looked up from his suspicious scrutiny of the pictures, and once his examination was complete he left the table, never having said a word.

"Why aren't you trying to talk to people?" Quamme looked over at me after the old man had left. He asked it in English, even though the rules required us to speak Russian 100% of the time.

"I thought . . . that we . . . teach . . ." What was the Russian word for together? "that we teach . . ." I gave up and finished in English, "together." In the MTC we had taught all our discussions together. But now I just sounded to myself like I was trying to justify and defend something unjustifiable and indefensible. I feared that now Quamme probably thought that I simply lacked the boldness necessary to open my mouth. I imagined that I could feel his frustration with how long I had taken to formulate that simple sentence, which I could not even finish without switching to English. I wondered if I should respond in English when he talked to me in English. But I knew that I'd never learn the language if I broke the rules and lost the Lord's help.

"No, we'd probably never get our thirty Ds if we taught together," he continued in English. "You said you had the first D memorized, right?"

I nodded yes.

"Well, just try your best to give them the 1st D."

If it were not for the language barrier, I would have felt completely prepared to give people the 1st D. In the MTC, I had spent hours and hours learning the proper way to give a discussion. Not only that, but I had acquired my tool for converting and I knew how to use it. My sickle for harvesting ripe fields of souls was to be the hallowed "commitment pattern." The commitment pattern had been presented to us as a divinely inspired method for teaching the Gospel, and I had practiced using this method ad nauseum on my fellow missionaries, teachers, and patient volunteers from the community who played the role of investigators. The first paragraph of nearly every chapter in the Church's divinely inspired step-by-by-step manual for converting, the *Missionary Guide*, defined the commitment pattern as follows:

> The commitment pattern is the process of (1) *preparing* people to feel the Spirit of the Lord, (2) *inviting* them to make commitments when they feel the Spirit, and (3) *following up* to help them keep their commitments.

These three steps of the commitment pattern were further broken down into about twenty sub-steps. The *Missionary Guide* not only explained in detail the theory and mechanics behind these sub-steps, but it also provided detailed instructions for what we missionaries should say in almost any situation. For example, the *Missionary Guide* helpfully provided us with numerous examples of how to accomplish the first sub-step of the commitment pattern in which we *prepared* people to feel the Spirit of the Lord by *building relationships of trust* (BRT) with them: if the investigator's home had a nice flowerbed in front then we should comment on the investigator's lovely flowers while discussing our own love of gardening, or if a bowling trophy sat on the investigator's mantel then we should relate to the investigator a story about the time we had bowled a 240 game. The *Missionary Guide* further instructed us that even once the discussion turned religious we should continue to employ this BRT process, the essence of which required us to build on common beliefs and interests and deemphasize differences.

I had all these steps of the commitment pattern down cold, at my fingertips, ready to whip out – my checklist for converting. I would talk to the next old man who came up to look at a picture of Joseph Smith and I'd start out with some kinship-inducing BRT, then I'd ease into *presenting the message*, then I'd *help him feel the Spirit* by testifying about the truth of that message, then I'd *find out* how he felt about what he was being taught, then I'd help him *to recognize the Spirit* as the source of the warm fuzzy feelings he would undoubtedly be feeling by that point, then I'd *invite him to make a commitment* to read the Book of Mormon by asking him a direct "will you" question, then I'd let him know that I would *follow up* in three days to make sure that he was keeping his commitment, then I'd baptize him, then Quamme would be proud of me, then I'd know I had the Spirit with me, then I'd baptize even more people, then. . .

And then came my chance. Another old man was approaching the table of pictures. I got ready to introduce myself, desperately trying to think of something I could say to *build my relationship of trust* with him. I had to wait, however. Quamme cornered the old man and jumped right into giving the discussion to him, completely bypassing the *BRT* step. I wondered at this and waited for someone else to approach.

Finally, a heavyset middle-aged woman with big red-plastic-framed glasses and a thick moustache waddled self-importantly up to the table.

"Good day. My name is Elder Young. I'm a representative of the Church of Jesus Christ of Latter-day Saints," I began. For nineteen years I'd waited for this moment. For ten long weeks I'd prepared for nothing but this moment. For fourteen hours on airplanes over here I'd thought of little else but this moment. It was incredible. I was ecstatic. I was doing it! I was making my first contact! I was a missionary!

"How are you?" I continued, my heart racing.

"Not bad," she mumbled without looking at me as she leafed through the pictures.

"What are your thoughts about God?" I asked. I knew that I was supposed to *BRT* before diving into religious waters, but there were no flowers or bowling trophies to comment on, and a comment about her moustache was obviously inappropriate. And besides, *BRT* meant spontaneity, and spontaneity meant better language skills and confidence than I had. And Quamme hadn't *BRT'd*, so I figured it must not be too bad to skip that step.

"Can I have this one?" She asked, holding up a picture of Christ descending in a cloud of angels.

"Of course."

"Thank you," she replied and quickly waddled away before I had the chance to think of something to say to detain her.

Flush with the thrill of my first contact, I turned back to look at Quamme. He was still talking to the old man who stood at the table. Quamme had worked his way into position in front of the man, blocking his path to the street. He had his Book of Mormon open and was showing the man the pictures in the front as he delivered the discussion.

No one else was approaching the table and so I simply listened as Quamme gave the first D, observing his tactics for keeping the old man engaged:

"Can I have this picture?" the man interrupted him, holding up a picture of a muscular Captain Moroni with a sword in one hand and the Title of Liberty in the other.

"Yes, as soon as I tell you about the Book of Mormon," Quamme answered, pointing to the Book of Mormon in his hand. He then continued to talk animatedly about Joseph Smith – he would only tell the old man about the Book of Mormon in the principle which conveniently came near the end of the discussion.

When he came to the part in the principle about Joseph Smith's First Vision, Quamme asked, "What do you think God the Father and Jesus Christ told Joseph when they appeared to him?"

"I don't know, I really should get going," the man said, as he restlessly shifted his weight from one foot to another.

"Just a minute, I would like to tell you about this book and give it to you to read." Quamme quickly responded, thrusting the Book of Mormon under the old man's nose and then continuing without so much as a breath:

"Joseph Smith was told that none of the churches were true."

I noticed that Quamme did not pause or ask any more questions of the man, probably in order not to give him an opening to ask to leave again. At the end of the D he asked:

"My companion and I would like to come by your house, give you this book, and talk to you some more about how God has a plan for your happiness. What is your address so we can come by at a convenient time for you?"

I was surprised to see the man give Quamme his address before grabbing his picture of a brawny Captain Moroni and hastily rambling away. I assumed that the Spirit must have been present at the discussion and touched the old man's heart and that I had just not felt it for some reason.

HARVEST

The 1st Ds I'd taught in the MTC, with all the *BRT*, testifying, personalization of the message, finding out how the investigators felt, and resolving concerns took forty-five minutes to an hour. Here, however, Quamme had recited all the words of the 1st D in fifteen minutes.

Quamme's D had seemed to me to be nothing more than a forced recital of the words. It just hadn't had the same feeling, the same spirit, the same ability to tighten the throat and water the eyes as the Ds in the MTC had. Whether I had given the discussion in English or Russian, the feeling there had been the same. My companion and I would knock softly on the heaven wooden door to the windowless MTC classroom which served as the home of the role-playing investigator. Initially hostile, he would tell us he wasn't interested or that he had his own religion. We would usually counter with questions about life or religion which would pique his interest, leading to dialogue and an invitation to enter. Or perhaps we'd counter with simple friendliness – a bit of off-topic *BRT* that would melt his stubborn heart into inviting us inside. Once inside, we'd sit down on cushioned chairs across from him and began our discussion as Christ smiled kindly upon us from His picture on the wall. The room was still and silent, warm and carpeted. Ethereally calm and motionless except for the gentle waves of palpable fervor that flowed into the room from the collective energy of thousands of young men and women passionately dedicated to carrying out the Lord's work. I would look directly and compassionately into the investigator's eyes. My voice would become sincerely and quietly plaintive and my chest would swell and burn as I bore witness of the truth of what I was teaching. This burning had made me feel sure that I was teaching with the Spirit.

I had felt nothing like this during Quamme's D.

Quamme turned back to me after writing down the man's address: "Why aren't you stopping anyone on the street to talk to them?"

"I thought we wait for them to come up to the table," I said sheepishly, embarrassed once again.

"No, we can't just stand here and wait or we'd never get 30 Ds."

"How should I stop them?"

"Yell out 'Free Pictures!'. Or just go up to them and ask them if you can talk with them about God."

"Ok," I said. "Thanks."

So, like the operator of a carnival game, I begin calling out "Free Pictures!" to people passing by. "Free" was a four-syllable word in Russian that I had just learned that day by reading the signboard, and my tongue had some trouble forming the necessary sounds.

No one was responding to my stuttered pitch, and I felt a little silly, so I decided to start stopping people as Quamme was doing. After all, confidence was the name of the game.

In the MTC, confidence had been heavily emphasized. Not only the confidence to stop strangers on the street, but the confidence to testify boldly and absolutely. I had been taught to not appear to have any doubts about any doctrine, practice, or teaching. I had been taught to testify with confidence that: "I *know* that this Church is the only true and living church on the face of the earth today and that only by being baptized in it and living according to its teachings can we return to our Heavenly Father."

The confidence game. I mustered all the confidence I had, but I was still too timid to stop just anyone that walked past. So I waited until someone with a kind face who was walking slowly looked my way, and then I shyly, almost regretfully, approached him.

"Hello, can I talk with you about God?"

"No thanks. I have my own God."

His own God? His very own God? Was He in his pocket or what? Later in my mission, frustrated by this common response and too weary to care about coming across as a smart-assed servant of the Lord, I would actually ask investigators where I could buy my own pocket God. All I could think of to say now as the man walked away, however, was the first line from the first D: "Most people believe in a Supreme Being, even though they may call him by different names." This urgently delivered observation, informative as it may have been, was apparently not striking enough to get the man to stop and turn around, however, and so it was on to the next man.

"Hello, can I talk with you about God?" It was my best rehearsed opening line.

"God? No, I don't believe in God."

He didn't believe in God? So there really were atheists out there. Yet he seemed fairly normal. How could he go on living without any meaning to his life? I was too consumed with these thoughts to offer any coherent response as he kept on walking past. No matter, there were other fish in the sea. I continued with my opening line.

"Hello, can I talk with you about God?"

"No, I don't have the time. Excuse me."

No time for God? What could be more important? I wished I'd been able to say that in Russian as I watched the lady walk away.

"Hello, can I talk with you about God?"

"Why don't you assholes leave people alone?"

Poor people, I thought with sincere concern for the eternal welfare of their souls, if they only knew what an opportunity they were passing up to hear the truth. I did not understand the cursing, as that, of course, had not been taught in the MTC. My comprehension of the language on the street increased dramatically once I learned a good mix of swearwords.

I saw the people walking past me on the street as individuals, as souls who were seeking the truth but didn't know it yet, as lost sheep who needed to be saved from ignorance. Their refusals hurt me. I hurt for them when they refused. They were not yet just a faceless potential D, a statistic to be phoned in to the President.

As the hours of my first day of proselytizing slipped by, I started to feel a little desperate. I'd been approaching person after person, and no one had stopped for more than a few seconds. Quamme had already given three discussions according to my count. I wasn't doing my part. I was starting to wonder if I lacked the Spirit, if I wasn't worthy. Why couldn't people sense that I had an important message about the *truth* to share with them? Why wouldn't anyone talk to me? Maybe I needed to tweak my opening line. Maybe that was what the Spirit had been trying to tell me.

So I added a slight variation that I'd picked up from listening to Quamme. "Excuse me, can I talk with you about God for a little bit?"

"God? Who are you?" asked the man with what seemed like genuine curiosity.

God's Truth Goes Forth Boldly to Sound in Every Ear

"I'm a representative of the Church of Jesus Christ of Latter-day Saints." I pointed to my nametag so that it would be clear even if my accent was incomprehensible. The line had worked! Instead of running off, he'd asked *me* a question. "I have a message for you about the plan of salvation."

The man put his face right up to my nametag, reading. "Church of Jesus Christ . . . Latter-day Saints . . . Never heard of such a thing."

This guy is golden, I thought. "Maybe you have heard of the Mormons?"

"Ahh, the Mormons! Many wives!"

I was surprised, but nonetheless prepared for this one with a little pre-memorized statement from the MTC: "No, we don't practice polygamy." I wanted to add "anymore," but I'd been told that it was better to leave that word out.

"Ah, too bad, I would like another wife," he said and laughed. I eagerly joined in laughing, thrilled that I could understand him. I would have this little polygamy exchange hundreds of times before I left Russia. Ninety times out of a hundred, the few who had heard of the Mormons had heard of us solely because of polygamy.

"What are your thoughts about God?"

"I don't know. God is good. God loves us all, but He's sad at who we are."

"Yes, most people believe in a Supreme Being, even though they may call Him by different names. We know that God lives. . . ." I jumped right into the D, trying to sound natural. I didn't get far, however, before he cut me off and told me he had to get going. I was too inexperienced to have any ready ploys for detaining him and I let him go with a wistful "Dosvidanya."

A bit more confident now that I felt reassured that I was worthy enough to recognize the Spirit's promptings, I continued stopping people with my new opening line. My feet were getting cold and my back was getting tired, but I was proud to be doing the Lord's work.

Finally, a well-dressed, thoughtful-looking man stopped in response to my line: "Excuse me, can I talk with you about God for a little bit?"

"Sure."

HARVEST

"What are your thoughts about God?" I began with this well-practiced question.

"Well, [unintelligible] God [unintelligible] people [unintelligible]."

Not having a clue what the man had just said, but desperate not to lose his attention, I launched right into my recitation, speaking nervously and as quickly as I could: "Most people believe in a Supreme Being, even though they may call him by different names. We know that God lives. We want to share with you our feelings about him. God is perfect, omniscient, and omnipotent. He is also merciful, kind, and just. We know that we can have faith in him. We can love him with all our hearts." I felt silly speaking in such a formalized manner when my language was obviously rudimentary. I also felt pretentious for speaking so didactically to this intelligent-looking man twice my age.

I dared not stop to ask a question lest he respond with a question of his own which I would not understand, or lest he use the break to leave. He was extremely polite and did not once interrupt me. He shifted uneasily a few times and looked over my shoulder, but this man stood in the cold on a busy sidewalk for thirty minutes and listened to my tortured Russian telling him that his and his ancestors' beliefs were wrong and that a nineteen-year old American boy and an obscure American church knew the real truth about God.

At the end of my monologue, I asked the man if Wednesday at 6:00 or Friday at 7:00 would be better for him, but he politely declined either time. He thanked me for my time, and continued on his way. Despite this failure to secure a second meeting or to dispense any literature, I felt good. If nothing else, I consoled myself, I had planted a seed that some day might bear forth fruit.

We finished signboarding after about three hours. I had only given the 1 D to the extraordinarily polite man. I had started a couple of other Ds, only to have the investigator lose interest after a few minutes and get away. Quamme had given 5 Ds, but he seemed satisfied with my contribution on my first day out. One fifth of the way to our 30 Ds requirement with only three hours of contacting, Quamme was in high spirits. We packed up our signboard to carry it to the nearby room that the branch rented as a meetinghouse.

God's Truth Goes Forth Boldly to Sound in Every Ear

I silently followed Quamme through the streets of downtown Novokuibyshevsk. I felt like I was walking through a wall-sized painting of an urban dreamscape. The sun shone brilliantly on the snow and the reflection infused the city with a surreal lucidity. Linden tree skeletons lined the streets, their bony fingers clutching long dead leaves which fluttered in the breeze. There was a freshness in the air, and all the painted buildings and kiosks shone with a faint green tint. Each step brought a new wonderment for me: ice cream stands in winter, grocery stores inside apartment buildings, babies bundled in furry mittens and hats, handmade ads selling apartments pasted to street light poles, Celine Dion's theme song from Titanic floating from the open window of a third floor balcony, babuskas selling dried fish on street corners, shy giggles and glances from teenage girls. This dreamscape was strangely beguiling, and I felt like I never wanted to leave such a marvelous place. The thought of our recent signboarding surfaced, and I felt slightly uneasy, as if the painting was hung a bit crookedly, but I shrugged it off.

5

Knock, knock: Open and Ye Shall Receive

Quamme and I stowed our signboard and table in the meetinghouse room, and then wolfed down a quick lunch at a nearby workers' cafeteria, where a burly lunch lady slopped soupy *pelmenni* from a gigantic vat onto our tin plate. Ten minutes and eighty cents later, it was time to get back to work. Time to knock some doors. Time to keep proselytizing.

In accordance with the rule in the *Missionary Handbook*, more commonly known as the *White Bible* due to its white faux-leather binding, we had to proselytize for ten hours a day. The *White Bible* contained approximately 165 different rules which governed all missions. They ranged from the mundane, common-sense variety ("use deodorant," "say thank you to those that feed you"), to the highly significant, break-at-your-own-everlasting-peril type ("do not swim," "read only books, magazines, and other material authorized by the church"), to the paramount, prime-directive dictates ("never be alone," "never be alone with anyone of the opposite sex," "sleep in the same room with your companion but not the same bed").

All missionaries were enjoined to carry the *White Bible* at all times, and I, like most missionaries, carried a copy in the front pocket of my white shirt next to my breast so that I could always be reminded of the pledge which I'd carefully penned in neat red ink in the back of my *White Bible*: **I will be a perfect example of exact obedience.** We had all made the pledge. The General Authority at the MTC had thoughtfully paused his speech in order to ensure that we all had the time to take our *White Bibles* out of our breast pockets and formalize the pledge in writing.

My *White Bible* next to my breast, I broke into a half-trot to catch up with Quamme, who was striding purposefully towards what I assumed must be the building we were going to knock.

Russian cities were perfect for mass knocking since nearly everyone lived in Soviet-style apartment blocks. Novokuibyshevsk was no exception. It had been built from whole cloth beginning in 1947 with the construction of a large oil refinery, and it had the structured sameness characteristic of a company town. It lacked history, longstanding mercantile establishments, storied community institutions, narrow streets, and small blocks. It did have, however, plenty of unadorned five-floored apartment buildings built in the 1950s to barrack the petrochemical industry workers brought in to work at the refinery. Each five-floorer shared a city block with about ten of its concrete-paneled cousins, each of whom was painted in a faded pastel – chalky pear green, rose pink, slate grey, cantaloupe. The colors all looked thin and tired, like they would smear and wash away in the next rain.

We passed concrete-paneled building after concrete-paneled building, all of which looked to me like prime candidates for my first knocking session. But Quamme kept walking, and I kept breaking into ginger half-trots, trying to catch up without slipping on the icy sidewalks. I thought about my dismal performance signboarding that morning – only 1 D – and then I thought about the perfect discussion that Elder Stevens, Quamme's previous companion, had given the day before to the taxi driver who'd driven us and our luggage around as we had swapped out Stevens for me. I thought about how Quamme had hugged Stevens upon parting with genuine affection, and how they had seemed to have become good friends. I felt bad for breaking up their companionship. I wanted to apologize to Quamme for this and for my paltry 1 D, and for the fact that he was now stuck with a useless greenie, but I was not confident that I could express such a delicate sentiment in Russian.

But I hesitantly began in my elementary Russian anyways: "Excuse me that you are not with Stevens more, but with a green one who knows nothing, and who only receive 1 D," I said, pleased at being able to convey at least the gist of what I wanted to get across.

Quamme looked at me curiously. "Да ладно тебе," he replied.

As best as I could understand he had said, "Yes, it's fine to you." This didn't make a whole lot of sense to me, so I asked him what "Да ладно тебе" meant.

He switched to English. "How can I explain it? It's a really common expression that means different things depending on the context. Here it's kind of like, 'Oh, whatever,' or 'Give me a break.' It's just a way to let somebody know that what they said is kind of ridiculous."

"Okay. Thanks," I replied in Russian, determined to speak the language as much as possible to let him know that I intended to be obedient and dedicated – a baptizing missionary.

Finally, Quamme and I walked up to one of these five-floorers which, according to our regularly updated area book, hadn't yet been knocked. A cracked concrete slab lined by brightly painted wooden benches sat in front of each stairwell door. A few unblinking babushkas wrapped in floral headscarves and hand-knit wool sweaters sat in stoic silence on the first set of benches. We had almost made it past the sullen stares of these dowdy yet undoubtedly doughty babushkas when a particularly feisty one confronted us:

"What are you doing here boys?"

"Talking to people about God, babushka."

"Well God bless you then boys," she replied, apparently mollified by Quamme's matter-of-fact reply.

We climbed to the fifth floor and Quamme went up to the first door. Then he paused and pointed to the doorbell.

"We don't use these," he instructed me in English with a look of great seriousness, as if to signal that what he was telling me was so important that breaking the rule against speaking in English was justified. "You don't know if the doorbell works, you don't know how loud it is. If it's too loud it annoys people, if it's too soft they won't hear it. But the mechanical knock... We can control the knock. We know the knock." I nodded like an eager apprentice being exposed to crucial information for the first time.

"Besides," Quamme continued dryly, "you know what they say: the more doors a missionary *knocks*, the hotter his wife will be. It says nothing about ringing doorbells, and in such an important matter it's best to err on the side of caution, don't you think?" I hesitated a moment, unsure how to respond, then Quamme smiled, and I laughed.

Quamme rapped sharply on the door, and after a moment it swung open to reveal a harried-looking woman.

"Hello ma'am, my name is Elder Quamme, and this is my friend Elder Young, and today we're sharing a message with people about the wonderful plan God prepared for us. Could we come in and talk to you about it for a few minutes?" Quamme began speaking in a friendly, earnest voice. He carried a Book of Mormon in his hand which he pointed to when he mentioned the message we were sharing.

"I have my own religion," she said angrily and slammed the door.

We moved on to the next door.

"Ok, now you give the approach," Quamme told me. "It's good practice for you."

I nodded obediently and took a deep breath, then knocked firmly three times on the wooden door. My eyes were fixed, not without some fear, at the small peephole, looking for signs of movement, of life. My ears strained for the sound of footsteps. Finally, after what seemed like minutes, I heard the floor creak. As the creaking grew louder and nearer, I ran through what I would say in my mind. Finally, the creaking stopped and I saw the peephole darken. My heart surged with adrenalin from the suspense of not knowing what awaited me behind the door. I heard the metal grating sound of the bolt unlocking with a knot in my stomach. Finally, I saw the suspicious, hostile face of a housewife, a potential investigator, appear through a crack in the door. I started to speak:

"Hi, my name is Elder Young, and this is my companion, Elder Quamme. We are representatives of the Church of Jesus Christ of Latter-day Saints. We have an important message for you about God. May we come in and talk to you about it?" My words were high and rushed, stumbling over themselves to get out.

"No." The door slammed shut. Could she not feel the Spirit? Did I say something wrong? At the next door that opened I gave the same approach.

"Representatives of what?"

"The Church of Jesus Christ of Latter-day Saints."

"What?"

"The Church of Jesus Christ of Latter-day Saints." It seemed like it was taking me forever to spit out that long name, a name even longer in Russian.

"Huh? I don't understand."

I looked helplessly at Quamme. "The Church of Jesus Christ of Latter-day Saints," he said with a much better Russian accent.

"Ah, Jesus Christ. No, boys. No thank you. I don't need any Jesus Christ right now. Maybe later."

For an hour it was knock, wait, no response, knock, wait, rejection, knock, wait, no response, rejection, no response, rejection, rejection, rejection, until we had finished the first stairwell. We exited the building and moved on to the second stairwell.

A bunch of girls were sitting on the benches in front of the second stairwell, giggling as we approached.

"Hi! Would you be so kind as to tell us the time?"

I blushed and looked at Quamme, who glanced down at his watch. "Twenty-three minutes from two," he said without a beat, using the most difficult grammatical construction possible. The girls appeared surprised and impressed by his fluency, and one of them, a thin brunette with red lips and dark flashing eyes, got up to greet us.

"You wouldn't happen to have a light would you?" she asked with a smile as she held out a cigarette wedged between her dainty fingers.

I felt it was time to end the conversation. With fleeting, unformed thoughts of tobacco and sex I felt vaguely sinful. Quamme shook his head no and we went inside.

The second stairwell was more knocking, more waiting, and more rejection, door after door.

As we approached the third stairwell a gaggle of ragged kids playing in the courtyard came running over to the benches, marveling at the funnily-dressed foreigners approaching their homes. We played around with them for a few minutes, making silly faces and answering their questions about who we were and what we were doing and where we were from, and I was just as happy as the kids to have someone friendly to talk to.

Knock, knock: Open and Ye Shall Receive

Even though it was still the first full day of my mission, the knocking was starting to feel old hat. No one seemed to want to hear what we had to say in the third stairwell, either. I was starting to wonder if I was bringing bad luck with my approach and accent. Or worse, maybe I was not worthy and was keeping the Spirit from being with us. I *had* just had a vaguely sexual thought when we had talked to those girls. Knocking couldn't possibly be this full of rejection normally, I thought.

My lower back ached from standing all day on the street and knocking doors. The single strap of my MTC-approved handbag wrenched my shoulder awkwardly and I wished that I had a backpack. It seemed to get heavier and heavier the longer we knocked, and I began thinking about how I could cut weight. The single heaviest item was my leather-bound English edition of the Scriptures. Over the last several years I had carefully marked hundreds of verses which I had found particularly important, and I was really looking forward to deep conversations in which I would use these verses to explain the Gospel, God, and the Plan of Salvation to people. I was not confident in my ability to find these verses in my unmarked Russian scriptures when the brief golden teaching moment arose, so ditching these books was not an option. And once I did find the verse, I could obviously not read it in English, so I couldn't jettison my heavy Russian set of Scriptures that I was carrying, either. My trusty book of discussions with all the Russian words accented for easy pronunciation was absolutely vital, and Quamme had told me that we needed the new member discussions as well. The one area where it looked like I could cut some weight was the set of six Books of Mormon which I had optimistically brought to hand out to people.

Buoyed by the thought of eventually lightening my load, I continued giving my door approach until we had knocked out the third stairwell. One more stairwell to go and we would have knocked out the whole building – about eighty apartments. Half of the time we could see the peephole darken and hear the floor creak, but the door had stayed shut. We had even tried talking to people through the closed door but we were either ignored or told to get off their doorstep, out of their building, and out of their country. To go back to America and preach there. And when people had opened the door, they invariably had their own religion, didn't believe in God, or didn't have the time. Others hadn't even bothered with an excuse. A glance at the uniform and nametag and it was a slammed door and a leave-us-the-hell-alone.

I was starting to feel more like a pesky door-to-door salesman than an emissary of truth who was seeking to bring joy into others' lives by enlightening them with the special knowledge I had.

Dusk was falling when we approached the final stairwell. On the benches lounged a pack of teenage boys and girls, gnawing on sunflower seeds, spitting, laughing, staring, hugging, drinking, smoking, groping. I walked past these our peers, pondering my social isolation from them.

"Hello Americans! Fuck you American boys!" A couple of the boys called out in English, accompanied by a middle finger. I looked at Quamme, he shook his head, and we walked up to the top floor while he told me stories of homesick missionaries weary of constantly being the center of negative attention who'd responded to these provocations in a less than Christ-like manner.

As we were finishing up knocking the building, I began losing my hope that there was someone in this building, just *someone*, whose heart God had softened and who was seeking the truth we had to offer. The lower we climbed down the stairwell the more my hope sank that we would sit down in overstuffed chairs next to the fireplace, look into people's eyes, and teach them about the plan of salvation with the Spirit burning hot in our bosoms.

But, as it turned out, we did get that one person to listen to our message. It came at the end when Quamme was clearly growing impatient with our lack of success with my door approaches. Or maybe he was just tired after eighteen months of knocking doors and wanted to get the thirty Ds out of the way. I began again:

"Hi, my name is Elder Young. My companion and I are representatives of Jesus Christ. We have a message for you about his plan for us. May we come in and talk to you about it?"

"What? Who are you? I don't know anything, young men," said an old man as he started to shut the door.

Quamme jumped in before the door closed: "What are your feelings about God?"

Knock, knock: Open and Ye Shall Receive

"На Бога надейся, а сам не плошай." I had no clue what the man had just said, but Quamme later told me that it meant: "Have hope in God, but do everything you can yourself, just in case." I would hear this bit of wisdom tens of thousands of times before leaving Russia, as it was the most common response to our incessant inquiries into people's feelings about God.

"Yes, that's a very good saying." Quamme said, and then he immediately launched right into the first principle of the 1st D, again without so much as a breath. "Most people believe in a Supreme Being, even though they may call him by different names. We know that God lives. We want to share with you our feelings about him. . . ."

The old man stood there uneasily in his dirty white undershirt and greasy green jogging-suit pants. His skin was oily, dirty, leathery brown and craggy, his hair unkempt. His face told of a hard life of manual labor in the oil refinery. His eyes were full of confusion and fear. He reeked of alcohol.

When Quamme finished the principle, the old man looked at him submissively, as if Quamme's nametag and black trench coat gave him some kind of authority. "Ok. Thank you," he said, and his fearful eyes asked: "Can I close the door now?"

Quamme looked expectantly at me, and I knew I was supposed to continue by reciting the second principle. I hoped the man would get the courage to shut the door before I had to begin. Once again I was struck by how unlike the MTC my real Russian missionary experience was turning out to be. And on the very first day. What were we doing cramming a D down this man's throat through a crack in the doorway? He had said "no" when I first asked him. Shouldn't we respect that? Anyone could see that he had no interest in what we were saying – he probably didn't even understand most of it. He just seemed afraid of us for some reason.

So I stood there silently, hoping that I could feign ignorance about the practice of alternating teaching principles and act like I thought Quamme would teach the whole D.

Using the momentary discord to his advantage, the man pleadingly said "thank you" again and began closing the door.

"Wait," Quamme said forcefully before the man could shut the door, "my companion wants to tell you about Jesus Christ."

I could not play ignorant now, so I launched into my memorized spiel, my face red and sweaty with the embarrassment of what I was doing: "Without the help of our Father in Heaven, we could not benefit from the plan of salvation. In mortal life, each of us sins and falls short of perfection. Our sins make us unworthy to return to our Father in Heaven. In addition, each of us will die to end this mortal life. God provided a way for us to overcome sin and death so that we can return to his presence. The central figure in the plan of salvation is Jesus Christ." At this point, the discussion instructed us that we were supposed to "read and discuss John 3:16," so I began pulling my Bible out of my bag. Quamme, however, shook his head and waved me off. It took too much time to read the scripture, and a D still counted as a D for statistical purposes without it. So I finished the last line of my principle: "It is wonderful to think of the great love our Heavenly Father has for us."

I then tried to testify about what I had just said, hoping to bring the Spirit into the discussion, something that was sorely lacking, as far as I could tell.

"I want to say to you that I know that the plan of salvation can do us happy. . . . I know that Jesus Christ loves you. . . . I am so grateful because this gospel. . ." I struggled to form these few sentences, and I was frustrated that my language did not allow me to say more. I strained hard at each word, desperately trying to inflect my voice with such sincerity, urgency, and earnestness that the man would have to be moved by the power of my testimony. The man stood there with the same confused, fearful look, and I thought that if only my language skills were better I could get through to him.

Judging that I had said all I was going to say, Quamme started in on the third principle. I was hoping that he would stray from the script to do *something* to touch this man and to get him to listen to what we were saying. If I were he, I thought, with his language skills, I would wax so eloquent in the bearing of my testimony that the man would have to show some emotion besides uneasiness. Or, I would engage the man in conversation, find out what made him tick, and personalize the message in the way in which the Spirit directed me so that it touched this man's heart. But, at the end of his principle, Quamme bore a short testimony similar to mine, just more polished, and the man looked just as confused and fearful. In this uninspired way Quamme and

I continued to alternate principles until we had recited all six principles and given him the entire 1st D through the doorway.

All that was left to do was to give him a Book of Mormon, commit him to reading it, and set up a time for us to come back. The man agreed to meet us three days later at 3:00. But three days later at 3:00, the door remained tightly shut, as it did each subsequent time we dropped by when we were in the neighborhood with nothing to do on our weekly planners.

I was discouraged by my first knocking session. I felt like I had let Quamme down. Why had I been hesitant about giving the old man the D? I felt like I had let President Hatcher down. Had he not specifically emphasized the day before at orientation that we should not be afraid to open our mouths? I felt like I had let the Lord down. Why hadn't I been able to bring the Spirit into our discussion and touch the old man's heart? Why hadn't we had success with my door approaches? Was I not worthy? Was my accent so bad that no one could even understand me? And most profoundly, but buried deep inside and unrecognizable at the time, I somehow felt like I had let myself down. What was I doing?

6

To Serve and Prospect

That evening we went to visit a recently baptized member named Natasha. She lived all alone in a small apartment on the top floor of her building. On the way up to her apartment we passed an old drunk man lying in the landing of the stairwell. He was unconscious and lay in a puddle of his own urine, the stench of the urine mixing with vodka and sweated garlic. My first drunkard. Ever. I felt sick, and my heart ached. If only he knew about the Word of Wisdom, I thought. All this misery could be averted if people would just embrace the Gospel and live by its precepts.

We were going to share the fifth discussion for newly baptized members. This discussion, entitled "Redeeming the Dead," taught the freshly converted about the importance of conducting genealogy so that they could perform proxy baptisms in LDS temples for and in behalf of their dead ancestors who did not get the chance to get baptized in the LDS Church while they were alive on Earth. This way, their ancestors would be able to live with them for time and all eternity in heaven. The discussion also contained many suggestions to help build stronger families here on Earth, such as holding family home evenings every Monday, planning family reunions, and publishing a family newsletter.

It was still my first full day on the holy job in Novokuibyshevsk, but I'd had more thoughts, experiences, and emotions in that one day than in months of languid Idaho summers or weeks of fervid training at the MTC. I was still jetlagged and tired and my body was trying to adjust to the new time zone: the day had begun eleven hours earlier than all those days in Idaho and Utah. And time zone difference aside, I felt like I was also trying to adjust to a new flow of time. As if something was making the band of time reveal itself in excruciatingly slow motion while simultaneously stretching itself out. Maybe it was just psychological – something to do with the repetitive nature of missionary work or the newness of it all. Or maybe it was partly chronobiological – the jetlag and Russia with its Arctic dark and declination of the sun had delayed my circadian rhythms, messed with my biological clock. Or maybe since I was doing the Lord's work I was now on the Lord's time, the time of Kolob, and, as Church members were wont to repeat, the Lord's time is not our time. Whatever the reason, I could not help wondering with a vague panic just how long two years could be.

Natasha opened the door wearing nothing but slippers and a threadbare cotton robe that was open in the front, exposing her small naked body. She swayed unsteadily and looked at us defiantly, her white hair wispy and wild: "What do you want?" she asked with a sneer, her words heavily slurred. She was drunk. Her face was bruised, and one eye was black and swollen shut.

In shock, I followed Quamme into her apartment, feeling like this was all just some kind of bad dream. I watched as he laid her down on the sofa and covered her with a blanket.

"Did he beat you again, Natasha?" Quamme asked gently as I stood by helplessly.

She nodded. She then hid her face in the blanket and began to sob.

"Why did you let him in? I thought we agreed that he could no longer come here to visit you?" Quamme asked with concern.

She pulled the blanket from off her head: "We agreed to nothing. You know nothing. I didn't let him in." The words sloshed out, angry and thick. I could only make a rough guess at their meaning.

"How did he get in, then?" Quamme persisted.

"I let him in, you moron."

"Why?" Quamme asked gently.

"He would break down the door if I didn't," she wailed and hid her face again underneath the blanket, muffling her sobs.

Quamme softly placed his hand on her small delicate forearm. "I'm so sorry, Natasha. You deserve better than that. I'm so sorry."

She continued to cry. I felt so powerless. What could I have hoped to accomplish by reading from the new member discussions in my garbled Russian about baptisms for the dead and family reunions?

"We're going to go now and try to see if Anna can come over. Is that okay?" Quamme asked after a few minutes of silence, still kneeling at Natasha's side.

"Yes, that would be nice," she responded through sniffles.

"Can we get you something for the pain?"

"No, that's not necessary."

"We'll stop buy the pharmacy and get you something, ok?"

"Ok."

We left to go buy some medicine and to find the Relief Society President of the branch, Anna. We passed by the drunk in the stairwell, and Quamme told me that this was the man who had beaten Natasha. I looked at his ugly face and dumbly open mouth, and my earlier pity was replaced by revulsion and rage. I wanted nothing more than to grab him by his oily hair and bash his dirty face into the urine-soaked concrete.

"Man, what kind of freaking lowlife beats a woman like that?" I shook my head in disgust.

"The guy's a creep. He steals from her, he beats her. I don't understand why she let him in, why she still talks to him. She said she was done with him."

We walked out into the shadows of the dark courtyard lit only by the spattering of light emanating from the windows of the building's apartments.

"What do you think that we can do for her?"

"I think that instead of a family newsletter, what she could really use is a steel door," Quamme said.

I smiled despite myself. "You really think he could have broken her door down?"

"Yeah, of course. It happens all the time here. That's why everyone wants a steel door. Members, missionaries, everyone, but they cost like a hundred dollars. Some thieves busted down me and Taylor's wooden door in Saratov and stole our coats and shoes."

"Wow. Really?" I asked with what little disbelief remained in me. "Well, can we help her get one? I mean, mission rules say that we're not supposed to give money to the members, don't they?"

"I think I might be able to scrape up enough money from the fast offering fund to get her one."

Quamme was the branch president of the Novokuibyshevsk branch, a position that would ordinarily be filled by a local priesthood leader, but, since the Novokuibyshevsk branch was made up mostly of women and teens, a missionary had to fill the role. As branch president, Quamme was in charge of the branch finances. The biggest fund that he administered was the tithing fund. Every Sunday, women would proudly present him with crisp white envelopes stuffed with wrinkled rubles and carefully filled-out tithing slips that had been shipped over from the Church's state of the art printing press back in Utah. Once a month, we would go to the Sberbank in the city center where we would wire all these wrinkled rubles back to Church Headquarters in Salt Lake City.

In addition to giving ten percent of their income for tithing, members were expected to contribute fast offerings each month to the Church. The general idea was that the first Sunday of the month members would fast for two meals and then donate to the Church at least the amount that they had saved by skipping those two meals, although the expectation was that they should give more if they could afford it. Unlike the tithing money, this money stayed in Russia with the local branch, and Quamme was free to spend it as he saw fit. This fund was much smaller than the tithing fund, and the bulk of the money came from the missionaries who donated generously from our monthly stipend, as the *White Bible* instructed us to do.

That evening, after seeing Natasha naked, drunk, defiant, ashamed, and scared, I went home with a heavy heart and wrote in my journal before falling asleep. The *White Bible* instructed missionaries to write in their journal regularly, and I was resolved to write daily.

HARVEST

Even before I started writing it, I entertained a few fuzzy fantasies regarding the future of my journal. In one I sat in a resplendent living room with my future family during family home evening as I shared with them inspiring passages from my missionary journal about the incredible spiritual experiences I had witnessed. In another, however, I pictured myself lying in bed reading the journal by lamplight, in private, years down the road, reflecting upon a brutally honest account, the ups and downs, the rewards and blessings, the trials and tribulations, the good times and the bad. Balancing these two different conceptions of what my journal should be produced my initial mindset to write honestly and thoroughly, but only to a point, and always with a positive spin. So I began that first evening: *This is going to be an interesting two years.*

Wrapped up in my more immediate concerns of language, companion, and proselytizing, I wrote only a little about my first feeling of helplessness. But I would come to know this feeling well. It was so dispiriting to me, this frustrating feeling of not being able to offer the kind of aid that produced immediate, tangible results. I had come to Russia to help people and I felt like people here needed my help. I had led a sheltered life in rural Mormon country and I had never seen such poverty, such drunkenness, such vice, such violence and abuse, such despair, such pain, and such disregard for God as I had seen in just this one day. I wanted to do something about it, to help fix it, to make it more like the Southeastern Idaho I knew, to bring the light of Christ to the faces of people in Novokuibyshevsk. I desperately wanted to see that what I was doing, the service to which I was dedicating myself for two long years, was helping these people. But, that first full day, at least for the proselytizing part of it, I had felt more like a public nuisance than a public servant, and it really bothered me. It bothered me that despite the Church's vast financial resources we weren't even sure we could get Natasha a steel door. It bothered me that this steel door was seemingly more valuable than the message I had to offer. And it bothered me that even those who had accepted this message still led lives of pain like Natasha's.

7

Banya Heaven

Deet-deet, deet-deet, deet-deet! At six sharp my little travel alarm clock rang out, ungodly chipper with a trace of menace. Although the *White Bible* said 6:30, President Hatcher had instituted a mission rule that all new missionaries had to wake up at 6:00 in order to have more time to study the language. Since the *White Bible* forbade a missionary from arising before his companion, Quamme also had to get up at 6:00. I slapped the oversized snooze button on top. The room was dark. I was disoriented and lost. I felt as if I had been whisked away during the night to some sanitorium high atop a mountain in the clouds.

Quamme's voice brought me out of dreamland: "Young, are you awake?"

I got up off my mattress and went to the bathroom, lit the gas water heater, and took a quick shower with the handheld showerhead with the hose so short that I had to kneel to wash my head and shoulders. I put on my Technicolor Dreamcoat robe and the ratty slippers which came with the apartment, and went out to the kitchen where Quamme had breakfast ready – a big pot of grechka (buckwheat groats) which he had mixed with apricot yogurt. I'd been with Quamme for over a week now and he'd made all the meals so far, and I was starting to feel guilty. Thoughts from when I was a young child standing in the kitchen with my mother, helping her to crack the eggs for an omelette or grate the cheese for a casserole came to my mind:

"Your companion on your mission will be so glad that you know how to do this!" I wanted to show Quamme that I could contribute in the kitchen as soon as I got used to things a bit. For now, though, I just did the dishes.

I quickly ate the meaty grechka, sounding out between bites the new words from my pocket tablet that I carried with me everywhere so that I could write down the unfamiliar words I heard on the street. I then began the first item on my morning schedule – the hour of gospel study we had to do every day.

After struggling for about an hour to keep my eyes open while reading the Old Testament in English and the Book of Mormon in Russian, I saw Quamme get up from his mattress to sit at the card table littered with books and papers. This was the signal that it was time for the hour of companionship study. The rules were remarkably silent as to what constituted proper companionship study. The only real guidance was that it had to be done together and that it had to last an hour. As I was to later find out, creative missionaries counted *anything* done together as companionship study, including making breakfast.

To begin our companionship study, Quamme pulled out an illustrated Russian grammar book that he had been given by his "father," or trainer, when he had first arrived. He went through several of the grammatical concepts with me for half an hour before handing me a Priesthood lesson manual in Russian to study, telling me that I would be teaching the lesson on Sunday. While I studied the lesson manual, Quamme created a little written quiz to test my comprehension of the day's material. I was touched and grateful that he took his pedagogical role so seriously.

The final section of the morning study schedule was my favorite part of most days, the hour and a half of language study. I already loved the Russian language. I loved the lyrical way it bubbled out of the mouths of girls as a completely different language than the harsh, slurred speech of the drunkards. I loved studying it. It was like playing chess: the rules were clear and relatively simple to learn, but the resulting speech was exquisite in its complexity. I loved its nearly perfectly phonetic alphabet and its efficiency, and, in time, I, too, came to disdain articles, most prepositions, the verb "to be," several verb tenses, and sentences with needless subjects.

Banya Heaven

I studied Russian desperately. I saw it as my key to being a better missionary. All the doubts and frustrations I had felt my first week I attributed to my lack of language skills, and I was sure that once I was able to speak fluently, I would be able to do the things as a missionary that I had always dreamed of doing.

I took out my pocket tablet, looked up the meaning of about thirty new words, memorized them, and then spent the remaining time studying grammar.

It was Wednesday, the hallelujah day in the mission. Wednesdays were our "preparation days," or P-Days, our weekly breaks from proselytizing. We had the day off until six p.m., at which time we had to resume proselytizing until we returned to our apartment at nine-thirty. Even our time off from proselytizing could hardly be called free time, however. We still had to wake up at six and complete the full three and a half hour morning schedule of study. Additionally, the *White Bible* also required us to do all our preparation for the week on P-Day (and only on P-Day): wash our clothes, clean the apartment, polish our shoes, iron our shirts, get our hair cut, shop for groceries. This was also the only day we could write to our families.

In the free time that remained for us to blow off a little steam from a week's worth of work, the *White Bible* required us to plan safe, wholesome, and uplifting activities. It went on to enumerate a long laundry list of forbidden activities: no television, no radio or unauthorized CDs, no unauthorized reading material, no musical groups or athletic teams, and no contact sports, water sports, winter sports, horseback riding, swimming, basketball in leagues, basketball in tournaments, full court basketball, and so on. We could, however, play half-court basketball.

The *White Bible* said nothing about the banya, however, so after a half-hearted cleaning of the apartment Quamme and I met up with Elders Wilson and Smith, the only other missionaries in Novokuibyshevsk, at a local banya. Quamme and Wilson negotiated the rental of a private room, while I tried unsuccessfully to engage in a Russian conversation with Smith, a fellow greenie who'd been out for just over a month. Smith had a girlfriend waiting for him to return with honor to Provo, and he always had a certain blank enthusiasm that seemed somehow forced to me.

HARVEST

Once inside I followed Quamme's lead and stripped off my clothes and garments and walked naked into the wooden-paneled steam room. Wilson and Smith joined us and Quamme handed each of us a *venik*, a bundle of birch branches with the leaves still attached, which had been soaking in a bucket of water near the door. Wilson grabbed the bucket and started to ladle water over the hot stones of the stove.

The steam hissed out, tortured and angry, hitting my face like a wall of fire. The blistering air scorched the passages of my nostrils, and I felt suffocated and claustrophobic for a moment. But once the wave of steam had dissipated into a more obtuse heat, I began to breathe deeply, pulling the hot humid air infused with rich bass notes of cedar and birch deep into my lungs. My sinuses cleared, and my head felt incandescent. We began to beat each other's backs with the *veniks*, which brought the blood to the surface of our skin and stimulated our circulation. We were silent; it was too hot and transcendent for speech. The only sounds were the low electric cracking of the heated rocks and the swooping whooshes of hot air followed by the smack of wet leaves on bare skin. We sweated and sweated until every pore in our body had spit out all its ambient impurities.

Once we couldn't take the heat any longer, we left the sauna and jumped feet-first into a large pool of icy water that robbed me of my breath. The water was too cold to move, so we floated motionlessly, stupid and giddy with cold.

"My balls just went inside my body!" Elder Smith yelled out. "Seriously guys, they're like little turtle heads! They went completely inside!"

"I can't take it anymore, I'm going back to the banya," said Wilson as he got out.

"I'm seriously worried about my balls! What if they never come back out? My girlfriend would not be happy. I'm outta here, too," said Smith as he clambered up and out of the pool.

"Ok, Young, let's see what you got," Quamme challenged me playfully. "How long can you stay in? I've never been beaten yet."

"All right man," I said, always up for some competition, no matter how small. "You're on."

After a few minutes of remaining as still as possible in order to not disturb the thin layer of water that had been warmed ever so slightly by my body, I found that I could move about normally – I was so numb that the water seemed to have lost a temperature, the only remaining sensation being that of a fluid texture. A couple of minutes more and it lost its texture as well. I began shivering. Quamme was doing the same.

"I'm not getting out till you do," he said.

"Me neither."

My teeth started to chatter uncontrollably. Quamme had a lost, faraway look in his eyes. His pale skin was gooonefleshed and pallid. My mind felt like it was getting smaller and smaller, as if it were slipping away into the cold and dark of outer space.

"Let's get out together," I finally suggested.

"Ok," Quamme quickly agreed, "On three. One, two, three," he said and we left the pool together.

"Very nice Young, I'm impressed," Quamme told me with a hint of respect as we shivered our way back toward the sauna.

"Man, that was intense," I said with a laugh of relief. Relief to be out of the ice water, but mainly relief that I had just done something to prove myself, something to earn Quamme's respect, something that didn't depend on my knowledge of the language or on my worthiness to have the Spirit.

The heat didn't feel as strong the second time around since it had to first unthaw our bodies. We sat and hypothesized about the purpose of the *veniks* and the cold water, each of us coming up with different theories about their effect on the body.

"The hot and the cold are like the ying and the yang, man, they balance each other out," said Wilson. Before his mission he had been really devoted to some martial art that I'd never even heard of.

"It's good for the skin, to open and close the pores like that. Or maybe it's bad," Smith asserted tautologically.

"The drastic temperature changes have gotta be good for the circulatory system." I said. "Ok, so the *veniks* and heat bring the blood to the surface, and the ice water then chills that blood, so then all the blood vessels are expanding and constricting with the temperature changes. It's like exercise for them. It makes them supple and flexible." This had been my longest sustained speech since coming to Russia, 1st Ds aside. And it felt good. Good to express myself in my own words in my own language.

"Whatever the mechanism, this is incredible. I'm always so refreshed afterwards," said Quamme.

"Yeah, I know, man," said Wilson. "When I build my house, I'm gonna put one of these babies in for sure."

With this allusion to post-mission life at home we all grew silent. Wilson's mention of home had given me the uneasy feeling I got whenever I heard gossip and I looked uneasily over my shoulder in fear that the gossipee would overhear. Talk of home was definitely against the rule commanding us to center our minds on our missions and the violation of this rule was one of the most frequently cited reasons for why missionaries did not have more success with baptisms.

We continued to sit silently until the heat was too much again and it was time for the ice pool. We repeated this hot-cold cycle a few times, taking a break sometime in the middle to go into an antechamber next to the sauna and lie down on the table and benches and drink the peach nectar we had brought. I lay on my back on the bench and sipped the delicious nectar from a small glass. My body had never felt so awake, so refreshed; it tingled, glowed, hummed, purred. It was as if some hidden system deep in the center of my body had been activated and was now chugging along, emitting positive radiation and tangible good energy. I lay there basking in this sensation, feeling so happy and at peace.

Then I remembered the *White Bible*, and I started to wonder if this was an appropriate P-Day activity. What if jumping into the pool counted as swimming? And what about all of us being naked? I couldn't think of any rule against that in the *White Bible*, but I was sure that it couldn't have been okay. After all, there was the rule about not sleeping in the same bed as your companion, and it was pretty clear what that was getting at. Maybe this was the appearance of evil or something. But all the other missionaries were doing it, I rationalized, and Quamme and Wilson were both in leadership positions – testament, I assumed, to their obedience and missionary success. We must be all right.

But we had been speaking in English! How was I going to learn the language if I wasn't obedient in speaking it 100% of the time? I'd lose the Lord's help. But maybe He understood that we just needed to relax a little bit, and that we'd get back to Russian as soon as we got out of the banya, I thought. But I knew, and He knew, and I couldn't stop myself from knowing, that this was all just rationalization. We both knew I really wasn't dedicated enough to being obedient.

After our purification at the banya, Quamme and I went to get our hair cut. The barber shop was at the base of one of the five-floorers. Russian pop played on the radio, and a few women dressed in light blue frocks lounged around waiting for customers. One of them, a plump thirtyish woman with lively gray eyes and short chestnut hair, eventually came over and asked me how I wanted my hair cut. Quamme was at the other end of the room talking to his stylist, so I was on my own.

"Short, please." It was the only word I could think of.

Looking at me from the mirror the woman said something that, judging by its rising intonation, I assumed was a question. Panicked and unsure how to respond, I tried again.

"Just more short please. But same like now," I said, becoming a bit more verbose.

She sighed in exasperation and began cutting my hair. She began in the back, and the cool breeze on my head alerted me that something might be going terribly wrong. As she moved to the front, I watched in the mirror with horror as she proceeded to airily buzz my hair off to little more than fuzz.

"No! No that so short!" I protested.

She shrugged and kept cutting. She sheared off all my hair except for the bangs, which she left long, just trimming them slightly. I looked like a peach with a thin string of bangs glued to it. Quamme called it a "rib" haircut, in honor of all the "rebyata," or young Russian men, who wore this popular style.

The plump stylist more than made up for my "rib" haircut at the end when she shampooed my bangs and gently massaged my fuzzy scalp. I had literally not been touched for months, except for all the firm handshakes and the quick hugs with my family at the airport. Her warm fleshy fingers on my scalp made me feel so wonderfully human that even the angels, those disembodied spirits of celestial realms, must have envied me. I wished she would never stop.

But she did, and we stepped out into the cold wind again. My bare head made me envy the Russians, none of whom were thick-headed enough to leave home without a hat. We went to buy groceries, where I played my usual role of dolt and stood around helplessly since there were no self-serve supermarket-style grocery stores in Novokuibyshevsk. Instead, customers had to tell the clerks what they wanted and the clerks would retrieve it from behind the counter. Although I could have told the clerk that God is omniscient and omnipotent, I could not yet tell her that we wanted a kilo of flour, so Quamme had to handle everything.

That evening it was back to proselytizing, but in a new setting and with a new approach. We were going to have an open house. Quamme had come up with the idea of giving the first discussion in our meetinghouse, where we could control the environment, sing a hymn, begin with a prayer, have pictures of Christ on the wall, and eat refreshments afterwards. The idea was inspired by the great Mormon missionaries of the past like Parley P. Pratt and Wilford Woodruff, who back in the 1800s had baptized thousands in England by standing on soapboxes in a corner of Hyde Park and preaching to large crowds. For weeks the other missionaries had been handing out hundreds of invitations for the open house, or the "day of open doors" as it was called in Russian. Quamme had even posted some advertisements which he had made on dozens of bus stops around town.

Three people showed up, and we four missionaries took turns giving the principles. The people seemed interested; they stuck around for refreshments anyways, and I felt as if the Spirit was present during the discussion. It had certainly been more like the MTC.

It had been a good day, that first P-Day. Lying in bed in my garments, I wished Quamme goodnight, closed my eyes, spooled up my mind's reel with the day's events, sucked in a deep and contented breath, and gave myself over to the pleasure of watching the reel drowsily unspool. Random images and thoughts from a day full of them. Flashes of scenes in the banya, snippets of conversation with Quamme. It was fine, I was going be able to make friends and fit in. Haircut, flour, swimming pool, satisfaction, freezing, sunshine. Almost fifty words in one day – the language would come. The touch of fleshy fingers on my scalp, the post-banya body glow. Russia was pretty freaking amazing, two years here wouldn't be that bad. The open house and the MTC-like discussion. The attentiveness and interest on the faces of those present. I was doing the right thing by being there.

8

To Heaven by way of Banya

Baptisms, baptisms, baptisms. "Your purpose as a missionary is to help people come to Christ through the ordinances of baptism and confirmation." This was the first sentence in the divinely inspired *Missionary Guide*. Baptisms, baptisms, baptisms. Our purpose, our goal, our obsession. It was typically and ideally a quick process. Missionaries could go from contacting an investigator on the street to baptizing her in the banya in less than two weeks.

Some missionaries went several months before tasting the sweet baptismal fruit of their hard labor. Some never tasted it all. But serving as I did in the highest baptizing mission in Europe at the time – over seventy a month some months – there was a good statistical probability that I would soon have the pleasure of experiencing my first baptism. Add to that the fact that Quamme was considered one of the better baptizing missionaries, and it couldn't be long now. Or so went my hopeful reasoning when I was about two weeks into my mission, eager and impatient to experience that first baptism, to receive that joyous reward that would come from achieving my purpose as a missionary.

My role during those early days continued to be to mutely follow Quamme as we proselytized and visited our investigators in pursuit of those baptisms. I couldn't understand much of anything, and I mostly just opened my mouth to parrot out 1st Ds during signboarding and knocking.

To Heaven by way of Banya

One notable exception to this was our time with Nina. Nina was an eighty-five year old widow whom Quamme and his previous companion Stevens had found knocking. They had committed her to baptism after she had heard the first three discussions within the space of a week. Nina was a bustling, vivacious woman with a nimble mind who claimed that she did pull-ups every morning. She had been a student turned sniper in Leningrad during World War II, and had troves of stories, ribbons, and medals from that time. Her only son lived in Moscow and had not visited her in years.

When she opened the door to meet with us at the appointed time for her fourth discussion I felt like I may as well have been her son, judging by the look on her face. She lit up with pure delight and waved us in.

"Come in! Come in! Come in! I've been waiting for you boys!"

She led us into a small clean room filled with old-fashioned furniture, ornamental mirrors with well-burnished frames, cheap statuettes of Greeks bearing fruit, yellowing lacy tablecloths, and threadbare muslin curtains. I looked around the place, looked at her face still beaming with joy at our presence, and wished that I could have been there for the moment when she had first made the commitment to get baptized, that I could have felt that excitement as the Spirit testified to her that she was making the right choice. Still, I was very excited to teach her, and I was a little nervous lest I say or do something which might give her second thoughts. I asked God in a quick silent prayer to please help me to have the Spirit with me as I taught.

At Quamme's cue I began the fourth discussion by reading slowly from my book of discussions with the accented words. I read aloud to Nina about our premortal existence and how we had lived with our Heavenly Father as spirits before coming to this Earth. I could understand the gist of most of what I was reading, and as I uttered each sentence that so logically laid out the beautiful, simple plan of salvation I was filled with the joy of being the bearer of glad tidings. I marveled that this woman was eighty-five years old and had lived her whole life without ever knowing its purpose. That she had never heard about how we lived as spirits with our Father in Heaven before coming here to Earth. I looked at her nodding her head in agreement with everything I was saying, as if this was all just a confirmation of something that she had known somewhere deep inside all along, and I was struck by the thrilling thought that we might have even known each other as spirits in the premortal existence. Maybe I had promised her there that I would come to Russia and find her and teach her about the restored Gospel!

Quamme continued by explaining to her that our purpose on earth was to receive a physical body and to learn to become more like God by using our free will to make the right choices of how to best control that body. Nina continued to nod her head in happy agreement.

I carefully read the next principle, informing Nina that where we went when we died would depend on the choices about our bodies that we made in this life, and that there were three places where we could end up – the celestial, terrestrial, and telestial kingdoms. I finished with my testimony: "I know, Nina, that if we can be making the good choices, we can be returning to our Heavenly Father in celestial kingdom." This was a thrilling idea to testify to – to be able to assure someone that they could go to heaven. Nina seemed satisfied with the idea.

Quamme explained to her that only those with the right key could get into the celestial kingdom and that she would get that key when she got baptized next Saturday. He then told her about the doctrine of baptism for the dead, and how even those who had died without being baptized in the LDS Church could go to the celestial kingdom if we had performed baptism by proxy for them here in LDS temples.

Next up was the fifth principle about chastity, and as I began to read I suspected that Quamme had made me begin the discussion just so that it would be my turn to give this principle and he could sit back and enjoy watching me squirm as I explained the basics of what Mormon chastity entailed. I pushed on through and talked to Nina about sex and felt the blood rush to my face. It was the first time I'd said the "S word" in Russian; I'd rarely said it in English. After I'd finished emphasizing a couple of times how sacred the power of procreation was, my book of discussions told me that I was supposed to commit Nina to live this law.

Did I really need to ask this eighty-five year old babushka living all alone if she would refrain from sexual relations, I asked myself. I looked at Quamme for help, but he just looked back at me, amused and expectant, signaling to me that he would not begin his principle until I asked the question.

"Nina, will you live the law of chastity in your actions, your thoughts, and your speech?" I read with my burning face buried in my book. How was this sweet old woman going to break the law of chastity in her speech, I wondered.

Nina blushed and giggled shortly and nervously. "Of course."

Automatically, I testified: "I know that the Lord will bless you for this, Nina."

There was one more major commitment in the discussion: the Word of Wisdom. Quamme explained to her that the Lord forbids the use of tobacco, alcohol, coffee, and tea, and then listed a few reasons why, including the final one: "Perhaps most important, the Lord promises that this law can help us be worthy to receive the guidance of the Holy Ghost. Through the Holy Ghost we can know that the Book of Mormon is true and that Joseph Smith was a prophet of God."

He then made the invitation: "Nina, will you live the Word of Wisdom, beginning right now – including the commandment not to take tobacco, alcohol, coffee, or tea into your body?"

"Of course," Nina said simply.

Quamme seemed a little surprised by how easy it had been to get Nina to commit to live the Word of Wisdom. "You understand that you cannot drink tea anymore, Nina?"

For Russians, tea was like water – natural and necessary. It was a good source of low cost nutrition and its vitamins and minerals were an important supplement to the Russian diet. But it was more than just a healthy drink. It was warmth, comfort, hospitality, centuries-old tradition. Traditional Russia just wouldn't be Russia without the tea. Take *War and Peace*: Natasha, Nicholas, Countess Mary and crew taking their assigned seats in the drawing room for a formal tea, philosophical conversations over a pot of tea lasting late into the night, soldiers' breakfasts of tea and biscuits, hot tea served to guests arriving by sleigh through the biting cold, family-heirloom samovars merrily whistling that tea is to be served.

"Why can't I drink tea?" Nina asked.

"The Lord revealed to Joseph Smith that hot drinks are bad for the body, and this includes tea. You may, however, drink herbal and fruit teas," Quamme answered.

"Oh, I like herbal and fruit teas best anyways," Nina said with a healthy nod. When neither Quamme nor I said anything more she sat up straight and put her hands on her knees. "Are we done then boys?" she asked with a mischievous smile.

"Yes, that's it for today," said Quamme.

"Good, because I have something for you," she said as she got up to go into the kitchen.

"Nina, I told you that you don't need to feed us," Quamme protested.

"Nonsense! You poor boys go around all day, eating nothing but dry cold food. Sandwiches and food on the street. You have no mothers to cook for you. What did you eat for lunch today?"

"Pelmenni," Quamme said.

"Bought frozen in a store, no doubt. That's not pelmenni. Next time I will make you real pelmenni," she said as she disappeared into the kitchen.

A few minutes later she came back out carrying two steaming bowls of cabbage soup. She set one in front of me and one in front of Quamme. A big dollop of sour cream and freshly chopped green onions floated on the buttery surface. While we ate the soup Nina shuffled between the kitchen and the dining room. She brought in two pastries filled with fish and onions, and two big glasses of homemade cherry compote.

"Eat, eat," she insisted when we lifted our eyes to look at her. She sat down and watched us with obvious gratification, her hands clasped together in her lap, her head slightly cocked, her mouth smiling broadly, her eyes glazed with pleasure.

"Nina, you did not have to do this. This is too much. It tastes wonderful, though," said Quamme.

"Yes, this is very delicious. Thank you so very much," I added.

"Eat, eat, boys," she said, her smile growing even wider with our thanks and praise.

We ate silently for a while, and then Nina went to the kitchen to prepare the second course. Tender chicken braised in apricot preserves and a tomato sauce, and potatoes and garlic fried in olive oil. While she was in the kitchen preparing this, Quamme put his uneaten pastry into his bag, and motioned for me to do the same. "It's got fish in it," he whispered in English.

Nina didn't seem to notice that our pastries had quickly disappeared. Having served us the second course she sat down to watch us again, beaming and glowing with pleasure. I honestly don't know if I have ever seen a woman look happier. When we had finished the second course, she brought out a big samovar of tea, and a plate of cookies and hard candy. "Don't worry, this is herbal tea," she assured us with that same mischievous smile. We trusted her and drank up.

A few days later, we began the fifth discussion with Nina by stressing the evils of selfishness and the need to serve others. We then explained fasting to her as a way to demonstrate control over our physical bodies and make us more like our Heavenly Father. We described how the first Sunday of every month all the members fast together and donate money to the bishop to help those in need. Finally we explained tithing as a way to develop unselfishness and support the work of the Lord and the Church. Quamme made the invitation:

"Nina, will you live the law of tithing when you are baptized by contributing one-tenth of your income to the Church?"

"Of course," Nina said, and smiled her signature mischievous smile as she headed off to the kitchen.

Just like the first time, I was a little surprised that we had not talked more about doctrine. I still had not had the chance to use my big set of Scriptures that I'd been lugging around for that critical moment when I would need just the right verse to resolve an investigator's concern.

A couple of days later, we met with Nina for the sixth and final discussion. We explained the mission of the church to her as threefold. First she must perfect herself by living the commandments, studying the scriptures, coming to Church, and on and on until the end – death. Second, she must share the gospel with her friends and family – every member a missionary. Third, she must redeem the dead by doing genealogy and performing baptisms for the dead in LDS temples once she was eligible to do so after a year of worthy membership. Quamme again made the invitation:

"Nina, after your baptism, will you actively take part in fulfilling the mission of the Church to perfect the Saints, proclaim the gospel, and redeem the dead?"

"Of course," she said simply and was off to the kitchen again.

I was amazed at how easy it had been. Nina had had no concerns, no questions but the one about tea, no reservations, no hesitancy, no second thoughts, no doubts. She had readily made all the commitments, and had unquestioningly accepted everything we taught her as the plain and simple truth. In this respect, she was a perfect example of one of the golden investigators whom I'd dreamed of from my early days as a child in Primary singing *I Hope They Call me on a Mission*.

Only something seemed off. Something about how little interest she had shown in the discussions, and how her eyes had only really come to life when she went to feed us. It made me worried that she wasn't taking this process seriously enough, that she didn't fully comprehend what a big step she was taking, that she didn't realize that her baptismal day would be the most important day of her life. More than likely, though, I told myself, the problem probably simply lay in the fact that I had missed out on the first three discussions, so I never got to witness that transformative moment when the light first came on.

We added another baptism for the upcoming Saturday when Wilson and Smith happened to run into a strong, active member of the Church who had just moved to Novokuibyshevsk from Armenia. Her daughter, Stella, had already read the Book of Mormon and was ready to be baptized. Because she lived in the area assigned to Quamme and me, our companionship got the credit for the baptism on the monthly statistics.

The Saturday morning of the baptism I had trouble concentrating on my studying. I kept drifting into pleasurable daydreams about what it would be like to be part of, to be partly responsible for, a baptism, a changed life, a saved life. And I can't deny that a part of the daydreaming pleasure came from the thought of adding a notch to my sickle, proof that I was a good missionary, that I was achieving my purpose, that I was worthy.

The third paragraph in the *Missionary Guide*: "Your ability to help people become converted depends primarily upon what you are (your attributes) and what you do (your skills). You will need to develop Christlike attributes and effective proselyting skills." Baptisms were treated not only as proof of a missionary's effectiveness, but of his worthiness and obedience as well. A baptizing missionary could get away with a lot and still be considered a good missionary. Baptizing missionaries served in the leadership positions, and everyone knew how many people Elder Jones had baptized last month in Penza. Baptisms were the main standard by which we judged each other, and we did a lot of judging. After all, the number of baptisms a missionary had was presumed to be a direct reflection of who he was (his Christlike attributes) and what he did (his proselyting skills). So even though I knew that this baptism would mainly prove that Quamme was a good missionary, I couldn't help but feel like it would say something good about who I was as well.

We had rented the same banya for their baptism where we had soaked the week before on P-Day. Quamme went into the sauna to get dressed in his all-white baptismal clothing, while Stella and Nina got dressed in the antechamber in the heavy white jumpsuits that the Church provided for them. The rest of us missionaries and the ten or so members who had come to support Stella and Nina then joined them in the antechamber.

We first took photographs of everyone in their white clothes as mementos for Stella and Nina, and as proofs of success for the missionaries to send home in letters. Then we officially began the ceremony by huddling around and listening to an opening prayer by one of the members, a teenage girl. I choked up listening to the plaintive, enthusiastic but slightly off-key voices of the members echo off the banya walls as they sang "Come, come, ye Saints, No toil or labor fear; but with joy, wend your way," in Russian, and I wished that the warm feeling could last forever. Anna, the relief society president, followed the opening hymn with a talk about baptism, emphatically reminding Stella and Nina that their journey had just begun and that they must come to church every Sunday and keep all the commandments. By this time, sweat was pouring down all our faces from the heat of the sauna and all the bodies packed tightly into the small room.

Finally, Nina and Quamme entered the water. Quamme raised his right arm to the square, and Nina grabbed on to his left arm with both hands. "Antonina Dmitrieva Michaelovicha, having been commissioned of Jesus

65

Christ, I baptize you in the name of the Father, the Son, and the Holy Ghost. Amen." With this, he placed his right hand on her back and immersed her completely into the water. As he lifted her from out of the water, I searched her face for signs of a transformation. And Nina's clenched eyes, perturbed brow, and sputtering mouth did transform into a self-satisfied smile as the missionaries and members congratulated her as she exited the pool, the wet jumpsuit pasted clammily to her body. I was relieved to see that she seemed pleased at least.

I had the odd feeling I always got after some beautiful musical performance in church and I would expect applause, but no one, of course, would applaud pursuant to church etiquette and instead there was just the empty sound of silence, muffled coughs, and people moving in their chairs. My first missionary baptism. I had achieved my purpose as a missionary, and it had been nice. A bit anticlimactic perhaps, but really nice.

The fact that I could only describe my first baptism as really nice didn't worry me too much. This had been more Quamme's work than mine. All I had done was read to Nina alternating principles from the discussions in my halting Russian. I hadn't first seen her face transform from a hostile one peering through the doorway crack to the one that had just come up out of the water. I hadn't shared with her my favorite Scriptures that I'd memorized in Seminary. I hadn't pleaded with her in prayer for God to give her an answer to her burning question about whether or not Joseph Smith was a prophet. I had eaten her food, however, and I had made sure to shower her with sincere compliments and gratitude, and I had made sure to smile at her a lot. Maybe I *had* helped. At any rate, she now had the key to the celestial kingdom and I had probably helped give it to her. And that was what being a missionary was all about.

9

The Women of Zion: Behind the Iron Curtain

Woman is God's supreme creation. . . . Of all the creations of the Almighty, there is none more beautiful, none more inspiring than a lovely daughter of God . . . God will hold us accountable if we neglect His daughters. He has given us a great and compelling trust. May we be faithful to that trust. President Gordon B. Hinckley.

We need you to work hard with your companion Elder Quamme and find some men to baptize. President Hatcher's instructions to me in our first interview.

Despite being God's supreme creations, women could not hold the priesthood and were therefore barred from holding most leadership positions within the branch. The Novokuibyshevsk branch had about eighty members, only about twenty of whom attended regularly, and most of these were women. Thus, if the branch was ever going to grow and become self-sufficient, we really did need to find some men to baptize, some men who could be faithful to that great and compelling trust to look after the Almighty Father's daughters.

In the meantime, the priesthood-bearing male missionaries had to run the show. So, the day after Nina's baptism, during our regular Sunday service, I assisted Quamme in giving Nina and Stella the gift of the Holy Ghost, passed the Sacrament, and taught the priesthood lesson to the one male there that held the priesthood – fourteen year old Kostya. Quamme presided as branch president, led the meeting, and played the piano. Wilson and Smith blessed the Sacrament, and Kolya passed it with me. Wilson taught the Sunday School lesson, and Smith gave a talk in sacrament meeting. I liked feeling useful.

Except for the girls too young to have yet married, most of the women in the branch were divorcees or widows. The husbands of the couple of women who were still married were largely indifferent about their wives' involvement, as far as I could tell. Or maybe they were just indifferent about their wives in general, an impression I frequently got. Or maybe they weren't really all that indifferent about their wives' involvement in what was perceived in Russia as a dangerous American cult, but their wives had convinced them to exchange their hostility for a look of indifference on the rare occasions when we met.

I couldn't speak the language well enough yet to carry on a decent conversation with these women, let alone to build any kind of relationship with them. I mainly just observed them. How they faithfully attended every Sunday meeting despite the not-insignificant cost of the bus fare to the meetinghouse and the greater cost of a lost day at work. How they always welcomed me and Quamme with a hot bowl of soup and a warm smile when we came to visit. How they could always manage that smile even in the most difficult of circumstances.

These middle-aged women who had seen more hardship than I would probably see in three lifetimes looked to my twenty-year old companion as their spiritual leader. They enthusiastically embraced the callings that Quamme gave them in the Relief Society and Young Women's organization. They prepared lessons from the *Gospel Principles* book, teaching each other about Brigham Young, Nephi, and the Word of Wisdom. They regularly visited each other's apartments as Visiting Teachers, and they went out of their way to give help to a Sister in need. They brought vegetables from their dachas to elderly Galina who couldn't make it out to her dacha anymore. They cut back their much needed hours at their job in a kiosk so that single mother Lyudmila could work there, too, after she had been fired from her job at the bank. They visited Irina to offer her sympathy without judgment when she and her husband started drinking again. They watched Elena's children when she needed to go into Samara. They donated a few spare rubles to the Fast Offering fund so that Quamme could buy food for those members who needed it more.

They had come to revere the temple endowment and temple marriage as the apogee of earthly life and the culmination of their spiritual journey, and they faithfully paid 10% of their meager incomes to Salt Lake City in tithing and saved the few rubles left over in the hope that they could someday visit the temple in Sweden. They strove to share the gospel with their friends and acquaintances and to bring them to church, and they lovingly fed and fussed over the missionaries whenever they got the opportunity.

These women also made me ache with sadness. Beautiful red-headed soft-eyed Elena with the two young girls would look so pitifully hopeful when Quamme would translate letters for her from the old-men subscribers to mail-order Russian bride services, and she would be embarrassingly adolescent with excitement during the phone calls from these men that we helped her with as interpreters. And then there was the Young Women's Evening in Excellence which Elena had planned.

Elena was the Young Women's President, and she was perfect for the calling. She sweetly, patiently, and lovingly did all she could to make the teenage girls in the branch feel like they were special – like they were daughters of their Heavenly Father. She prepared great lessons, made little handouts for them to take home, invited them over to her apartment, and was like an older sister to them, giving them advice, taking an interest in their lives, spending time with them. Tuesday evening was to be the Evening of Excellence which she had planned for these young women.

I had never been to an Evening of Excellence, but I remembered the excitement in our house as my mother and sisters put on their best Sunday dress, my dad shaved and put on a suit and cologne, and they all went off to the church with twenty other families from the ward. And I saw the photographs afterwards – smiling girls with cheeks flushed from all the attention sitting down to a potluck dinner next to their proud parents, a dignified emcee behind a wooden podium handing out ribbons, medals, and golden certificates to all the girls as the audience applauded. Girls playing the piano, girls singing, girls displaying the quilts they had made.

Elena and the young women had put a lot of work into making cute little invitations to give to their parents and friends, inviting them to come and celebrate with them and share in their accomplishments. They'd given one to me and Quamme as well, since Quamme was the branch president.

Quamme and I arrived a few minutes late to the warm, brightly lit meetinghouse room. Forty chairs were neatly set up in five rows of eight for the audience. The walls had been decorated with framed pictures of Christ and Joseph Smith. Frilly daisy-yellow curtains had been hung over the usually bare windows, protecting the room from the dark and cold of the night outside. In the front of the room was a long table covered by a white linen tablecloth, on which rested fresh flowers and handmade certificates. Behind the table sat Elena and six nervous, embarrassed teenage girls, ranging in age from thirteen to sixteen.

Quamme and I were the only ones there. We sat down in the front row, the other thirty-eight seats accusingly bare. I felt sick inside. I was horrified by the thought that we almost didn't come. Where were these girls' parents? Their grandparents? Their friends? How were they going to feel with no one but us in the audience?

Elena smiled wanly at us, and I wanted to cry. She came over and handed us two copies of the evening's program, and then returned to stand behind the table. She faced the room and began.

"Hello. Welcome to our Evening of Excellence. We'd especially like to welcome President Quamme and his companion Elder Young. We have a very special evening planned tonight. These girls have worked very hard to prepare for this evening, and I am very proud of them. We'll begin first by reciting the Young Women Theme, after which Nastya will give the opening prayer."

The girls all stood up and began reciting from memory: "We are daughters of our Heavenly Father, who loves us, and we love him. We will stand as witnesses of God at all times and in all things, and in all places as we strive to live the Young Women Values, which are . . ." I looked into their eyes, wondering how they were feeling inside. Some looked at the floor with embarrassment, some smiled and looked proudly at Quamme and me, some looked insecurely at each other for reassurance. This mixture of embarrassment, pride, and self-doubt continued throughout the evening as the girls presented their colored pencil drawings of Jesus, sang hymns, played classical music on the piano, read stories they'd written, told of service projects they'd undertaken like babysitting the neighbors' kids for free, and were awarded certificates attesting to their self-worth.

I sat there wishing that I could let these girls, these daughters of God, know how special and inspiring they were to me for living the gospel so valiantly without the support of family and friends. I wished that they could attend one of these evenings back in America, where the Church worked like it's supposed to. I wished that their parents had been baptized and were there to support them. I wished that I could marry Elena so that she didn't have to put her picture in the mail order catalog. I wished so badly to fill those empty chairs.

10

The Remoteness of Goals

Late one evening we arrived back at our apartment after visiting members all night. We removed our winter clothing, put on our slippers, and, just as I was getting ready to grab a glass of milk and some Russian gingerbread cookies called pryaniki and retreat to my mattress to look up the words I'd gathered on my little tablet throughout the day, Quamme told me, in English:

"All right Young, time for companionship inventory and planning out our week."

The *White Bible* required us to take time "at least once a week" for "companionship inventory." Companionship inventory, as the business-like name suggests, was a time for companions to take stock of their relationship and to discuss any shortcomings. I'd been introduced to the practice in the MTC. Some missionaries there had thought the whole idea, from the cheesy name to the formalized discussion, to be a bit ridiculous, and they would make a joke out of inventory sessions by satirizing the model examples of proper companionship inventory found in the *Missionary Guide*:

"Hey Elder Scott, I think it's high time that we had a talk about our *feelings*. I feel, and I mean, I may be wrong now, but I feel like you don't really respect me as a *missionary*. I mean, I feel like all I am to you is eye candy with a nametag."

"I'm very glad that you feel comfortable enough about our relationship to share that with me, Elder Christensen. I really think that we are making good progress with being open in our communication. And I want you to know that I respect you immensely as a missionary, although I must admit that you do make it hard to concentrate on the work sometimes, especially when you wear that gray suit. Rrrrar!"

Our teachers had touted companionship inventory as the key to maintaining a good relationship. The married ones told us that they still conducted weekly companionship inventory with their spouse, noting that if you could learn to get along with someone you might not particularly like but were still required to be with for every single minute of every single day, then married life would be a breeze. I'd liked the idea of learning to get along with companions as preparation for marriage, but I'd never been quite comfortable with the formal, sit-down, talk for fifteen minutes about the relationship, ready, set, go, business. I was never one to joke around about it, but I had never had much to say either, just my usual "I think things are going pretty good, how 'bout you?"

But this time, I was actually really looking forward to having a deep, serious conversation with Quamme about our relationship, and I'd been disappointed when my first week we had skipped the talk.

I had literally spent every second of the previous two weeks within fifteen feet of Quamme. I was getting to know his mannerisms: the way he would force a thin smile and stick his head out bird-like when he would stop someone on the street with "Excuse me, can I share with you a message about God?" and the deflated way his smile evaporated and his head retreated as soon as the person walked on past; the sanctimonious prayer-giving face he made; his confident, hurried, elongated stride; the way he would flabbergast random kids by forming his freakishly long index and middle fingers into a V and then splaying them out until they were almost horizontal; the way he gave out one final giant sigh every night before he went to sleep. But this was Quamme on the silver screen. I knew his character a bit, but there was no real relationship between us to speak of.

I knew Quamme was a good missionary and a great trainer because everyone told me how lucky I was to be with him. He was generally obedient, but he was not obsessed with obedience. He was easy to live with, considerate, flexible, easy-going. He was one of the best Russian speakers in the mission, and he seemed to have a great sense of humor from what I'd observed. So I knew that Quamme must be good for me, and I respected and liked him, but he seemed preoccupied, wrapped up in his own thoughts, remote. I was pretty wrapped up in my own worries and thoughts too, but I couldn't afford to be. I needed to relate to someone.

I was feeling lonely and homesick. Quamme was all I had. And he could only be so much, especially considering my persistence in trying to speak only Russian. Fortunately, companionship inventory was a widely, if not officially, recognized exemption from the rule requiring us to speak only in Russian, and so we would hopefully be speaking in English without any guilt.

I had no idea what Quamme thought of me. Did he like me? Why didn't he ever really talk to me? Was I doing everything I should be? Did he blame me for our lack of success? I wanted to know what Quamme was thinking, how he felt about the work we were doing. To me it felt like we were getting rejected a whole hell of a lot. What did he think? How did he deal with the rejection? How did he deal with the loneliness? How had he dealt with the language frustration when he was a greenie? When did he start understanding what people were talking about? I probably should've just asked him these questions and not waited for a formal companionship inventory session. But I did so partly because I was reserved by nature, but mainly because I feared that the verbalization of these questions would constitute an admission that I was having a tough time of it, which would mean that the Lord wasn't helping me, which would mean that I lacked faith and wasn't worthy of His help, which would basically mean that I wasn't a very good missionary.

I took Quamme's aloofness as a sign that I might be doing something wrong, and I guess more than anything I wanted reassurance that what I was doing was okay, that the work always involved this much rejection and that it wasn't my fault, that you got used to the rejection after a while. I wanted someone to put his hand on my shoulder and tell me that he had been in my shoes, that he knew how tough it was with the new language and culture shock and rigor of missionary work, but that I was doing a good job, and that things would get better. So, when Quamme mentioned companionship inventory, I was happy to put off my milk and pryaniki for the chance to *talk* to someone. I excused myself to use the restroom and while there I tried to think of ways to broach the topics I wanted to talk about. When I came back out, Quamme had two sky-blue sheets on the table.

He handed me one. I read: *The Church of Jesus Christ of Latter-day Saints. Missionary Weekly Planner. Use this side of the form at the beginning of each week to set proselyting goals and activities with your companion. Use the reverse side to record all current families in your teaching pool and proselyting results as they occur. Carry this form with you each day. Include all contacts by you and your companion.*

Quamme reached into the breast pocket of his white shirt and pulled out a well-worn blue sheet which had been folded in quarters. "So, first I like to see how we did on last week's goals before we set new ones."

"Okay," I responded, my enthusiasm slightly waning.

"*New families you plan to add to your teaching pool.* We said Four." Quamme must have been using the royal we because I had said no such thing. He turned to the back side of the sheet where a bunch of names and addresses were written down. "Well, we have a return appointment with Sergei, and, umm, nobody else, so that makes One.

Next up. *Potential converts you plan to have at sacrament meeting.* We wanted Six. Vera and Masha showed up, so that makes Two.

Discussions you plan to have resulting in return teaching appointments or baptism. We were shooting for Twenty 1st Ds and Ten 2nd-6th, we had Twenty-Seven 1st and Three 2nd-6th.

Nonmembers you plan to schedule for a firm baptismal date. Two. We were trying to get Lyudmila and then somebody else to commit to baptism, but no luck, so Zero.

Potential converts you plan to baptize. Two, and we baptized Two, Stella and Nina.

Potential converts you plan to baptize in the next 3 weeks. Four. We'll have to wait and see on this one."

I was concerned that I had not been part of the planning process the week before, and I was even more concerned that we apparently had only met one of our goals for last week. Quamme, however, had read off our failures matter-of-factly, showing no sign of distress. He moved quickly to the next item on the agenda – setting new goals.

"*New families you plan to add to your teaching pool.* How does Four sound?"

"Sure, I guess."

"*Potential converts you plan to have at sacrament meeting.* How about six?"

"Sounds good," I said.

In this way we quickly set our goals, which just happened to be identical to the goals of the week before. The trick, evidently, was to set the goals just above what was reasonable to expect from past experience so that we could exercise faith, but not to set them so high that we would fail miserably and get discouraged. In my experience, once missionaries had figured out what those numbers were, they pretty much stuck to them throughout their mission, making minor variations for circumstances.

Then we turned to the back of the sheet. Quamme had about ten names and addresses written down – investigators from prior weeks and contacts we had made this week. He neatly rewrote all this information onto his new weekly planner, telling me a bit about each investigator as he wrote.

"Tamara's an old babushka that me and Stevens knocked into a couple of weeks back. We gave the first two Ds, but haven't been able to get back in touch with her. Igor's a fifteen-year old kid I met on the street – I gave him the first D and he seemed pretty excited about coming to the meeting, but he never showed. Ivan's the brother who dogged us. Remember him?"

When Quamme was done, he turned back to the front of the sheet which had a weekly planner broken up into thirty-minute time slots. We were supposed to plan out every one of these slots for every day from 6:30 a.m. to 9:30 p.m.

I decided then that these blue sheets would make an excellent record of my mission. Ten years hence I would be able see exactly what I was doing that very day ten years ago in Novokuibyshesk. I would be able to see the progression of each investigator from when he'd first entered my teaching pool as nothing but an address and an annotation ("old happy dude"), to his being blocked out for biweekly meetings for the discussions, to his final baptismal date punctuated by exclamation points. So I bought a two-ring binder and a hole-punch and filed away each blue sheet at the end of the week.

The Remoteness of Goals

These worn blue sheets now help me to summarize an average week: Twenty-one hours a week for language, gospel, and companionship study. Twenty hours street contacting, reciting twenty-five 1st Ds verbatim, yielding maybe four or five addresses, one of which might not be a fake. Twelve hours knocking, teaching three or four Ds, yielding one or two investigators. Ten hours for preparation and consumption of meals. Eight hours for visits to members and branch activities. Seven hours visiting inactive members. Five hours teaching investigators 2nd-6th Ds. Five hours in travel. Four hours doing service at hospitals and orphanages or giving English lessons. Four hours for Sunday meetings. Three hours teaching the new member discussions. Three hours to clean the apartment, do our laundry, shine our shoes, print out photos, buy our groceries, get our hair cut, and take care of other errands. Three hours for recreation – chess, banya, soccer, basketball, Monopoly, and sleeping. One hour for district meeting. One hour writing letters. All this amounted to a grand total of 105 hours of planned, blocked out time each week. Major variations to this schedule were baptisms, zone conferences, and monthly cultural evenings. Off the clock in the morning until 6:30, we sometimes woke up at 5:30 to go outside and exercise by jumping rope or playing soccer with the members. And off the clock in the evening from 9:30 to 10:30, we would write in our journals, snack, study, and read.

My contribution to the weekly planning session that first time was simply to write down whatever Quamme told me to on my blue sheet. This was fine by me. I considered myself to be too new and inexperienced to have any opinion as to how we should spend our time. And besides, as a new missionary and a junior companion, I was more absorbed in my own progress than anything – the work was more Quamme's than ours. My work, as I saw it, was to be obedient, learn the language, testify when I could, and not be too big of a burden on Quamme. Plus, I wanted to get the planning session over with as quickly as possible so that I would have more time to talk to Quamme during companionship inventory.

Having blocked out our 105 hours into planned thirty minute segments, Quamme folded up his new blue sheet and put it in his pocket. I did the same. Then Quamme stood up from his chair, walked over to the wardrobe, and begin to undress by loosening the knot on his tie and slipping it over his head.

"How do you feel about things so far?" he asked with his back to me.

"Good, I guess. I'm starting to understand a little bit more of the language, but still… it's hard," I said, relieved and happy that we were going to finally talk.

"You're doing a fantastic job, though. Another couple of months and you'll be able to get by just fine." He was taking off his shirt now, his back still turned toward me.

"Yeah? You think?" I was already starting to feel better from this little bit of encouragement. "How long did it take you?"

"By about my third month I could get the gist of what people were saying when we were talking about the gospel, and I could say all the gospel stuff I wanted to. Not as well as I wanted to say it. But I could get my thoughts out there. You're never going to feel completely comfortable, though. There's still times when I can't understand what people are talking about, and if I get into non-gospel conversations, it can get pretty rough pretty quick. But you're coming along really well. You'll be fine sooner than most."

"Yeah." A voice inside me had told me many times to just be patient and that I was learning the language more quickly than most, but it felt so good to hear someone else say it.

"Any problems or anything you want to talk about?"

Problems? Problems? I didn't want to have or cause any problems. "No, no problems."

Quamme finished removing his pants. "That's good. Well, that's it for tonight then, I guess. I gotta go see a man about a horse." He turned from the wardrobe and walked into the bathroom, wearing only his garments. It was strange to be living so close to someone that I was aware of every single time he was urinating, but rarely ever of what he was thinking.

I was left unsatisfied, wanting more. My hunger for a good heart-to-heart had only been piqued. I was only slightly less lonely, slightly less insecure about how I was doing, and slightly less worried about the future. This was not the textbook *Missionary Guide* companionship inventory which I had been expecting.

The Remoteness of Goals

I still wanted to know how Quamme felt. About me, about the mission, about our companionship, about our investigators, about the branch, about the Gospel, about President Hatcher, about being away from home for two years, about the struggle to not think about girls, about all the rejection.

I sighed and took out my pocket tablet from behind the *White Bible* in my breast pocket and grabbed Quamme's big red dictionary. Возвеличивание. Exaltation. *Sigh.*

11

Persecutions May Rage

The Church has become one large family scattered across the earth. There are now more than 13 million of us in 176 nations and territories. A marvelous and wonderful thing is coming to pass. The Lord is fulfilling His promise that His gospel shall be as the stone cut out of the mountain without hands which would roll forth and fill the whole earth, as Daniel saw in vision. A great miracle is taking place right before our eyes. . . . This work has reached out to the Baltic nations and on down through Bulgaria and Albania and other areas of that part of the world. It reaches across the vast area of Russia. President Gordon B. Hinckley at the 178th Semiannual General Conference.

Growing up in Idaho, every October and April there was a weekend when we changed our clocks and I was struck by the arbitrariness of time and the seasons changed and I was struck by a sense of timelessness. In October golden aspen leaves fell to the shimmering birth waters where brown trout turned coppery red had returned to spawn, and in April sage buttercup bloomed in meadows where the newborn grasses smelled of melted snow. It was these weekends when we stayed home from church and snuggled under blankets in front of the television to watch General Conference broadcast on the NBC affiliate out of Utah. And every Conference, without fail, the leaders led off with an impressive barrage of statistics: 10,752,986 members in 160 nations, 6,066 Church-owned satellite sites broadcasting this conference in 83 nations whereas in 1982 there were only 300 satellite sites, 242,118 convert baptisms this year, 58,593 missionaries serving in 333 missions throughout the world, temples dedicated in Helsinki, Finland and in Sacramento, California (the 7th in that state and the 123rd in the world), a new conference center that could accommodate over 100,000 people over the four sessions but which was still not big enough to meet the demand – more than 370,000 tickets had been requested. We were flooding the Earth with the Book of Mormon. The truth was sweeping across the globe. We were the stone cut out of the mountain. No unhallowed hand could stop the work from progressing until it had penetrated every clime and sounded in every ear. We were all witnesses to a remarkable latter-day miracle – the Church's rapid growth. We started with just six members in 1830 and look at us now. Millions.

Quamme and I were doing our part to keep the momentum rolling forward, and we continued to signboard over the next couple of weeks. We were having decent success, handing out hundreds of pictures and dozens of Books of Mormon and piling up loads of 1st Ds.

We began to encounter a bit more friction on the street, however, or, as I considered it then, persecution.

"Excuse me sir, can I talk to you about God?" I addressed a passerby.

"I don't want to hear about God, I want to hear about why your Clinton is murdering Serbs," a handsome middle-aged man responded.

My Clinton? Murdering Serbs? "I'm sorry. I don't know what you're talking about."

"Don't play dumb with me you American bastard. You arrogant pricks think you own the world." I still wasn't very good at understanding Russian swearwords, but his anger and aggression made it easy for my imagination to fill in the gaps.

"I don't know anything about that, but I have a message for you about God's plan for us."

"To hell with you and your plan."

"Excuse me, Ma'am, can I talk with you about God?" I moved on to the next passerby.

"Murderers!"

"Excuse me?"

"Murderers! Bombing our Serbian brothers!"

"Can you tell me why America is bombing them?"

"I don't know. Ask your Clinton. Ask Monica Lewinsky."

I felt guilty for having strayed from my message, so I abruptly asked: "What are your beliefs about God?"

"Oh no! Goodbye."

"Wait!"

From what Quamme and I could gather from our conversations on the street, our only source of information since the *White Bible* forbade access to any media, the U.S. had started bombing Serbia. But neither of us knew why other than because our Clinton was the devil and America was the world's bully. I developed a few phrases to deal with the hostility.

"We're not representatives of America, sir, we are representatives of Jesus Christ."

"We are not here to discuss politics, but we have a message for you about the plan of salvation if you would like to listen."

I finally got an illicit clipping from the *Idaho State Journal* that my mom sent which gave me some idea of the rationale for the bombing. I looked up the word *genocide* in the dictionary, determined to try out a new tactic on the street. The next time a man asked me why my Clinton was bombing the Serbs I was ready with an answer:

"To stop the genocide happening there."

"What genocide? There's no genocide. You want to talk about genocide," at this point the man got visibly upset and launched into a lengthy tirade of which I could make out little other than that it involved America's slaughter of the Indians. It ended with: "So, don't preach to me about genocide."

Despite this first angry response I still thought that this tactic held some promise – maybe I could *BRT* with people by talking about politics long enough that they would want to listen to what I had to say about God. But I soon found that I couldn't shake the uneasy feeling that I shouldn't be talking about anything but the gospel. And deep inside I couldn't shake the even uneasier feeling that told me that I actually preferred discussing politics over the gospel, and that calling this strategy an attempt to *BRT* was just a dishonest justification. So I abandoned the approach, which wasn't working well anyways. My language skills were too poor to talk politics and I didn't know enough about the situation, and so I just found myself repeating: "I don't know. I heard that it is genocide."

In response to the increased anti-American sentiment, the local police began to regularly stop by our apartment to make sure that we were all right and to warn us to keep a low profile. Not being familiar with the visa registration requirements I was surprised that they knew where we lived, and I was touched by their apparent concern for us. We contemplated following their advice to remove our nametags, but ultimately decided against it, feeling that it showed a lack of faith.

One morning after signboarding, Quamme and I went to stow the signboard in our meetinghouse. We walked into the inner courtyard of the building containing our meetinghouse, and there, on the outside door, pasted with the same watery paste we had used to paste posters advertising our open house, was a handwritten sign which read, in the elegant English letters of my mom's letters:

Yankee Aggressors, Go Home!!

"Evil Russian Orthodox women," Quamme said, telling me that the sign must have been put up by the women who rented a room just down the hall from our meetinghouse where they sold icons, candles, and religious books for the Russian Orthodox Church. These women were virulently opposed to a foreign religion invading their turf, and they did everything they could to make life miserable for us, hoping, I guess, that we would leave. They went so far as to take to loudly banging pots and pans in the adjacent room for the entire duration of our Sunday services.

"C'mon, let's scrape this off before any of the members see it," Quamme said. "Hopefully it hasn't been here too long."

"Hold on just a second," I said, "let me take a picture."

I pulled out my camera and took my first photo since I'd arrived to the Russia Samara mission. This picture seemed like the perfect way to start my mission scrapbook which I was sure my future wife or I would make one day. The hostility in the sign gave me some pleasure, for the martyr's mentality and persecution complex so prevalent in the Church had shaped my thinking: the more we were persecuted the more it proved we had the truth.

I'd heard this theme many times in all those Aprils and Octobers spent watching General Conference wrapped in my blanket in front of the television. It was the backside to all the rejoicing in the Church's growth. The more success we had, the bigger and stronger that we grew, the harder that the adversary, Satan, would work to stop this growth. Any unfavorable press coverage, any dip in convert baptisms, any "anti-Mormon" rhetoric, it all became proof that the Church was true: we were being singled out for persecution because Satan was desperate to stop the good work.

> We can keep faith, in part, by helping the Church to grow in numbers and also in spirituality. We can count our growing membership. We can count the increasing numbers of stakes...

> We can also tell that we are making progress by the attention we get from the adversary. Do not falter nor be distressed when others misrepresent us, sometimes deliberately and sometimes in ignorance. This has been the lot of the Lord's people from the beginning, and it will be no different in our time. . .

> This work, which Satan seeks in vain to tear down, is that which God has placed on earth to lift mankind up! ...

> Persecutions may rage, mobs may combine, armies may assemble, calumny may defame, but the truth of God shall go forth boldly, nobly, and independent... President Spencer W. Kimball in the Church's Sesquicentennial General Conference:

And it wasn't just General Conference talks. Persecution was perhaps the predominate theme running throughout the Church's presentation of its history to me growing up. The Church history films shown in the Legacy Theater on Temple Square spent an astonishing amount of time focusing on this persecution in all its violent and tearjerking detail. It began when fourteen year old Joseph Smith first told other people about his having seen God the Father and Jesus Christ in a grove of trees and grew from there: Joseph was tarred and feathered and ultimately shot by an angry mob, the Saints were driven from their homes in the dead of winter, raped, plundered, massacred, hounded by governors, hunted down by armies, and despised by governments.

And fast-forward to Quamme and I being sworn at in the street and called Yankee aggressors and told to go home.

If persecution did prove truth, then probably only the Jehovah's Witnesses had more truth than us in the Samara region at that time. The Jehovah's Witnesses, along with the Seventh Day Adventists, were our main competitors for souls in that region of Russia. They faced the same disdain and hostility from the Russian Orthodox Church that we did, and they were "persecuted" even more by the registration officials and the bureaucracy than we were.

One of the ways in which we were all being persecuted was by the arguably unfairly targeted enforcement of registration laws. The Russian registration and visa laws mandated missionaries' compliance with a myriad of complex rules and regulations. These rules varied slightly by *region*, the most common administrative subdivision in the Russian Federation, and by *republic*, a nominally autonomous subdivision which was designed to be home to a specific ethnic group and had its own constitution and president.

The Russia Samara mission spanned five regions and three time zones, and included one republic, Tatarstan. The capital city of Tatarstan, Kazan, was a majority Muslim city which refused to register the Church as a religious organization. Because of this the missionaries serving there could not talk to people on the street or knock doors for fear of being caught proselytizing. Elders (the Church did not allow Sisters in Kazan) were still expected to get their thirty Ds a week, however, so they proselytized in taxis, where a fifteen minute ride guaranteed them a D safe from the eyes of the police and registration officials.

When I first got to Russia, there were rumors that the whole mission was about to become like Kazan, and that we wouldn't be able to signboard and knock doors and proselytize anymore. There were also rumors that we were about to get kicked out of the country, ostensibly for registration violations. The problems stemmed from a 1997 law that forbade the registration of dangerous cults and religious organizations that had not been legally recognized in Russia for 15 years. Since most foreign religious organizations were not legally recognized prior to the breakup of the Soviet Union, this law threatened the registration of most Protestant and foreign religious organizations, including the LDS Church. The real harassment and problems, however, came at the regional administrative level, where registration officials had considerable autonomy in the enforcement of this law.

I soon witnessed firsthand the application of this autonomy. One evening Quamme got off the phone and turned to me, his face serious.

"We have to leave for Samara first thing tomorrow morning."

"Why?"

"There's some problem with your registration. You might have to leave the country."

"What?! Why?

"That was Lebedev – he's a member that works for the Church to handle all the registration issues – he said that there's some problem with your registration and that we need to go to Samara and try to fix it or you'll have to leave."

I hadn't even known that I was registered. I knew I had a passport and visa and thought that was enough. I had trouble sleeping that night; I couldn't tell if the thought that I might soon be banished from Russia was more exciting or troubling to me.

The next morning we took the train into Samara and met Lebedev at the mission home. He was the first Russian man I'd met who was active in the Church. He was extremely thin and did not smile. He shook my hand and introduced himself hurriedly but with an earnest warmth, as if to communicate that any other time he'd like nothing more than to sit down and get to know me but that these were serious times and we had serious business to attend to.

Lebedev turned to Quamme and started speaking rapidly. I caught something about taking a taxi and registration, and that Lebedev knew some lady. Lebedev continued to speak to Quamme as we went outside to catch a taxi, and I heard something about Kazan. I wondered if that was where I was headed. I drifted into pleasant daydreams of minarets and Muslim girls and not having to contact on the street, and I tuned out the conversation, of which I could only really understand Quamme's short replies and questions.

After about twenty minutes we stopped in front of an apartment building that had one stairwell with an official looking seal over it and the imposing word registration. I still had no idea what was happening, and thought that I might be getting some stamp to go to Kazan. As we approached the building, Lebedev turned to me, and said, in English: "You must tell that you were in Kazan."

I looked at him quizzically. He blushed, and turned to Quamme and said in a Russian which even I understood: "Tell him that he must tell them that he was in Kazan."

Quamme relayed this to me in English, and I asked Lebedev, in Russian, "Why?"

Lebedev just shook his head and repeated Quamme's English: "You have to tell them that you were in Kazan." We were walking up the stairs now.

We entered the room, where a tired-looking woman sat at a desk, leafing through some papers. We stood and waited deferentially. Is she the one I'm supposed to tell that I was in Kazan? How long was I supposed to have been in Kazan?

I couldn't believe that I was about to lie. I was wearing the nametag. I introduced myself as a representative of the Church. I told people that I was a representative of Jesus Christ Himself. How could I be asked to lie in that capacity? What would the Russians do to me if they found out I was lying? What was a Russian jail like? Did President Hatcher know I was doing this?

After about a minute of ignoring us, the official asked a single question, without even looking up from her papers:

"So, Jacob Young, you were in Kazan, is that correct?"

"Да." Yes. Such a small word. It wasn't even my word – it was Lebedev's. It wasn't even my language. This wasn't even my country. But it was shameful all the same. At least I hadn't had to meet her eyes.

She stamped some paper and handed it to Lebedev, still not looking up.

And that was it. Registration problem averted. I'm not sure if the Kazan story was meant to actually deceive the registration official or if it was just a necessary part of some "agreement" that Lebedev had arranged with a "sympathetic" registration official, bribery being just the cost of doing business in Russia.

On the way back to Novokuibyshevsk with Quamme, I was trying to shake the uneasy feeling:

"I can't believe I was asked to lie as a missionary!" I said in English.

"Yeah, it happens. I had a friend who served his mission in Mongolia a couple of years ago. All his paperwork said that he was an English teacher affiliated with 'Deseret International Charities.' When asked, he couldn't tell people that he was a representative of the Church, he could only say that he was an English teacher for 'Deseret International Charities.'" Quamme answered in English, seeming not to mind the chance to talk for a bit without the frustratingly long pauses and the many "how do you say's" that were unavoidable when we spoke Russian. We weren't proselytizing on what should have been a proselytizing day, so the rules were already partway out the window.

"Really? Well, that at least sounds legal and technically ok. This, though, this was pure fraud," I said.

"That's just the way Russia works. Everyone bribes the bureaucrats. Everyone bribes the cops. I was in a taxi last month, and the cop pulled the driver over for speeding. The driver just pulled out his wallet, handed the cop 100 rubles, and that was it. No ticket. We were on our way. Have you noticed how people won't give you a receipt unless you ask for it?" I nodded even though I hadn't. "Well, they're trying to get out of paying taxes. That's just the way it works here."

"Do you think the Church bribes government officials?"

"I don't know. I've wondered that before. I asked Hatcher that question one time. He just looked at me with that look of his and said: 'The Church obeys the law.' Which law he was talking about, I'm not sure."

There's a well-known concept in Mormonism called the higher law. It dates back to Adam and Eve in the Garden of Eden. God had commanded them not to partake of the fruit of the tree of knowledge of good and evil. However, they had also been previously commanded to multiply and replenish the Earth, and this commandment was considered to be the higher law. Thus, when Eve was deceived by Satan into partaking of the fruit of the tree of knowledge of good and evil and was subsequently banished from the Garden of Eden for her disobedience, Adam was faced with an ethical dilemma similar to mine. If he partook of the fruit so that he could join Eve he would be breaking God's commandment to stay away from that tree. If he did not partake of the fruit, then he could not join Eve and would not be able to multiply and replenish the Earth. Because the commandment to procreate was the higher law, Adam did not sin by partaking of the fruit – he merely transgressed.

The higher law concept also appears early on in the Book of Mormon, in a story that caused some moral perturbation for some of our investigators who actually started to read the book. Nephi, the heroic early protagonist and prophet, was commanded by the Lord to murder a man named Laban in order to obtain some brass plates containing genealogical records. Nephi does not question why the Lord could not have made some other arrangement to obtain the brass plates that did not require him to kill another man. Instead, he obediently takes the sword from a drunken Laban and slices off his head. This murderous act was accorded to him as great obedience and righteousness.

And the Church's concept of the higher law was not just theoretical; it was pressed into service early on in the history of the Church when it was used to justify illegal practices like polygamy, for example.

"So, maybe I was just lying to fulfill the higher law?" I asked Quamme.

"Yeah, that's possible," he said unenthusiastically.

This rationalization didn't feel right to me, either, but at least it was something. And I needed something to try to somehow justify what was happening. I needed to preach the gospel to the Russians and so it was ok to lie to stay in the country; there was genocide and so the U.S. was justified in bombing innocent Serbian civilians.

Later that year the Russian Constitutional Court ruled that the 1997 law forbidding the registration of dangerous cults and new religious organizations did not apply to religious organizations that had been legally recognized prior to 1997, or to any congregations that had a legally recognizable presence in at least three regions. This ruling notwithstanding, registration problems at the local level continued for minority religious organizations like the Church and the Jehovah's Witnesses.

HARVEST

But not in the Samara region. A few months after my lie about being in Kazan, Hatcher arranged to fly Samara's Minister of Religion on an all expenses paid trip to Temple Square in Salt Lake City to demonstrate that the Mormons were a fine people. The Minister of Religion must have been impressed, because the registration problems died down after that. The problems persisted for the Jehovah's Witnesses, however, suggesting that perhaps persecution does correlate with truth, or at least to baptisms, since the Jehovah's Witnesses had by some estimates grown at over twenty times the rate of the LDS Church in Russia since 1990, despite having deployed a much smaller full-time missionary force.

12

Happy are we!

We are all enlisted till the conflict is o'er;
Happy are we! Happy are we!
Soldiers in the army there's a bright crown in store;
We shall win and wear it by and by.
("We Are All Enlisted"; Hymns of the LDS Church no. 250).

We stood in front of Natasha's new steel door. *Our* steel door. Solid, substantial, shiny. I could still smell the burnt welding rods. The honest-day's-work smell of a job well done. Quamme had scrounged up the money from the fast offering fund and made all the necessary arrangements, but I couldn't help feeling like I too had somehow helped to do a good thing. Quamme rapped sharply on the steel with his knuckles. No way that drunk guy is breaking this down, I thought. I imagined Natasha snug and secure behind this steel, and I was happy in a self-satisfied way.

But my happiness dissipated as soon as the door opened. In front of me stood the old drunkard, the man whose face I'd wanted to bash into the stairwell concrete that first night at Natasha's.

He looked at us smugly, victoriously. The gloat of ownership. Of the new steel door, of the apartment, of Natasha.

"Get out of here kids," he said. Quamme or I could have easily taken him, the old weaselly coward. "She doesn't want you here anymore."

"Let us talk to Natasha," Quamme insisted.

"I said get lost," he said and slammed the door.

HARVEST

We kept trying to visit Natasha, and each time I stood before the door half-hoping, half-fearing a violent encounter with the weasel. But the steel door never opened, even though we could hear stealthy footsteps and see the peephole darken. Finally, Natasha opened the door to tell us that she didn't want to see us again. When we asked for an explanation she shook her head: "You boys would not understand." We kept trying, but our knocking tolled hollow.

In this way, Natasha had joined the long list of inactive members. She'd gotten baptized, added her number to the Church's 13 million plus membership rolls, attended a couple of Sunday meetings, and never come back. And she was right. I wouldn't have understood why she let the weasel back in her apartment. And I wouldn't have understood what it was like to become a new member in Russia, to lose old friends.

Most newly baptized members lasted about as long as Natasha. Some branches in the mission hovered at a ten percent activity rate, an abysmal figure which must have been at least partly attributable to the rapidity of the conversion process: we were instructed to commit people to baptism during the 2nd discussion, and people often got baptized within two weeks of meeting the missionaries, not having read more than maybe a chapter in the Book of Mormon, and having attended Church only once. The fact that the baptism usually schismed the family couldn't have helped either: though we would have preferred to baptize complete families, such opportunities were rare.

The reactivation of these inactive members was the only work emphasized nearly as much as baptizing was, so we spent dozens of hours each week going after these lost sheep. I'm surprised at how well I can still recall sitting in their apartments and looking into their faces, searching hopefully for signs that they were feeling the Spirit.

There was Sergei and his wife and two young boys – the only complete family in the branch – all of them thin in their loose clothes and with dark hair and tired eyes. My first time there, Sergei's wife complained for two hours to Quamme about her life while Sergei hung his head in shame. I couldn't understand more than a few words here and there, but Quamme filled me in on some of the details later. Sergei had just sold a pint of his blood to buy vodka. The kids had no school supplies. Her job required her to work twelve hours a day and the pay would be laughable if it weren't the only thing standing between her family and starvation. The next time we came we brought school supplies and gave the kids a haircut with some clippers we'd bought at the local department store. They all hadn't been to church for over a year, but they sometimes came to the picnics and soccer games that Quamme organized.

There was serious Aleksey with the newish furniture and the wavy salt-and-pepper hair. His nonmember wife hated us. He was polite but obviously weary of our visits. He never smiled when we came, but would always let us in and sit down with us to talk for half an hour while his wife made her presence known by rattling dishes in the kitchen. Quamme asked him why he never came to church and he said that he was busy. Quamme asked him if he read the Book of Mormon and he said that he sometimes did. Quamme asked him what had happened to the man who was so excited about the Church last year that everyone had him pegged to become the first native branch president in Novokuibyshevsk and he just shrugged his shoulders and looked down at the floor. He sometimes inquired about some of the members he used to be friends with.

There was Sasha and his old nonmember father, who looked near death. Sasha had gold teeth, charisma, and a salesman's smile. Every time we came he had a story about a vocational course he was going to take or some disease that he or his father had just come down with. He was always about to start coming to church again – he just needed a little bit of money to pay for the course or the medicine. Usually depending on whether Quamme gave him money, Sasha would sometimes come to Church the following Sunday.

There was Galina with her stretched-out exhausted face and her frazzled weak-tea hair falling off in clumps. Her oldest daughter thought we were a cult. Her husband was dead. She was an honest woman who worked long hard days, every day, into provide for her two daughters. Quamme told her that the Lord would provide if she paid tithing and came to Church, but she would just smile wearily, shake her head, and tell us that she would lose her job if she took Sundays off and that she could barely make ends meet even without the tithing to pay.

There were three or four such members for every active one. Most couldn't have cared less about our messages of Lamanites, baptisms for the dead, tithing, or temples. Most simply wanted nothing to do with us. And for those who would talk to us, it wasn't religion they wanted to discuss. They wanted to talk about the cold, about having the heat shut off in their apartment building, about the new expensive treatment that promised to cure them of their alcoholism, about the price of cabbage at the market, about not getting paid at work, or about not having a job at all. It was early 1999, in the midst of a devastating Russian economic crisis, worse than the American Great Depression by many accounts. More than half of Russians were living under the official poverty line (set at a meager $25 a month). Alcohol-related deaths, suicides, murders, drug abuse, and the spread of infectious diseases like AIDS were all on the steep rise. The number of deaths far outstripped the number of births. People were looking to get out.

But what could we do about a failing economy? We had naught but the Spirit to work with, and so we kept visiting these inactive members, trying to help them to feel the Spirit again.

I was still pretty much useless for anything but reciting the discussions verbatim. Quamme flipped on my switch at the beginning and out came my greeting: "Hi, my name is Elder Young. I am from Idaho." Then it was back to hibernation mode until the end of the meeting when I might be flipped back on to give the closing prayer or utter a few sentences of testimony about something that I'd happened to understand in Quamme's lesson.

I couldn't wait to learn the language better and become senior companion so that I could do more talking and convince these people that the Gospel had answers to all their problems and that all it took was faith and a willingness to turn their lives over to the Lord. But, as it turned out, I didn't have to wait until I became senior companion to prove to these inactive members the power of the Lord. This opportunity arose at the end of a visit with one of these inactive members, Irina, when she made a special request of me.

Irina was the former Relief Society President, an intelligent and capable woman. She was married to a nonmember but had a fourteen-year old daughter, Olga, who was still active. Irina and Olga had been very good friends with Elder Kerr, the Novokuibyshevsk branch president from a couple of years back. In the early years, Irina had been the glue that held the branch together. She had given all the lessons in church, visited other members, planned activities, brought investigators to church, and always been the first to bear her testimony at fast and testimony meetings. Recently, however, she had stopped coming to church. She was in danger of losing her job as an accountant, and she was starting to fight with her husband who had just lost his job and was now spending his time on the couch with a bottle of vodka.

On top of all of this, her mother had recently fallen very ill. Irina's response to the stress was like that of many Russians and she started drinking. Quamme and I visited her often. Rather than push hard on her to stop breaking the commandments, Quamme was wise and experienced enough to just simply be there for her and show her that we cared. I, however, had my blind and simple faith that her problems would be resolved if only she stopped drinking and started to come to church again. One evening we were sitting in the living room talking to precocious and highly-strung Olga while Irina was in the kitchen boiling sausages.

"Kerr has not written me for five months. Five months, Quamme! He probably already has had a beautiful wedding in the London temple with some faithful Mormon girl. They probably have an adorable baby missionary boy on the way by now. I don't get it. He promised he would come visit me before he got married."

"I'm sure he'll write, Olya. Life can get busy for returned missionaries. Now, what can we do to help your mom come to church?" Quamme asked.

"No one can help her, Quamme. You shouldn't even try. She just likes the attention. Maybe if you stopped visiting her she would come back to church so that she could get her weekly dose of missionary dotage. Who knows? Who cares? Maybe she just sees my dad there drunk on the couch, remembers the good old days, wants to feel that camaraderie again, so she goes and drinks with him. Who knows? Who cares? All my friends at school keep asking me where I go on Sundays. What should I tell them?"

"Well, maybe you should invite them to come with you," Quamme suggested.

"Quamme, Quamme, Quamme," she shook her head in adorable exasperation with Quamme's naivety. "How little you understand. You don't realize how tough life is for me, do you?"

"Do you pray for help with your situation?"

"No. What good would that do?" This was somewhat shocking to me, to hear a member say such a thing.

Irina came into the room, setting down a plate of pink-orange boiled sausages.

"Why don't you say the prayer, Elder Young?" Quamme turned to me.

I thought for a moment before starting. What I wished for most was that Irina and Olga would have the faith to turn their problems over to the Lord. With that thought in mind I began:

"Our dear Heavenly Father, we are so happy to be here with Olga and Irina," I paused, vaguely anxious as always when praying publicly, particularly when I had to speak in Russian. "We know that Thou wants to help them in this difficult time. Please help Irina to have the faith to stop drinking and to come to Church. Please help Olga to not have pride and to have the faith to see that Thou can help her if she will pray to Thee. In the name of Jesus Christ, Amen."

When I looked up, I faced Olga's vicious glare, "Who are you to tell me I have pride, Young?"

I wasn't prepared for such a response and mumbled an embarrassed "Sorry." I'd learned the word pride that morning during language study and I'd been eager to use it. So much for trying to improvise and say more than my usual lines about faith, prayer, and coming to Church. For the rest of the meeting I played chess with the husband, who claimed to have played with Anatoly Karpov, and who, despite his inebriated state, beat me soundly.

As we stood in the doorway putting on our shoes and coats, Irina asked us if we would give her nonmember mother a priesthood blessing so that she would be healed from her illness. She looked directly into my eyes: "I would like you to give the blessing, Elder Young."

I solemnly signaled my assent by slowly bowing my head.

Happy are we!

"Dear Heavenly Father," I prayed to myself as I closely followed Quamme through the dark on the icy path home, "Please help me to show Irina and Olya that all it takes is faith. Help me to bring comfort to this family. Help me to know Thy will concerning Irina's mother so that I may be an instrument in Thy hands and bless her."

13

Speaking of God, Speaking for God

I am called of God. My authority is above that of kings of the earth. By revelation I have been selected as a personal representative of the Lord Jesus Christ. He is my master and He has chosen me to represent Him—to stand in His place, to say and do what He Himself would say and do if He personally were ministering to the very people to whom He has sent me. My voice is His voice, and my acts are His acts; my doctrine is His doctrine. My Commission is to do what He wants done; to say what He wants said; to be a living modern witness in word and in deed of the divinity of His great and marvelous Latter-day work. How great is my calling! ("My Missionary Commission" by Elder Bruce R. McConkie, often recited in unison by missionaries at the start of weekly meetings).

Quamme had set up an appointment for the next day to visit Irina's mother, and Irina met us at her mother's apartment, introduced us to her, and then slipped out the door, leaving us alone with the tiny old woman. She lay on the bed, wheezing shallowly. Her face was ashen and her eyes distant. She seemed oblivious to our presence.

I knew it was wrong to do so, because one is not supposed to test or poll the Lord, but I could not help but view a priesthood blessing as the ultimate measuring stick for my faith, worthiness, and spirituality as a missionary.

I had received the Aaronic priesthood when I was ordained a deacon at age twelve, along with the hushed reminder that I was receiving the power to act and speak in God's name. I knew then that I was being given an awesome power, and I tried hard to grasp its full might and significance. Its pedigree was impressive. It originated in Exodus, when God ordained Aaron the Levite and his sons to be priests for the Lord and decreed that only those priests could perform holy ordinances such as daily sacrifices and grain offerings. Its highpoint, at least in my mind, came when John the Baptist used this power to baptize Jesus Christ. This power was soon taken from the Earth during the Great Apostasy, however, and was not restored until 1829 when John the Baptist laid his hands upon the heads of Joseph Smith and Oliver Cowdery in the woods near the Susquehannah river and uttered these words: "Upon you my fellow servants, in the name of Messiah, I confer the Priesthood of Aaron, which holds the keys of the ministering of angels, and of the gospel of repentance, and of baptism by immersion for the remission of sins."

The lofty language about the ministering of angels notwithstanding, in practice the Aaronic priesthood simply enabled me to become an administrative agent of the Church: As a twelve-year old deacon, I passed the sacrament in my white shirt and tie and collected fast offerings by going door-to-door to members' homes. At fourteen, I was adjudged worthy to receive my automatic promotion to the office of teacher, and I visited members' homes as the junior home teaching partner and prepared the sacrament by filling the small plastic cups with water. At sixteen, I became a priest and could bless the sacrament, baptize, and ordain others to the Aaronic Priesthood.

Despite the rather routine nature of these ordinances, I always had a feeling of reverent importance when performing them. At the same time, though, I eagerly anticipated the day when I would be given the higher priesthood, the one with the power to perform miracles – the Melchizedek Priesthood.

Ever since 1978, when the ban on giving the priesthood to men with any visible or otherwise ascertainable African ancestry was lifted, the Melchizedek Priesthood has been given to all worthy adult males who have been members for at least a year. And so, upon turning eighteen, I was given the Melchizedek Priesthood following a searching interview regarding my worthiness. I now held the same power by which the Prophet led the Church, received revelation, and had been inspired to call me on a mission to Samara. I held the same power by which the Holy Ghost was conferred on new members, the same power by which sacred binding ordinances were performed in the temple, the same exclusive power to act in God's name which distinguished this Church from all others.

Unlike the Aaronic Priesthood ordinances, few of the ordinances performed by Melchizedek Priesthood holders are formulaic in nature. Many involve what is known as "giving a priesthood blessing," in which the giver speaks as an inspired conduit to pronounce God's blessing on the recipient. These blessings are frequently used to heal the sick or dying, and when blessings are given for this purpose the recipient is first anointed with consecrated olive oil.

I remembered the warm feeling of lying next to our fireplace while my mom read to me faith-promoting stories about priesthood blessings from books like *Shining Moments*. In one story a Mormon pioneer family crossing the plains was in desperate straits – winter's cold breath was breathing down their necks, they were miles behind the rest of the wagon train, and the sole ox pulling their covered wagon had just collapsed from sickness. But after the man of the family anointed the ox with oil and gave him a blessing, the ox miraculously arose and proceeded to pull the wagon with remarkably renewed vigor. In another story, a non-LDS doctor told the grief-stricken LDS family that there was no cure for their young daughter's illness and that she had but weeks to live. But two weeks later, the dumbfounded doctor could only shake his head in disbelief when the girl returned after a priesthood blessing and there was not a single trace of the illness in the vivacious girl. The underlying implication of all these stories was that the greater the faith and worthiness of the priesthood holder, the more likely that he would be inspired to truly speak in the Lord's name when pronouncing the priesthood blessing. It followed, then, that the greater his faith and worthiness, the greater the chance that the blessing would be efficacious.

A portion of one of the talks which I had heard repeated as a young man succinctly illustrated the principle of priesthood power being a function of obedience, and it also spoke to the unlimited power of the priesthood:

> I know of a great man who held his dead son in his arms, and said, "In the name of Jesus Christ and by the power and authority of the

Holy Melchizedek Priesthood, I command you to live." And the dead boy opened up his eyes.

This great brother could not have possibly done that had he been looking at a pornographic piece of material a few nights before or if he had been involved in any other transgression of that kind. The priesthood has to have a pure conduit to operate. (Bishop Vaughn J. Featherstone, May 1975 Ensign)

I had never before given a priesthood blessing, and I was nervous and excited to be the Lord's conduit, to feel how the Lord would speak through me, to speak with His voice, to feel what it was like to be truly inspired. I was glad that I had been trying so hard to keep the commandments; I felt worthy; I felt as pure as I had ever been. I looked at the old woman lying in bed wheezing, and I wondered what God had in store for her.

"Do you have the oil, Young?" Quamme asked me.

I reached into my pocket and pulled out a small gold vial full of consecrated olive oil that I had purchased in the MTC for just such an occasion. I handed the vial to Quamme, and he placed a few drops on the sick woman's head. He then laid his hands on top of her head and said firmly and with quiet authority: "Yekaterina Vyacheslavovicha Preobrazhensky, by the power of the holy Melchizedek priesthood I anoint you with consecrated oil. In the name of Jesus Christ, Amen."

Quamme had apparently just pronounced Yekaterina's name, but for all I knew he had suddenly been blessed with the gift of tongues and started the blessing by prophesying in some unintelligible spiritual language.

It was now my turn to seal the anointing and give a priesthood blessing. So I approached Katya's bed and asked her to state her name again. And again. And again. Finally, Quamme wrote it down for me. Of all the things I'd been worrying about ever since Irina had asked me to give the blessing, not being able to pronounce the woman's name had never crossed my mind.

I remained silent for a few moments, pronouncing her name over and over in my head. I also rehearsed for the nth time the words to the sealing portion of the blessing which I had earlier memorized. I didn't want to have to open my eyes to read anything while I was giving the blessing. I wanted them closed so that I could block out all distractions and concentrate on the whisperings of the Spirit.

I laid my hands, first my right, then my left, on top of her head. Her hair was thin and falling out, and I could feel the hot skin of her scalp and the buttery olive oil mixed with sweat. Her head was so small, and my hands completely engulfed this cradle of life and consciousness. I felt the warm glow of power. Quamme placed his large sweaty hands on top of mine, and their heat and pressure morphed head, hands and olive oil into a feverish fusion of flesh.

"Yekaterina Vyacheslavovicha Preobrazhensky, by the power of the holy Melchizedek priesthood I seal this anointing. Yekaterina, at this time, your Father in Heaven also wishes to give you a blessing," in a trembling voice I reverently spoke the memorized portion of the blessing.

It was now time to speak for the Lord. Maybe He wanted her to be healed. Or maybe He would direct me to simply give her some words of comfort as she approached an imminent death.

I stood there, silent. I wanted this blessing to come from the Lord, and not from myself, so I cleared my mind of all thoughts and sensory impressions until it was a blank slate waiting for the Lord to make his mark.

I continued to stand there meditatively, with an open focus, not directing my mind anywhere, letting my mind's currents flow freely.

Snippets of thoughts drifted through my mind, and I let them float on through.

I hope our hands aren't too heavy for her head.

It's so hot in here.

She smells old, like a rest home.

Still I stood, silent.

A full minute passed. The silence was becoming heavy and sticky.

Finally, a raw impulse, not yet a thought, spurred me to speak.

I have to say something.

Whether that impulse was a divinely inspired leap of faith or simply the pressure of Quamme shifting his weight uneasily and the knowledge that I had to begin giving a blessing at some point, I did not know.

"Katya," I continued, and then I paused again. I had still received no inspiration about what I should say next. So I began speaking, knowing that it was I who had formed the sentence I was about to say next. I hoped, however, that once I began speaking the inspiration would come.

"Your Heavenly Father loves you very much."

I paused.

A thought about giving comfort came into my head, and I felt a slight panic that I did not know the Russian word for comfort.

"God wants you to be happy and to feel good, but He gives us bad things sometimes, so that we can have faith. If you will have faith in God, Katya, this sickness will not have the power to make you feel bad. Pray to God with faith, and he will bless you. I bless you, as well, Katya, that your family will feel God's love in this time. In the name of Jesus Christ, Amen," I finished with relief.

When I lifted my hands off her head, Katya feebly thanked us, and we sat down on her couch. Quamme made small talk while I contemplated what had just happened. Katya could have just as easily arisen from her bed healed as she could have died that very instant for all I knew. I had felt nothing regarding the Lord's plans for her. How could that have been? Why had I spoken in generalities? Why had I hedged? Why had I not felt any inspiration? Was I not worthy?

But I was more worthy than I had ever been, I reminded myself. But still, we had not been doing a full hour of companionship study in the mornings. And I had looked at girls on the street with lust in my heart. But I was trying as hard as I could not to lust, I thought in my defense. But to lust in your heart was to commit adultery. Deep inside I knew I wasn't worthy. It was my fault that the Lord hadn't spoken to Katya. It would be my fault if she wasn't healed. I wished Quamme had given the blessing instead.

We left Katya's stuffy dark apartment and came out into the crisp spring air. The sky was cobalt blue, the snow was starting to melt, buds were appearing on the trees, and it smelled like mittens wet from building a snowman. The Lord works in mysterious ways, I thought; maybe I had said all that He had wanted me to say.

14

Missionary Modeling

It seemed impossible. I was in a new country doing new things. Eating new foods, meeting new people, speaking a new language, trying on a new extroverted personality, and devoting myself to the most important work there was. But it had somehow happened. Life had become a stultifying routine.

Wake up. Shower. Eat breakfast. Study for three and a half hours. Get dressed in the same suit and tie I'd worn the day before. Leave the apartment and signboard until lunch. Eat lunch. Knock doors and follow up on addresses until dinner. Eat dinner. Visit inactive members, active members, and investigators until 9:30. Go home and eat a snack. Write in my journal. Go to bed. Repeat.

Many days I literally said nothing beyond asking people if I could share a message about God with them, and then trying to recite that message. I sometimes felt like that's all I was – an enormous, annoying, ambulatory tape recorder with a huge nametag whose sole function was to walk around asking people to press my play button so that they could hear my recorded message about God and Joseph Smith.

P-Days and the banya were a refreshing break, and the gradual gratifying process of coming to understand and speak Russian kept the stagnation at bay. And I was starting to build little relationships with some of the members, and it was cheering to see them, whether at home or during Sunday meetings. And the baptisms were nice, I supposed.

Missionary Modeling

But still, the unavoidable fact of missionary life meant that we spent most of our time proselytizing: invading people's personal boundaries and tapping all our ways and wiles to get them to listen to our fifteen minute presentation, getting rejected and scorned over and over, and trying hard to think about anything but the rejection, the boredom, girls, and home in the intervening hours of silence between doors or passersby. It was all becoming rather wearisome and lonesome, and I needed something to inspire me and fire me up to keep proselytizing. For this reason, I was looking forward to my first zone conference.

Zone conferences were our monthly reunion with other missionaries and President Hatcher. They were our chance to socialize with someone other than our companions, about something besides our proselytizing goals, and to do it guilt-free in English. To feel intelligent and substantive again. To remind ourselves that, yes, we still had a personality.

Zone conferences were also our chance to visit the big city. To buy Frosted Flakes and eat at McDonalds, and, for the questionably obedient missionaries at least, to visit the only store in the mission with a good selection of American music and buy $2 CDs to send home.

They were our chance to get updates on the legal and political situation. To load up on proselytizing supplies from the office. To sit down one on one with President Hatcher for an interview. To be issued new mission rules to fret about for the following month and sometimes beyond.

Our chance to receive proselytizing training from the President and his Assistants to the President (APs). To fill our spiritual canteens with inspiring stories and testimonies.

Our chance to pick up a month's worth of mail and devour it in one greedy, otherworldly session.

In short, zone conferences were a big deal.

Each month, all the missionaries in the nearby Samara region, about forty or so, traveled to the mission home in Samara. The other missionaries stationed further from Samara gathered on later dates in Togliatti and Saratov, where the President and his APs would meet with them in some unreconstructed Soviet community hall that the zone leader had rented for the occasion, forty homesick kids sharing the latest gossip about their girlfriends and the Utah Jazz underneath scarlet banners with hammers and sickles and pictures of Lenin.

The day before zone conference, Quamme, Wilson, Smith, and I took several buses and four hours to make it to the zone leader's apartment in Samara so that Smith and I could take the test to become Alphas, the first of the three missionary rankings designed to provide an indication of a missionary's mastery of Russian and the craft of proselytizing. Alpha, Beta, and Omega. Being an Alpha was a prerequisite for moving up to the power position of senior companion, but it was certainly no guarantee of advancement. Time in field and number of baptisms also played a big role, as did the inspiration of President Hatcher. Same story with other leadership positions: to be a district leader the Elder usually had to be a Beta, and in order to become a zone leader or AP, the Elder had to have received the little personalized wooden plaque awarded to Omegas.

My hard work and talent for rote memorization paid off, and I became an early Alpha. We stayed to sleep on the floor of the zone leader's apartment, and early the next morning we took the bus to the mission home, piling into the office with our suits wrinkled and dirty, but our faces cleanly scrubbed and shaven.

When the room had filled up with dark suits and conservative dresses (there were about a dozen Sisters in the mission) we commenced zone conference by standing up and passionately reciting the words of Joseph Smith – the creed we had all memorized in the MTC. Forty voices rippling with conviction trumpeted the rousing words, sending chills down my back. I stood more straightly, and I sounded off with enthusiasm and pride:

"The Standard of Truth has been erected; no unhallowed hand can stop the work from progressing; persecutions may rage, mobs may combine, armies may assemble, calumny may defame, but the truth of God will go forth boldly, nobly, and independent, till it has penetrated every continent, visited every clime, swept every country, and sounded in every ear, till the purposes of God shall be accomplished, and the Great Jehovah shall say the work is done."

It was thrilling. I felt like I was back in the MTC again, singing *Called to Serve* with thousands of other missionaries, all of us feverish to embark upon our great work. How I'd missed that Spirit, that esprit de corps.

Missionary Modeling

The zone conference theme this time was centered on a one-page handout given to all the missionaries. On the front side was a top ten list. David Letterman sans humor and with a heavy dose of guilt.

Top Ten Missionary Pitfalls Which Limit Effectiveness

Common errors made by missionaries which hinder effectiveness: These are things that some missionaries have trouble giving up.

1. The habit of ignoring certain mission rules with which they don't agree, as found in the white handbook
2. Not speaking with everyone
3. Not scheduling regular time for "contacting"
4. Visiting the same investigators over and over who are friendly, but don't keep commitments
5. Visiting members to reach a quota of hours or visits, rather than to address specific needs and problems
6. Staying longer than the Spirit
7. Inconsistency in scripture and language study
8. Losing too much time to travel because of poor planning
9. Not having a backup plan
10. Talking about home, excessive letter writing, talking about the things of the world, and the desires of the flesh. Collecting "things".

Do you find anything on this list that is keeping you from that strong commitment and strict obedience necessary in those who follow the Savior?

Yes, I did find things on the list that were keeping me from the strong commitment and strict obedience necessary to follow the Savior. Hatcher and the APs spent a few hours going over each item on the list in detail and I sat feeling guiltier and guiltier as I listened to them. Our companionship had problems with each of these items to some degree. There were some *White Bible* rules we had ignored entirely: We never wore our "missionary uniform in public on preparation day while not engaged in recreational activities," and we didn't "always address [our] companion as Elder." And all the time we spent on buses, and we'd never once tried to speak with anyone about the Gospel. And we never went into member visits with a specific need in mind – we just went to chat it seemed like, and sometimes, if we didn't have any appointments that evening, we'd stay for hours. And we didn't always do a full hour of companionship study. And we traveled inefficiently, from one side of the city to another for a single appointment. And...

But along with the guilt came relief. Here was the key to reducing all that rejection, the recipe for success: Blind obedience. Sure, I'd known the recipe before. But this top ten recipe was great: each ingredient was specifically spelled out, and Hatcher and the APs were providing us with incisive, practical, and detailed step-by-step instructions for putting the whole thing together. It was encouraging to have some concrete things to work on that would make us more effective as missionaries.

Moreover, my guilty conscience was somewhat assuaged when each companionship stood up and read aloud their monthly statistics. The four of us from the Novokuibyshevsk district had had 4 baptisms, had spoken Russian 90% of the time, had taught over 30 Ds each week, had woken up and went to bed on time every single day that month, had left from and returned to the apartment on time every day, and so forth. All of which made us one of the most obedient and highest baptizing districts.

On the back side of the handout with the top ten list was a crude illustration of a model missionary: Dark suit. Shiny polished shoes with a white-square gleam. Short, neat, meticulously combed hair. Square chin. Jaw clenched resolutely. Lips set in a straight, no-nonsense line. Determined eyes looking to the horizon. And carrying a *briefcase*.

Yes, the big change for the month was that missionaries were now expected to carry briefcases instead of handbags.

"The baptizing missionary must look confident and inspire confidence in people. Handbags don't inspire confidence, briefcases do. Handbags make you look like students, briefcases make you look like professional servants of the Lord," Hatcher explained, while the APs, like two male *The Price is Right* models, demonstrated this principle by unveiling their own new, expensive, leather briefcases and opening them to reveal the neatly stacked brochures inside.

President Hatcher, who presided over the roughly one hundred and twenty young missionaries in the Samara mission, was a mix of Hammurabi, Donald Trump, Og Mandino, Stephen Covey, Dr. Phil, and a standard Mormon bishop. Giver and enforcer of rules, promoter, demoter, mid-level manager, life coach, motivational speaker, therapist, surrogate father, spiritual leader, ultimate source of authority.

I knew enough talk to know that the type of mission president you drew made a huge difference in determining the type of mission you would have. Some were angry hard-nosed disciplinarians who liked to conduct surprise raids on their charges, showing up unannounced at missionaries' apartments at all hours of the day or night to see if they were following the rules. Others were softies who let the missionaries watch Disney movies and listen to Enya on P-days. Most, though, like President Hatcher, probably fell somewhere in between and were well-intentioned men who did the best they could at balancing the demands from above for more baptisms and better retention numbers, and the needs from below for emotional and spiritual assistance. Mission presidents were former doctors, dentists, lawyers, businessmen, oilmen, pharmaceutical men, salesmen, any man who'd been relatively successful in life, professionally speaking. They volunteered their time for a few years and relocated their family to the country, although they often did not speak the language.

Hatcher was a self-made millionaire. He had made his money in real estate and sales, and he loved to talk about it, especially relishing the opportunity to recount the story of how he had sold shares in prize breeding bulls to rich lawyers and businessmen, always laughing a deep belly laugh when he got to the part about how he would give these city slickers a framed photograph of the bull for them to hang in their downtown offices. He taught us about the Rule of 72 (a quick way for estimating the doubling time of an investment), and how to use money to make money. He also loved to preach about how money was not an evil thing, but was rather a blessing from the Lord – he frequently taught us that the richer we became later on in life, the more power God would have to do good works through us. One of his favorite phrases, often repeated, was: "I've been rich, and I've been poor. Rich is better."

After Hatcher had waxed eloquent about the advantages of briefcases for a few more minutes, that was it for the handout. After lunch and a short message from Sister Hatcher about the dangers of drinking unpasteurized milk, it was time for testimony meeting. The APs commenced the bearing of testimonies when Elder Gibbons, a short, baby-faced, and rather supercilious AP, stood up and walked the narrow path to the front of the room and began:

"I would be truly remiss if I didn't stand before you and bear my testimony today. As most of you know, I'm going home next week. I've been thinking a lot about my mission over the last few days. As I look back over the last two years I can truly say that they were, without a shadow of a doubt, the best two years of my life. I am so grateful for having had the opportunity to serve the Lord here in Russia."

At this point he began crying. "I know that this work is the Lord's work, that we are here to give this people the knowledge and ordinances they need to return to our Heavenly Father. I have had so many incredible experiences here that there is no way I could ever deny the truth of this Church. I want you young missionaries here to know that it is worth it. Every door you knock. Every street contact you make. Every morning when you get up when all you want to do is sleep in. If you serve the Lord with all your heart, might, mind, and strength I testify to you that He will bless you for this, not just with more baptisms, but with a stronger testimony of the importance of this work."

The tears were coming down hard now. "I know with all my heart, with every fiber of my being, that this Church is true. I know that Joseph Smith was a prophet of God and that he saw God the Father and Jesus Christ with his own eyes. I know that the Book of Mormon is the word of God, and the most correct book on Earth. I know that we have a prophet today who speaks with the Lord, even Gordon B. Hinckley. I know that the power of prayer is real." He took out a handkerchief, wiped his cheeks and eyes, dabbed at his nose, took a deep breath, and composed himself.

"Part of me is afraid to go home. I'm afraid that people won't recognize the new me. I'm afraid that I won't fit in back in the real world. And I don't know if I even want to fit into that world anymore.

But one thing I do know is that I will never be the same, and for that I am eternally grateful to my Father in Heaven.

I love you guys, and I love you, President Hatcher. Thank you for all your examples to me. I will miss you more than you know.

I say these things in the name of Jesus Christ, amen."

Testimonies continued in this vein for over an hour. The atmosphere was emotional and charged. Most missionaries cried. Some talked about struggles which they'd overcome with the Lord's help. Many told stories about their latest baptisms or investigators. Lots talked about the importance of obedience to the mission rules. Everyone said that they *knew* the Church was true.

I was edified, uplifted, inspired, recharged, and motivated by the testimony meeting, but I was one of the few who did not stand up and make the walk to the front to bear my testimony.

15

Obedience

After testimony meeting, each missionary had to interview with President Hatcher. Because there were forty of us, the interview was typically a quick affair unless there was some problem that needed to be discussed.

"Elder Young, good to see you again. How's Novokuibyshevsk treating you?" Hatcher greeted me as I walked into his office, stealing a glance at the big white board with pictures of all the missionaries grouped by location and leadership position.

"Great, it's been wonderful," I said as I took a seat in one of the two chairs at the corner of his wooden desk. It didn't even occur to me to think his question over and then answer it sincerely. It had been an automatic response; everything was always coming up roses in the Russia Samara mission. When I sent in my weekly letters with the big letters describing how well things were going, I would usually include a non-rosy sentence. Something mildly non-rosy, like: "It's really hard, but I'm learning a lot." Something with a touch of honesty that made the rest of the letter more believable. But I knew that it was to my benefit to remain reflexively positive in face-to-face interactions with President Hatcher. Particularly so early on, when Hatcher was still trying to form his impression of me, to decide where to put me on the big white board.

After I had given the opening prayer, Hatcher smiled, congratulated me on getting my Alpha, encouraged me to soon get my Beta, congratulated the companionship on our baptisms, and encouraged us to baptize some more, preferably men next time. He continued the interview by asking me how Elder Quamme was doing, and when I said "great," he affirmed that Quamme was indeed a "real champion." Then he asked:

"How is your worthiness, Elder Young?"

I had undergone countless interviews with priesthood leaders over the years, most of which focused almost exclusively on my worthiness. Searching question after searching question about the details of how I'd lived my life. As I answered President Hatcher – "I am worthy, I'm doing good" – I recalled my first interview as a twelve-year old boy preparing to visit the temple in Logan, Utah to do baptisms for the dead.

I had been singing songs every Sunday in Primary for the preceding eight years about how it was my sacred duty to prepare myself to someday visit the temple, the House of God, a place of love and beauty. I was so excited that the someday had finally arrived, and I could not wait to enter a house of God for the first time and to feel His presence.

Besides the fulfillment of the spiritual dream of being in the Lord's house there was another reason to be excited about passing the interview with the bishop: all my friends were going, which meant a two-hour ride in the bishop's Chevy Suburban to Logan together, followed by dinner in some restaurant, probably JJ North's Grand Buffet where I could gorge myself on chicken wings and tapioca pudding. I rarely made it to the city to eat out, and almost never with friends, so this was heady stuff.

But before any of us could eat chicken wings and feel the Lord's presence we had to pass an interview with the bishop. I sat in the hallway outside the bishop's office with about a dozen other girls and boys waiting for my turn to be interviewed. There were two rooms set up for interviews, one on each side of the hallway. On one side was a classroom with the first counselor in the bishopric, and on the other side was the bishop's office. I was hoping to get called into the room with the first counselor, Brother Rasmussen, since he was less intimidating. He was the father of one of my best friends, and a science and math teacher at our small school.

I was in luck. Brother Rasumussen began by asking me several questions about my faith, and then continued with several questions about my obedience in keeping the Word of Wisdom, paying my tithing, honoring my parents, not taking the Lord's name in vain, listening to good music, etc. I considered myself to be a good enough kid who was trying hard to be loyal to his sacred duty by preparing himself to go to the temple someday and I was proud to be able to truthfully answer every question in the right way. Then Brother Rasmussen's voice changed and he started speaking slowly and carefully:

"Now, Jacob, I am going to ask you some questions about the law of chastity. If you don't understand any of the terms, please let me know."

"Okay" I agreed.

"Are you modest in your dress and actions?"

"Yes," I said readily.

"Have you engaged in sexual intercourse, including oral sex?"

"No," I answered. I was starting to feel hot and sweaty.

"Have you ever engaged in petting or necking?"

I had heard these words before in lessons and talks about chastity, but I was not sure exactly what they meant. I assumed necking meant kissing a girl's neck. I wasn't sure why this was so bad, but I hadn't kissed any necks and so I was glad I could answer, "No."

My voice had trembled just a bit, and I was afraid that he would think I was hiding something.

"Have you ever masturbated?" Brother Rasmussen inquired, looking at me intently.

"Umm…" I mumbled.

Brother Rasmussen read the confusion on my face. "Do you know what masturbation means?"

"No." I was relieved that I didn't have to ask. My curiosity was piqued.

"Masturbation means to arouse yourself sexually, usually by touching your penis."

Absolute mortification. I *had* touched my penis before in a way that made me feel really good, many times actually. There was no doubt about it, I realized, I must have been sexually arousing myself. I had been masturbating.

In a small withered voice I murmured, "Yes."

Obedience

Brother Rasmussen raised his eyebrows, but he quickly regained his equanimity. He informed me gently:

"Jacob, this is something that you must talk to the bishop about. Our interview is over. I'll let the bishop know that you need to talk to him."

What?! No!! What had I done? Was this really something so serious that only the bishop could deal with it? I could feel my heart start to pound rabbit-like, sending a rush of blood thumping up into my head, burning my ears and cheeks, making me dizzy with dread.

I sat there, dazed, until Brother Rasmussen escorted me from the room into the hallway where my friends were sitting on benches, waiting for their turn. I avoided their eyes, and cursed my red face. I sat down at the far edge of a bench, isolated, and waited for the bishop, who was busy interviewing someone else.

I stared at the floor and desperately tried to regain a look of normalcy and nonchalance. I prayed that Brother Rasmussen would wait until all the interviews were over before informing the bishop that I needed to speak with him, so that my friends wouldn't see me go from one room into the other. I had no such luck, however. The bishop soon opened his door, shook my friend John's hand and thanked him for his time. Just as John, who was all smiles, left the bishop's office Brother Rasmussen walked in. Fifteen seconds later, the door opened again, Brother Rasmussen walked out, and the bishop called me inside.

Bishop Kipling was a farmer and the father of a girl in my sixth-grade class. I looked at him across his thick desk, and I felt sick with nervousness. His hooknose, graying hair, and black horn-rimmed glasses gave him a rather austere air.

"Why are you here to talk to me, Jacob?" he asked sternly.

He was going to make me say it! But Brother Rasmussen must have told him. "Because I have a problem with, with," I thought about my friends just outside the door, worried sick that they could hear me, "with masturbat... with touching my penis," I finished quietly, utterly ashamed of myself.

His non-reaction confirmed to me that he must have been told.

"The Lord is pleased that you told us about this. This is a very serious sin, Jacob, and we are here to help you overcome it."

A very serious sin?

Bishop Kipling pulled out a pamphlet from his desk, and turned to the section on sexual purity. He handed it to me, and directed me to read part of it aloud:

"The Lord specifically forbids certain behaviors, including all sexual relations before marriage, petting, sex perversion (such as homosexuality, rape, and incest), masturbation, or preoccupation with sex in thought, speech, or action."

There it was. The proof. That ugly word masturbation leered at me from off the page, right after horrifying words like rape and incest. I couldn't believe that what I had done was wrong. It had felt so good.

Bishop Kipling then pulled out his Book of Mormon and turned to Alma 39:5, and bid me read aloud again:

"Know ye not my son, that these things are an abomination in the sight of the Lord; yea, most abominable of all sins save it be the shedding of innocent blood or denying the Holy Ghost?"

Next to murder?! I was completely stunned, shell-shocked. This was a nightmare.

"Do you look at pornography when you masturbate?" he asked me next, his eyes hard behind his glasses.

"No," I replied truthfully, wishing I could shrink and shrink until I disappeared into the chair.

He seemed slightly surprised, and continued asking me questions. "What do you think about when you masturbate?"

"I don't know, just how good it feels, I guess." Later on I would look at pornography and I would think about sex, but up to this point I had just liked to explore my body and think about how good it felt to touch myself. I had not yet experienced ejaculation.

"What time of day do you usually touch yourself?"

"At night, in bed," I answered, hoping that the interrogation was about over.

Bishop Kipling turned around and reached into his filing cabinet to retrieve a copy of a talk by Apostle Boyd K. Packer entitled "For Young Men Only" and a copy of a talk by Apostle Mark E. Petersen entitled "Steps in

Overcoming Masturbation." We went over Elder Packer's talk first. He likened the body to a factory that produces a life-giving substance. Normally, the factory works slowly and unnoticed, and it has its own automatic release valve in case an oversupply of the substance is produced. However, if a boy fondles himself and tampers with the factory's release valve, then the factory speeds up and the boy will be tempted to release it again and again. All of this was terribly fascinating to me, despite my embarrassment, and I wondered what the automatic release valve was, but I dared not ask.

We then went over Elder Petersen's talk, using it to map out a strategy for me to overcome my masturbation problem. His talk was full of suggestions: never be alone; break off your friendship with others who have the same problem; don't ever mention the problem to anyone so that it won't be in your mind; don't admire yourself in the mirror when you bathe; pray; exercise vigorously; be outgoing and friendly; read Dale Carnegie's book "How to Win Friends and Influence People"; reduce the amount of spices and condiments in your food; wear pajamas that are difficult to open; hold a Book of Mormon firmly in your hand when you go to bed at night; and, in severe cases, tie your hand to the bedpost at night.

In the midst of my mortification and consternation I was starting to feel a bit more optimistic. Apostles of the Lord had specifically addressed this problem and how to overcome it, which meant that it must be fairly common, and that I wasn't alone in suffering from it. And all the suggestions made the struggle to overcome it seem like an adventurous challenge, a test of my manpower and resolve, a rite of passage of sorts.

But then Bishop Kipling dropped the bombshell: "I'm afraid that I can't allow you to attend the temple until you have quit masturbating and have fully repented."

These words hit me like a punch to the groin. I stopped breathing. I felt sick. My stomach knotted and swirled. I was such a sinner! I would be the only one out of all my friends not worthy to go to the temple. My parents would know!! At this thought, I panicked and began to plead with the bishop.

"But my parents will know that I have seriously sinned! Isn't there some way that I can still go to the temple? I didn't realize that it was wrong. I won't do it anymore now that I know. Can't I repent before the temple trip? Please let me go!!"

But the bishop would not budge.

"What will I tell my parents? Do I have to tell them that I have masturbated? Are you going to tell them? Please don't tell them," I begged desperately.

The bishop mercifully agreed not to tell them and told me that I could simply tell them that I was working on some things with the bishop. I used this line on my mom a couple of days later when she asked if I was going, and, to my surprise and great relief, she didn't pry or express any disappointment in me.

I continued to have a few interviews every year with the bishop and his successor up until I left for my mission. Masturbation would always be at the forefront of our discussion. Sometimes I would be proud to report that I had been doing well and that it had been many months since I had last masturbated. More often I would have to tell them that I was struggling. It was always awkward afterwards to run into them at school, church, home teaching, or at the post office, an unavoidably frequent occurrence in my small town. As I shook their hands and looked into their eyes there was uneasiness, and I had to look away. I knew they knew how unclean and unworthy I was – what a hypocrite I was for putting on the white shirt and passing the sacrament on Sundays.

I liked Hatcher's approach. Twice now he had simply asked me if I had any problems with worthiness, without getting into specifics. At the same time, I felt kind of let down, like when you have put a lot of work into making dinner and no one even comments on it – I had worked hard to stay worthy, to not have unclean thoughts, to not masturbate, and he didn't even ask. Even without receiving explicit recognition for my virtuous forbearance, however, I felt good about things. It had been several months since the last time, and I had been doing a lot of praying, scripture reading, and other God-pleasing activities since then, so I felt as worthy as I had ever been. Maybe as worthy as I could ever get.

On the train back to Novokuibyshevsk that evening, I asked Quamme, in Russian now that zone conference was over:

"Think you that we must stop to drink the fresh milk, because maybe it has, umm, how do you say, 'tuberculosis'?"

"Nah, I've been drinking that babushka's milk off and on since I got to Novokuibyshevsk, I figure that if it was contaminated I would have gotten sick by now."

I agreed. I had no health objections to drinking the milk. I had only asked in order to show Quamme that I was concerned about obedience, even though it didn't appear to be an official rule. Then I thought about what did appear to be a newly instituted mission rule, and asked Quamme:

"Will you buy a, how do you say, 'briefcase'?"

He laughed. "No, I've been using a handbag for a year and a half and it's done me fine so far."

I smiled.

16

Lessons in Normal English

Zone conference had revived my flagging vigor and I was anxious to start following the recipe for success with more exactitude. I started waking up fifteen minutes earlier, at 5:45, more of a symbolic gesture towards renewed obedience than anything. And I resolved to start talking to everyone, even on the bus, and to try to not entertain any thoughts about home or girls. It wasn't long after going back down into the trenches of missionary work, however, before I was mucking through the routine and drudgery again, and the model missionary and the top ten list were nothing but a small burr in the back of my mind.

One of the things we started doing that broke up the routine was to give free English lessons. The *White Bible* limited us to four hours of service a week, so on Tuesdays and Thursdays we held two-hour lessons. These lessons quickly became my favorite time of the week. For those few hours I felt like I was a normal person again, and normal had never felt so good. Instead of being the bumbling foreigner spouting a stilted spiel about God and Joseph Smith to drunks and crazies I could just talk in English about normal things with normal people. With people who didn't despise me and look at me as if I was some poor deluded religious freak, some brainwashed cult member. With people who had actually sought *me* out.

Quamme had a penchant for advertisement, so we made a bunch of signs that we pasted on streetlamps and bus stops all over the city: "Free

Lessons in Normal English

English Lessons!! Speak with REAL Americans!! Tuesday and Thursday evenings at 55 Kirova Street, on the second floor. Absolutely Free!!"

All four of us missionaries attended, and we each taught a different ability group. Wilson and Quamme spoke mainly in Russian and taught grammatical principles and vocabulary to the beginners and intermediates. Smith and I each taught an advanced group. Most knew English from the book really well, but had never had the chance to use it, so we just talked with them, helping them work on their accents and book-formalism oddities, just giving them a chance to practice speaking and listening with a "REAL American."

These English lessons were my first independent ventures out from under the shadow of Quamme and I relished the freedom to run the lessons as I pleased without a senior companion controlling everything and dominating the conversation. And since I spoke in English, I wasn't inhibited by the lack of confidence and frustration that came with trying to express myself in Russian. It was a taste of what I imagined it would be like when I was a senior companion who could speak the language.

We had upwards of forty people at each lesson, and I had five or six regulars in my group who spoke English exceptionally well. When I first started giving lessons I came to class with only some general ideas for discussion topics, but the conversation was often halting and awkward so I started to come up with some games to grease the gears of social interaction. Spin the Bottle turned out to be a hit, and so I'd come to class prepared with a coke bottle and slips of paper with questions, some serious, some silly.

One evening, one of the questions required the person to tell the story of their first kiss. As I'd been writing the question earlier that morning, I'd hesitated, thinking that it might be a mistake and could make the conversation a bit too risqué for an Elder, but I'd put it in anyways, thinking that it would be a topic that would get people to speak.

The bottle landed on Nastya, one of the two cute twenty-year old girls who came every week. Both Nastya and her friend Oksana spoke English well but with heavy accents. They looked like sisters with their high Slavic cheekbones, arched eyebrows, and pixie noses.

Nastya read the question aloud and then puckered her lips and shook her head playfully at me. "I do not want to talk about *my* first kiss, Young. I want to hear about *your* first kiss."

I looked around the room nervously to see if any of the other missionaries were listening in, but they were engaged with their groups. Although I was worried about appearing un-missionary-like, I was secretly pleased with the attention and had been half-hoping that something like this would happen. "No, the rules of Spin the Bottle are that *you* have to talk about it," I said.

"Yes, please, Young, tell us about yourself. We do not know anything about you," Oksana chimed in. "We do not even know your first name!"

"Yes, tell us your first name," pled Nastya.

"My first name is Elder," I joked – the standard missionary response to this line of questioning.

"What kind of first name is Elder? Why cannot you tell us your name? Is it some big secret? Big secret spy Young," Nastya teased me.

"No, it's not secret, it is just that we are not supposed to tell people our first names in order to maintain a more spiritual relationship and not get too familiar with people." I felt silly talking about maintaining a spiritual relationship with my English students and I wanted to change the subject.

"We will not tell anybody, will we Nastya?" Nastya shook her head and smiled flirtatiously.

"No, I can't. Sorry."

"And why can't you get too familiar with people?" Oksana asked.

"Can you date the Russian girls?" Nastya asked.

"No, we can't date girls while we are on our mission." I liked this question, expecting that it would lead to some nice sympathy.

"No girls!! How can you live like that? Do you not like sex?" asked Nastya.

"No, I, I mean we, we like sex, but we will have sex when we go home after two years and get married." I was blushing furiously now. The few other people in the group, all older by a generation, seemed to be enjoying this conversation immensely.

"No sex for two years! Have you ever had sex?"

"No, I haven't."

"We can help you with this, Young," said Nastya.

I was embarrassed and flustered. Her naked, challenging eyes and playful smile fanned the hormonal fire I was constantly trying to smother.

"Ok, I think that that is enough of this topic, let's spin the bottle again." I was trembling; the brief exchange had been the most raw excitement I'd had in months.

Of course, the main motive of holding English lessons was to convert those who came. To this end, we announced after every English lesson: "We will be holding a short meeting afterwards so that we can talk about the reason why we are here in Russia, if anyone is interested." This, of course, meant: "If you stick around, we will give you a first D."

One of the people in my group who regularly attended the English lessons, but never the discussion afterwards, was a middle-aged man named Vitaly. Every time I saw Vitaly, the word *patrician* came to my mind. He looked like he belonged in the Senate of Rome wearing a striped tunic and debating the virtues of democracy. He was tall and lean, with curly black hair, a high forehead, an aquiline nose, and a dignified bearing. He moved with an aristocratic grace and spoke flawless English with a beautiful British accent. I loved to talk to Vitaly; he could talk intelligently and articulately about seemingly any subject, and I admired him greatly.

Over the course of a few weeks, I felt like I had built a good "relationship of trust" with him, so one evening after the English lesson I decided to make my move in the hall outside the meetinghouse room.

My heart was pounding against my garments, and drops of cool sweat were trickling from my armpits down to my belted hips. I had by now made thousands of contacts and approaches on the street, but this was different. Vitaly was as close to a friend as I had in Russia, and I didn't want to offend him. This was somebody I really liked and admired, and I wanted to be liked and admired by him in return. Additionally, there was the importance of the moment. This wasn't just a drunk on the street I was approaching. This was clear branch president material – Vitaly was intelligent, moral, responsible, neat – he even looked like a bishop from back home. This could be it. The fulfillment of the mission Hatcher had given me to find priesthood leaders for this branch. If I could just make the right initial approach, handle this with grace and delicacy, speak with the Spirit.

"Hi, Vitaly." So far so good.

"Oh, hello Young. Thank you for class tonight, it was very beneficial."

"Thank you for coming, Vitaly." I said, determined to get right to it before I lost my courage. "Um, you know, my companion and I would love to come talk with you at your apartment some time, if you would like."

He appeared a little surprised, perhaps because I had just invited myself to his apartment, but he quickly recovered and graciously replied: "Yes, that would be delightful."

"When is a good time for you?" I pressed the point.

"Well, I suppose that next Wednesday at five o'clock you could come over."

I proudly told Quamme that we had a meeting for next Wednesday with a man who was great branch president material. Quamme looked skeptical. He had been dedicating the last five months in Novokuibyshevsk to finding a good potential branch president to baptize.

Climbing the stairs to Vitaly's second floor apartment in one of the nicer buildings of Novokuibyshevsk, I was extremely anxious. Stomach-higher-in-the-throat-with-each-step kind of anxious. Securing a meeting with Vitaly was the first truly independent work I'd done as a missionary, and I hoped badly that everything would go well.

Vitaly answered the door and led us into his living room. He wore an olive plaid blazer with a light olive V-neck wool sweater over a black cotton turtleneck. Quamme and I sat down on a plain black upholstered sofa and Vitaly sat across from us in a matching armchair. A Kazak carpet lying on the hardwood floor separated us. I scanned the apartment. Besides the sofa, armchair, and carpet, the room was bare except for some potted plants by the windows and a bookshelf full of books on one wall. The apartment was ascetically clean, and white sheer drapes let in a natural light that perfectly accentuated the wholesome and clean ambience of the apartment.

A container of Nestle Quick Strawberry Milk mix on the windowsill stood out from the furnishings. This impressed me greatly. I had seen this mix during zone conference in Samara in one of the modern supermarkets there, but I had not bought it because it was too expensive. I wondered if he had put that there to impress us. None of the other investigators whose homes we'd been in could have afforded Nestle Quick, nor had their homes been this clean, this comfortable, this light. I liked the spirit here.

After the initial exchange of pleasantries, Vitaly excused himself and went into the single bedroom. He returned with his wife and eight year old daughter, both of whom wore clean, freshly ironed dresses. They greeted us shyly and timidly. His daughter then went back to the bedroom, and his wife to the kitchen, from whence she immediately returned with a platter of food. Big orbs of grapes, sappy slices of peaches, crumbles of aromatic cheese, and pomegranates. Where did he get grapes, peaches, and pomegranates from, I wondered. I hadn't seen them at the market. This was too much, he couldn't afford this, I worried. I hoped that he wouldn't be disappointed with our conversation after all the work he had obviously gone to preparing for our meeting.

His wife gave the tray to Quamme and then returned to the kitchen to retrieve the tea.

"No thank you, we don't drink tea," Quamme refused her hospitality when she came back out with three small cups of tea on a tray with cubes of sugar and cookies.

"You don't drink tea? Because of your religion, I presume?" Vitaly asked in English, with that fine British accent.

"Yes, it's called the Word of Wisdom. We don't drink alcohol, smoke cigarettes, do drugs, or drink tea and coffee," Quamme explained in Russian. It seemed to me only natural to respond to Vitaly in the language which he was speaking so fluently to us. But Quamme emphatically spoke his basic Russian, as if to say: "This isn't a free English lesson anymore. We're here for a different purpose."

"I can perfectly understand the rationale for abstention from alcohol, cigarettes and drugs. I abstain as well from these vices as a matter of principle and good health. But tea mates! What is wrong with tea?" Vitaly asked with a trace of a smile on his lips.

"That's a good question." Quamme nodded. "The first prophet of our Church, Joseph Smith, received a revelation saying that tea is bad for the body," Quamme said, switching reluctantly to English. I was a bit annoyed that Quamme was taking the lead and doing all the speaking again, just like in all our other discussions. This discussion was in English. This was my contact, maybe even my friend. I could lead!

"Yes, I have heard of Joseph Smith," said Vitaly.

"What have you heard?" I jumped in and asked.

"I have heard that he founded the quintessential American religion, complete with an American Bible, American prophets, and, of course, the prototypical American corporate and hierarchical organization." He had just said quintessential and prototypical! He also seemed to know quite a bit about the Church. He would make such a perfect branch president. If only. . . .

"Yes, that is partly true. But it is not an American Bible, it is called the Book of Mormon, and it is another record of Jesus Christ," said Quamme, a bit too defensively for my taste. "In fact, we have a message for you about this book and about Jesus Christ that we would like to share with you."

"No thank you mates," Vitaly said, waving his hand in refusal, as if he'd known that this was going to happen. "I am not interested in any of your dogmatic messages about God." Oh no! No! I was afraid this would happen. I wished I had made it clear that we were coming to talk to him about God. . . . Dogmatic! I'd never heard anyone use that word before. Is that what I was doing? Being dogmatic? I'd never thought of it like that. Vitaly continued: "I am interested in hearing you talk about yourselves, about America, about what it's like for you to live here, about your opinions of the world, about your ideals, about your goals."

Please, please, please Quamme, I thought to myself. Please just do me this one favor. Let's just be gracious and talk to this man in English about America and politics and school for an hour. Please, let's just try and be friends – it's obvious he's not at all interested in religion. Don't offend him. He went to all this work. His daughter dressed up for us. He put Nestle Quick on the windowsill and fed us grapes and pomegranates. Just talk to him. Please!

Quamme looked at me accusatorily, as if to say, "Why didn't you prepare this guy?" He then told Vitaly: "I am sorry, but we are here to share a message with people about God, and if you aren't interested in that message then we'll have to leave."

No!

"Well, go ahead and share your message with me, then," said Vitaly with inscrutable evenness.

"Why don't you start, Elder Young," Quamme told me.

I decided to speak in English, hopeful that this way the evening wouldn't be a complete waste of time for Vitaly and that he'd get some language practice. It was a little strange translating back into English the words I'd memorized only in Russian. Quamme gave all his principles in Russian, presumably since it had been a long time since he had taught a discussion in English. I could kind of understand that, but I was annoyed that he would not even testify in English, despite the fact that Vitaly had not said a word of Russian all evening and clearly spoke English better than Quamme spoke Russian.

Vitaly listened to us with nothing but indifference in his eyes. He asked no questions and didn't try to challenge any of our statements. As soon as the discussion was over, we got up and left. I was too ashamed to look Vitaly in the eye as he escorted us out.

Quamme and I did not speak to each other the rest of the evening. It was the first discussion we'd taught together where there had been tension between us. Different styles. Different ideas about the best way to go about teaching. Competition over who should take the lead. Before the roles had been clear: Quamme, by virtue of his experience and language ability, controlled everything and I spoke whenever and about whatever I was told to.

The silence gave me plenty of time to think. Why had I told Quamme that this guy was good branch president material? Why wouldn't Quamme just talk to him like a regular person and not like a missionary? But, on the other hand, why did I care more about Vitaly's opinion of me than about doing the Lord's work boldly and confidently?

Vitaly stopped coming to English lessons, and I never saw him again. I thought about the old man on my newspaper route to whom I'd tried to give a Book of Mormon when I was ten years old, and it hurt. I wished that I didn't have to try to convert *everyone* I met, and that I could treat some people as just friends. Maybe *I* could learn something from *them*.

17

Touched by an Ache

It was the end of April. I had been on my mission for a month and a half. The weather was schizophrenic. Some days the sky sank to the ground in depression and became the grey heavy air we breathed. Arctic winds whipped across the steppe, the dirty slush and oily water froze into ugly grey-brown ice, and winter's dead-blue hand tightened its grip on the city. And then some days the sky lifted, the sun shone brightly, the air stood still and fresh, and the warm lazy days of backyard barbecues and chlorinated swimming pools seemed right around the corner (but a continent away).

On those spring days, women shed their long fur coats to reveal their tight black miniskirts, transparent gossamer blouses, and distressed leather boots. Russian women seemed extremely fashion and image conscious to me, and I was constantly amazed at how so many of them would artfully apply layers of cosmetics and perfumes and array themselves in an elegant buttoned blouse, high-heeled pumps, and faux designer jeans or a nice skirt just for a quick trip to the market.

I might have remained obedient if the parade of sexy nylon legs and flirtatious lashes-lowered glances was all I had to avoid. But it was the buses that got to me. My lower back constantly ached from all the time on my feet, and I savored the longer bus rides as a chance to sit and rest. Apparently I was not alone in wanting simply to sit, because Quamme and I would both grab any open seats we could find, which meant that I frequently found myself sharing a seat with a woman. With a woman's soothing shoulder. With a woman's soft thigh.

The seats were narrow enough that body contact was unavoidable. The casual and unintended touch of a woman's thigh and shoulder made me hurt with pleasure, nostalgia, and loneliness – I felt like burying my head into her lap and crying, it felt so good to be touched. The rest of my body and mind faded away, and those small spots on my leg and upper arm were all that remained: my entire being, nerves, hopes, desires, senses, thoughts, were packed breathlessly into those small points of contact. The warmth alone also invariably caused me to get aroused. Each time the bus hit a bump in the road our legs would rub, and my arousal would become unbearable. I fought to block any sexual thoughts, but I could not block the raw physical response. And it seemed like I could not think of anything but how good it felt to be touched. I wished the bus rides would never end.

The crowded rush hour buses, sardine cans on wheels, were far more dangerous, however. Human flesh crammed into every molecule of available space, until we were all packed so tightly that it was hard to breathe from the crush of people. Just when I was absolutely certain that there was no possible way that one more person could cram in, the bus's doors would open and two tenacious babushkas would push, shove, claw, grunt, and cuss their way onto the bus, the doors gasping mechanically behind them in a herculean effort to close. No one held on to the bars, not even those that could reach them. The bus could abruptly brake and the solid wall of people would stay upright and immovable, a smashed up mass of entangled arms, legs, breasts, pelvises, armpits.

The danger here was obvious. I often found myself thrust up tightly against a woman. When I had my handbag I would swing it from my back to my stomach to create some room. If all I had was a Book of Mormon I would hold it in front of me. If I lacked either, I would try to angle my body to create some free space, but when the bus became too crowded this was impossible and my pelvis sometimes found itself molded to a woman's spongy butt. My eyes found themselves inches away from the pale virgin skin peeking through where her hair parted and fell away, an image which before the mission I wouldn't have found all that alluring, but which I now found irresistibly erotic.

My nose inhaled the damp overripe-fruity smell of her hair and scalp. I could feel her lungs through her back as they expanded and constricted with each breath. I imagined I could feel her blood pulse with mine. I could feel her body's rhythms. I could feel a palpable electrifying sexual energy buzzing excitedly between our bodies, and I wondered if she could feel it, too.

To shield myself from the embarrassment of an erection, I wore only my more restrictive brief-style garment bottoms and tried to remember to carry at least a Book of Mormon everywhere we went. And I would recite the discussions in my head, convert numbers from Base 10 to Base 2, reel off the names of the U.S. Presidents in order, anything to keep my mind occupied. But it didn't always work.

I never felt guilty for these incidences on the buses, though, since I did not actively entertain any sexual thoughts and tried my best to avoid them. But one night, long after we had retired together at 10:30, while Quamme was asleep and I was still lying awake, contemplating with dread how much time was left before I could go home and be normal again, one of the more intense incidences from the bus crept into my mind. I made a bare acknowledgement of its occurrence. But instead of pushing it quickly out of my mind, like I had been doing, I let myself recall the feeling. Slowly, my mind began to recreate the situation in all its sensual detail. The feel of the unknown woman's body, the way she had turned and smiled at me, the way she had seemed to welcome the contact and willingly press herself even harder against me. Once I allowed that to happen, the floodgates burst and I was deluged with cascades of images and sensations from the past few days. The come-hither stares of the starry-blue-eyed girl who hung out on the bench by the stairwell to our apartment. Nastya from the English lessons: "We can help you with that Young." The heat and softness of the woman from the bus. I was lying on my stomach, thrashing around, pretending to myself that I was fighting with the demon of these evil thoughts. In reality, though, I was rolling around so that I could rub myself against the mattress. I continued until I convulsed with the pleasure of an incredibly powerful orgasm.

Immediately after the pleasure had subsided the horror descended. What had I done?! I'm so sorry God, I cried out inside as I clutched at my head. I'm so sorry! Please forgive me! Please!! I couldn't believe that I had been so weak. I couldn't believe that I had worked so hard to stay worthy – for months – only to throw it all away for a cheap thrill. I beat at the sides of my head. Why was I so weak, so sinful? How could I continue to be a missionary?

Then a glimmer of hope: Perhaps it didn't count! After all, I hadn't touched myself. And then a dark flood of despair snuffed out the hope, a false hope, a distinction without a difference. Of course it had counted. I had committed a most serious sin, I had grievously offended God, and I had done it as a missionary.

I started to panic. What was I going to do? I knew that I wasn't worthy enough to be a missionary. I started to plead again desperately to God for forgiveness, but I knew that it was futile. I knew that I had to tell Hatcher in order to receive forgiveness, that this sin was serious enough that I couldn't deal with it on my own.

But what if Hatcher sent me home?! I couldn't take the disgrace. I would rather die. I couldn't tell him, the risk was just too great. But I couldn't stay and serve either. If I hadn't been worthy enough to go to the temple how could I possibly be worthy enough to represent Jesus Christ?

The next few days were filled with episodes of self-loathing masturbation. In the shower, on the toilet, in bed at night. I had convinced myself that since I had already sinned, the damage was done – I was a sinner, and that was all there was to it.

But I could not push the guilt out of my mind. Like Russia's grey winter sky sunk to the ground in depression, this heavy guilt hung all around me, shackling itself to my thoughts, weighing down any lightness of soul, worming its way deep inside me and then sucking everything into its darkness.

As I stared at the pages of my Scriptures in the morning without reading, as I walked up to people on the street without smiling, as I recited the words of the discussions without feeling, as I tried to ignore the fact that I hadn't prayed in days without succeeding, and as I lay in bed without sleeping, I felt so sick and hollow and hypocritical and disgusted with myself that I knew I could not go on serving a mission like that. Finally, I decided that I had to tell President Hatcher at the next zone conference what I had done, even if it meant running the risk of getting sent home. I hated myself for the mess I had gotten myself into.

18

Despair

I had started out drinking the unpasteurized milk simply because it was the milk that Quamme bought for us, and because it tasted better than the sterile boxed milk. But after Sister Hatcher's warning about the risk of tuberculosis associated with this milk, I began to wonder what would happen to me if I got tuberculosis. Then Quamme told me that he had heard through the missionary grapevine that a sister missionary had just been sent home after contracting tuberculosis, and I began to entertain the fantasy of getting sent home sick. And then I found myself drinking lots of milk.

It wasn't a big deal at first – just a little thought that danced seductively through my mind as the cool sweet milk slid past my tongue at the end of a long day of dirty streets and charmless buildings. Something to bring a smile to my lips and a dreaminess to my eyes for a moment. But the thought soon turned into more, a minor addiction maybe. My little helper to make it through the day. A way to avoid facing my fear that I could not make it as a missionary for two years, and that, even if I could, it would only be as a sinful, hypocritical missionary unworthy of the Spirit.

The gossipy consensus around the mission was that, although in our mission the figure was probably only about ten percent, worldwide almost a quarter of all missionaries didn't make it through the full two years but rather ended up coming home early. Some returned because they'd gotten sick from the poor nutrition and substandard living conditions. Some because they'd been physically injured. Some because of an unrepented-for sin they'd lied about in their pre-mission interviews but which they felt the urge to confess once they'd gotten a taste of missionary life. Some because of a sin they'd committed while on the mission, usually a law of chastity violation. Some because they'd sank into a deep, suicidal depression or snapped psychologically.

It was hard to know exactly how many were sent home. It was done quietly, shamefully. Sometimes the only indication came from a comparison of the missionary phone list to see who was missing. But sometimes an AP, a zone leader, or a close friend to the departing missionary would be privy to some inside information, and he might tell a friend, who would tell a friend, until the story made its way into mission culture as a kind of perversely fascinating cautionary tale.

Getting sick was the only plausible scenario in which I could imagine going home. Choosing to go home was out of the question. To do so would be to quit, to admit defeat, to fail. I knew I wouldn't be able to face myself in the mirror if I failed like that; I wouldn't be able to face the Lord on my knees; and I wouldn't be able to face my family and community when I got back. And I was convinced that if I failed in something this big I would be setting myself up for a lifetime of failure – that each successive time life got hard it would be that much easier to walk away again.

Getting shipped home for disobedience was another way out, but the thought of coming home in disgrace was terrifying, and so an act of intentional disobedience was out of the question. I was already sick with worry that I might be sent home when I confessed my masturbation to Hatcher at the next zone conference. In order to maintain my resolve to confess, I was trying to push this thought out of my mind and convince myself that I would not get sent home: All my friends back home did it, I reasoned. I've read that something like 95% of men do it regularly. I can't be the only one to have done it on a mission. I haven't heard of anyone being sent home for this. So, either (1) missionaries get sent home for this and I just don't know about it, (2) missionaries here are just more obedient than me and don't masturbate, (3) they do but don't tell Hatcher, or (4) it's not a sin for which I'd get sent home. The last one had to be right, I decided.

HARVEST

Malingering was the final option – a cop-out ticket home. I knew of a missionary who'd been sent home for a mysterious back pain that must have been geographically induced since it disappeared once she got back to America. But I was too proud to ever feign an illness or injury like. Besides, that would still be a private admission of defeat; it just lacked the public shame. There was a second definition of malingering, however, one used by the military: the intentional infliction of self-injury.

Drinking the fresh milk and entertaining thoughts of "what if" was nearing malingering territory, thus defined. But I never thought of it like that. I was simply living normally, drinking the milk that Quamme drank, the milk that tasted good, and God could intervene if He wanted to. The thought of getting sick was just that: a thought. One that gave me comfort on particularly rough days: Well, maybe I'll get tuberculosis and all this will end and I'll be back in Logan reading a biography of Lenin next to the heater in the student lounge at Utah State. But eating a piece of pig that had been putrefying for days behind the couch was another thing altogether. I was no longer flowing normally through life, buoyed by the occasional thought about how God might intervene and send me home. I was firmly in malingerer territory. I was taking action. I was forcing God to play His hand. I was trying to poison myself.

I didn't know what my chances of getting trichinosis were. I didn't know if it could kill me or cause permanent damage. I didn't care. I just knew that it was a way home – a more honorable way than choosing to go home, or coming home for depression or psychological problems, or being sent home for disobedience

Looking back through the gauze of ten years, it's hard for me to fathom that I was so unhappy, so desperate. I now read my journal in an attempt to understand this despair, but the words in my notebook only scratch the surface. I was still writing in English, and I was still writing with posterity in mind. Even then, amidst all the forced positivity about how well things were going, and buried in the dozens of pages of prosaic retelling of haircuts, plumbing failures, apartment hunting, weather reports, cultural tidbits, culinary curiosities, and perfunctory reports on the status of our proselytizing efforts, there emerges here and there a timid understated comment that triggers the memories of how I really felt.

Despair

There was the homesickness: I missed my family; I missed hearing their voices and seeing their faces. I missed reading a good book; I missed learning; I missed being able to satiate my curiosity with knowledge. I missed my friends; I missed flyfishing; I missed my privacy and solitude; I missed my independence. I missed girls. I missed being touched. I missed music. I felt so isolated from all that I had loved growing up – all that was left were the Church, the Lord, letters, and a remote companion. Apparently for me they were not enough. And I blamed myself for this.

There was the language barrier. I had spent most of my time up to that point feeling helpless and worthless. I could only make a rough guess at what people were saying, and that was only if they were talking about religion. I couldn't say what I wanted to say, how I wanted to say it, so I didn't say anything most of the time. And when I did say something, it was so rudimentary that I was left feeling like a child

There was the feeling of being an alien, an outcast, a pariah, a public nuisance, a thing to be pitied and despised. Not only did I not fit into the new culture I had been plunked down into, with my funny clothes, ever-present twin Quamme, and strict rules of obedience, but I felt like I spent my time antagonizing that culture, trying to convert people out of that culture and into some idea of Mormon culture that was becoming chimerical and laughable the more time I spent in Russia. I tried not to think about how I must appear to others, but the characteristically blunt Russians told me that without my ever asking.

There was the rejection inherent in proselytizing. And it wasn't just the psychological displeasure inherent in being so frequently rejected by others that got to me. I cared deeply for the souls of the Russians. I fancied them my brothers and sisters. It hurt to see them lose their chance at eternal life

More than anything, though, there was the guilt. The guilt from having fallen asleep some mornings when I should have been studying, the guilt from having spoken in English to Quamme, the guilt from having had thoughts about home and thoughts about girls, the guilt from having masturbated, the guilt that came from the awful knowledge that I was screwing up what might be my brothers' and sisters' only chance at salvation because I too weak and sinful and given over to the natural man to ever be worthy to have the Spirit.

HARVEST

Again, through the gauze of years it is hard for me to understand this guilt. Sure, I can pinpoint its sources, I can identify the ways in which it was used by those above us as a tool, I can see its effects, and I can even kind of feel what it felt like when I close my eyes and let myself turn back into that nineteen-year old dejected kid climbing the cold dark stairwell to his cramped, cockroach-infested apartment after a full day of indifference, rejection, slammed doors, anger, condescension, and pity – the kid who had just spent eleven hours trudging from door to door, scrunching up his face into his best missionary look of joy and serenity to show people how happy the Gospel could make a person – the kid who had just spent eleven hours squashing his stomach's fear of speaking to strangers and straining to inflect each stumbling foreign word with sincerity, quiet conviction, and a comprehensible Russian accent – the kid whose sole driving thought, from waking before dawn and dressing in a white shirt and tie to sit at the table and work through his Russian Book of Mormon to wearily slumping on a cold seat on the last bus home at night, was how to best serve the Lord and please Him – the kid who removed his raincoat, boots, hat, and suit coat, laid down between his hunter green sheets, pulled the top sheet over his head, fought back the tears, and blamed himself for their lack of success that day because he knew inside that he was not obedient.

It was ironic. To non-missionaries like the members we were spiritual giants, obedience incarnate, sterling examples of righteousness and dedication to the Lord. We had forsaken college, families, jobs, girlfriends, country, everything, in order to serve the Lord, without receiving any earthly reward in return – no financial remuneration, no educational assistance, nothing. In fact, we paid for the privilege to the tune of almost $400 a month. To ourselves, however, we were simply and eternally inadequate. No baptisms that month and the branch members were going inactive? It certainly wasn't the Prophet's fault. Not the Apostles'. Not the General Authorities' who came to visit the mission and promised us in the name of Jesus Christ that if we would talk to twenty more people a day then the number of baptisms would double. Not the Mission President's. Certainly not the Message's nor the Spirit's. No, it was the missionaries who could not follow the simple rules laid out in the *White Bible*, it was the missionaries who thought about home too much, it was the missionaries who bought CDs and had not cast off the things of the world, it was the missionaries who stayed longer than the Spirit, it was the missionaries who failed to have the Spirit with them strongly enough for people to feel Its presence. After all, the formula was simple: The Church is true; the Spirit will witness this truth to people; missionaries will have the Spirit according to their faith and obedience.

So, I guess that the part of this guilt that is the hardest for me to now understand is why I could not recognize it for what it was, why it had such power over me. For it was only some time after this guilt had passed that I could diagnose its destructiveness. And then only after some change had occurred that made the guilt lose some of its power.

That change began, slowly, for me, I believe, when the last of the bloody juices of the pig meat had slithered down my throat, leaving my mouth dusty and coppery. As I sat on the hard wooden bench of that orange couch and turned my thoughts deeply inward, there arose up a vague realization of the absurdity of what I had just done, a dim understanding that the universe was a silent, cold, clocklike place, that fate was blind and indifferent, that the *Trichinella* roundworm was either in the pig or it wasn't, that I was either worthy or I wasn't, that I would either get sent home for masturbation or I wouldn't, that no one could change these things, that there was no *reason* for anyone to change these things.

In the aftermath of this vague realization, my despair, instead of continually resonating as guilty despair over my weakness, began, sporadically and almost imperceptibly, to be met by defiance, by a dash of self-confidence, by a streak of independence. I inchoately sensed that freedom, the chance to find significance, to find meaning, lay in that vague realization that all I could do was to go on and discover whether I would get sent home and whether it really mattered, mattered to me.

19

The Good News with the Bad

The nebulous feeling that I had turned some kind of corner propelled me into my second zone conference. I was surprised by how calm and resolute I felt about my upcoming confession to Hatcher. The thought of being one of those whispered-about missionaries who had been mysteriously sent home no longer gnawed at me. I felt like I would do what I had to do to serve a mission the right way or I wouldn't serve at all.

The four of us from the Novokuibyshevsk district made it to the mission office about an hour earlier than anyone else, giving us time to read our mail, which was not sent to our individual residences, but to the main mission office. I grabbed my letters from the big wicker basket by the office door and rushed off to a corner of the room to devour them.

First I read the four letters from my mom. She wrote faithfully every week. She always began by commenting on things I'd written about in my last letters, asking me questions. She'd then give a nice detailed account of happenings in the family and community, and I would be transported back to the world of grandparents and greenhouse tomatoes, a world that seconds before had seemed so far away that I wasn't sure at times if it even existed anymore.

She would usually follow this with some news from around the world that she'd gathered just for me. This tender gesture somehow made me feel closer to her than when she wrote about the more personal stuff. I could just picture her combing the Idaho State Journal for articles that would interest me, knowing how much I liked to stay informed. And the fact that it was sort of against the rules, or at least the hard-line interpretation of them, for me to read the articles she'd send, made me love her even the more for it.

> *The Jazz finally beat Sacramento in a five-game battle. The fourth game Stockton put one in at the last second to give them a one-point win. We got them pretty good at Utah for the fifth game. I even got into it! ☺ I'll send you the article and another one for you to read.*
>
> *The U.S. bombed the China Embassy by mistake about a week ago. That didn't sit too well with China at all. We have enough problems as it is. Yugoslavia says they're willing to put an end to all this and withdraw, we'll see what happens….*
>
> *I've been very interested with the bombing that Moscow has done on Grozny. Do you know about this? I just read that they were going to send ground forces in to the area to stop them trying to break off to independence. I guess there was a war from 1994-96 something like that over the same thing. Is that right?*
>
> …
>
> *I think of you always and when I have any doubts, Heavenly Father is right there to whisper peace to my heart and let me know that He is mindful of you and that I shouldn't fear. What a comfort and blessing that has been to me. Take care and may you be blessed constantly.*

She always closed with her love and testimony and then attached a few spiritual thoughts and stories.

I moved on to the other letters. My dad told me about how it was taking almost a month to get the crop planted as the weather had been cold and rainy, and about how much he loved me and knew that I was doing the Lord's work. My older sister had sent me a note about the status of her wedding plans and a package with some homemade tapes of her favorite classical music, the only kind of music besides Church hymns the mission rules allowed us to listen to. My brother wrote about the Jazz and all the girls he was dating and how proud he was of me. My younger sister wrote about track, school, and driver's education.

I finished up with letters from my friend Dave and my former girlfriend Christy. Dave had written a travelogue from his road trip across

America to pick up a new sodcutter in Illinois, and Christy had written a friendly, but strictly friendly, little letter.

I didn't have a girl waiting for me at home like many of the missionaries, and I told myself that I was glad for it. The way I told myself I saw it, the only way to make it through the mission was to jump in with both feet. Those who had left girls with promises to "see them in white" in two years often left a foot back there, too, and so they straddled both worlds but lived in neither. I'd already seen some bad cases. Smith from our district with his girl waiting for him, wearing his promise ring, writing him every other day, sending him pictures, cookies, cassette tapes, and scented letters. I'd seen the forlornness on his face at district meeting as he pretended to be taking notes in his little black book, although it was obvious to all of us that he was writing his girlfriend. I had seen him give out two boxes of Book of Mormons in two weeks to people on the street just so that he and Wilson would have an excuse to make a supply trip to the mission office in Samara to pick up more books, and, oh, there's the mail there in the wicker basket, might as well grab that.

No, I wanted none of that, or so I told myself as I tried to quash the jealousy that inevitably arose whenever we all opened our mail together and I caught the smell of perfume or homemade cookies and saw the bliss light up the face of the missionary who was so obviously loved. I dealt with the homesickness by compartmentalizing. I tried to think about home only during the time I spent reading letters and the hour on P-Day when I wrote them. As soon as I finished the letters from home, I collated them in a two-ring binder and read them no more.

"Good morning, Elder Young," my old companion from the MTC, Elder Viska, interrupted my reading and snapped me back from a truck stop in Amarillo with Dave. Missionaries were starting to file in.

"Mornin'. How's it goin'?" I replied.

"Good, good. Hey, I heard you got your Alpha last month. Congratulations."

"Oh, thanks," I replied and stuffed my letter from Dave into my handbag. I felt my stomach briefly knot when President Hatcher walked in, knowing that he would decide my fate in a few short hours, but I soon relaxed.

I don't remember the spiritual lesson or the proselytizing training that took up the bulk of the conference. I remember the news. Hatcher gave an update on the situation in the country. Things were coming to a head. The war in Yugoslavia was fueling anti-Americanism. The Russian Orthodox Church wanted us out of Russia. The registration authorities were harassing the Church into paying bogus fines and were trying to strip the Church of its religious status. We might all have to go to Moscow to get new registration. Armed masked men had burst in on a Sacrament meeting in Volgograd and had threatened the members there with violence if they kept attending. Missionaries in Moscow had been arrested for disorderly conduct while signboarding, and as a consequence, signboarding was now a forbidden proselytizing technique. And then the news that hit me the hardest: no more English lessons or we could lose our registration status.

After a lunch of soggy cardboard pizza that the zone leader had picked up from an American-style pizza place, we commenced with the bearing of testimonies. After not having borne mine last time, I was anxious to dispel any idea that I might be one of those missionaries who lacked a testimony and had come on his mission for the wrong reasons – because his parents had promised him a car when he got home or because his girlfriend had made it clear that she would only marry a returned missionary, for example. Nobody had said anything about it last time, although the zone leader had given me the eye when he had approached me and Quamme after conference was over.

"Thank you for your testimony, Elder Quamme. I was really edified by it," he had said as he smiled and shook Quamme's hand.

"Yeah, thanks. I enjoyed yours too," Quamme had replied.

"Elder Young," he'd said simply, nodding his head in acknowledgement and shooting me a meaningful look, as if he and I were in on some secret together.

I'd always thought of myself as possessing a strong testimony. I'd never doubted the fundamental premise that the Church was true. Yes, at times I'd questioned certain doctrines, practices, and historical occurrences of the Church that seemed rather incongruous with what I expected from *The Church* of the God whom I believed in. Yes, at times I was less than spiritually edified at Church and Church activities, bored even. And yes, at times I was less than enthused about following some Church teachings. But the Church was my foundation, my paradigm, my filter through which I viewed and understood life and the world. And there had never been any cracks in my foundation, kinks in my paradigm, holes in my filter, or moments when I was not infused with the thorough awareness and certainty that the world of the Church was the world as it truly was. I knew that the Church was true in the same way that I knew that I existed and that I was not the only one who existed: it simply was; it simply had to be.

No, it wasn't because I didn't have a testimony that I hadn't borne it. Stage fright had played a role. So had the fact that I saw testimony bearing more as a tool to reach outsiders than to preach to a choir of missionaries. Related to this was my feeling that a testimony was more personal than communal, more inner belief than outward display. And then I suppose I simply disliked repeating the few well-worn phrases that every testimony must have – perhaps because, as Goethe once said, I was afraid that "the phrases that men hear or repeat continually end by becoming convictions and ossify the organs of intelligence." I wanted convictions, but not ossifying ones. I wanted them limber, living. To live my convictions must be living.

Still, I knew I had a testimony, and everyone else was bearing theirs, so I felt that I should probably bear mine, too. So as I sat on my hard chair while missionary after missionary came up and bared their soul, I ran through different opening sentences in my mind and the butterflies started to flutter. Finally, when most everyone had borne their testimony and the pauses between bearers were becoming awkward, I stood up and walked to the front.

"I would be most ungrateful if I did not stand before you today and bear my testimony," I began, "and thank my Father in Heaven for his love and patience with me. These last few weeks have been difficult ones for me, and without His support and love, I don't know how I would have made it through them." I was trying to speak from the heart, but my words fell flat and false on my ears. The shining-eyed looks of expectant camaraderie spurred me on, however.

"I've been learning a lot about myself and about the gospel here in Russia. I've learned that I can't do this work without the Lord's help. I've learned that He stands ready and willing to give us that help if we will only ask Him. I've learned that there is no greater joy than to serve God with all your heart, might, mind, and strength." I had wanted to speak from the heart but found myself instead saying the things that I only wished were true. I transitioned into the traditional testimony:

"I know that Joseph Smith was a prophet of God and that the Book of Mormon is the word of God. I know that the Church is true and that we are doing the Lord's work here. I am so grateful for the opportunity to be a part of it. I pray that I will be worthy to be an instrument in the Lord's hands to bring about this mighty work and glory. This I say in the name of Jesus Christ. Amen." As I said these last few sentences I felt the old familiar burn – the heat rising from my chest into my face, making my eyes water and my voice choke. I sat down relieved and happy.

The relief didn't last long, however. My mind quickly shifted from listening to the last remaining professions of conviction to contemplating my upcoming confession to Hatcher and speculating about the consequences.

"Elder Young, come on in," Hatcher said warmly as he shook my hand and led me into his office. "How have you been?"

"Pretty good, things are coming along."

"Great! I appreciated your testimony today."

"Oh, thanks," I said, thinking again how I should have borne it at the first zone conference.

I said the opening prayer and then Hatcher began: "Well, let's get right to it. I have some news for you."

I leaned forward in my chair. Did he already discern what I'd done?

"I'm making Elder Quamme my assistant, which means that in a couple of weeks you'll be getting a new companion, Elder Enders. He's another Idaho boy and a real champion. I expect that you two will work really well together and accomplish great things."

"Ok," I said simply. I was not too surprised – transfers usually took place every couple of months. But still, the thought of Quamme leaving had never crossed my mind. We had finally started to develop a friendship, and things were comfortable – we knew each other's quirks and we weren't annoyed by them. I wasn't looking forward to the adjustment period again. I hoped my new companion and I would like each other. There was nowhere to escape if we didn't.

"How is the work going?" Hatcher asked abruptly.

"Well, we didn't have any baptisms last month, and some of the investigators that I thought were golden kind of fell away. And there are so many inactive members. We visit them all the time, but they just don't really seem to be all that interested in the Church anymore. But things are going well. We're working hard, and we have some promising investigators." I led with the bad and finished with the good.

"That's good. Keep up the hard work. The Lord really wants some priesthood leaders for the Novokuibyshevsk branch." He nodded his head.

"Yeah, I know." I nodded in agreement.

"I don't think I received a letter from you the past two weeks, Elder Young. Is there something wrong?" He looked at me with what seemed like genuine concern in his eyes.

"Well, actually there is something that I need to talk to you about, but I needed to do it in person, so I didn't send a letter." Having begun, knowing there was no turning back, all my prior calm fled, my heart raced, my stomach jumped, and my palms tingled.

"I see," he said and nodded his head understandingly. "In the future, though, make sure that you write me a letter each week, even if it is just to tell me that you need to talk to me. I read each one of my missionary's letters carefully, and I get worried when a missionary skips a week."

"Ok. I'm sorry," I said, growing more nervous. This was not a good start.

"It's not a problem. Now what did you need to talk to me about?"

I leaned back in my seat. Folded and unfolded my arms. Leaned on the left armrest, and put my right hand in my pocket. Reversed the position. The wave of shame had hit me, and I wanted to look down at the floor, but I forced myself to stare right into his piercing, slightly bulged eyes.

"I'm so sorry," I blubbered, bursting into tears and hanging my head, staring at the industrial blue carpet. "I'm so sorry. I've been trying so hard to be good, but I messed up bad."

Hatcher handed me some tissue from his desk. "Can you tell me what happened, Elder Young?"

I looked up at him. He gave me an uncomfortable smile.

"Yes." I hung my head again. "I masturbated."

I was so disgusted with myself. I was such a freak. I may as well have wailed to this spiritual, wise, grandfatherly man: "I can't help myself – I drink my own urine."

Hatcher, however, did not seem disgusted or even disturbed. He seemed relieved. "Have you quit?"

"Yes."

"That's good. The devil is working on you overtime, Elder Young. He knows that you are one of the valiant spirits. He is afraid of the good that you can do, and he is throwing everything he can at you to try to weaken you. You know what you need to do to stay strong. Are you doing a full hour of gospel study?"

"Yes. Most of the time anyways."

"That's good. Keep at it, and remember that prayer is power, Elder Young. I encourage you to develop your relationship with your Heavenly Father so that when you have these urges you are able to turn to him, unashamed, for help."

"Thanks," I said, still sniffling. "I'll try to do that. It just seems like I'll never be able to stop this."

"See? That right there is stinkin' thinkin' and you need a checkup from the neck up. Of course you can stop. With God all things are possible."

I laughed with relief. "Yeah, you're right."

"Good. Anything else you need to talk to me about?"

"No, that's it I guess."

"You're a real champion, Elder Young. The Lord is really pleased that you are trying so hard to do the right thing."

"Thank you, President Hatcher. That means a lot," I said. And it did mean a lot.

"Keep up the good work," he said. "Are you going to be a Beta next time I see you?"

"Yeah, I plan on it."

"Good. Because a failure to plan is a plan to fail."

"Heh. I like that."

I walked out of the room lightheaded with euphoria. That sky parting, sun bursting, birds into song breaking, and butterflies a flitting kind of feeling. I wasn't going to get sent home! I wasn't going to have to live with that shame. I wasn't even that terrible of a sinner, that wicked, judging by President Hatcher's mild reaction to my confession. I was still a champion. It had been such a contrast to other priesthood interviews where I'd left feeling like sinful scum. At that moment, I was so relieved and impressed with President Hatcher and his graciousness that I would have goose-stepped through a brick wall for the man had he but asked.

20

Less Grave New World

Maybe Hatcher mentioned to Quamme that I was having a tough time of it. Maybe I had started to relax after having committed the worst sin I could have imagined possibly committing yet surviving to proselytize another day. Maybe Quamme had started to relax after having climbed all the way to the top of the leadership ladder when he received the call to be AP. Maybe Quamme had picked up on my loneliness, or maybe he was getting lonely, too. Or maybe it had something to do with the fact that now that we knew we would only be spending another couple of weeks together we realized that we actually kind of liked each other. Whatever the reason, we started speaking English more and more frequently. And with English came something that resembled friendship.

One late afternoon we had just knocked out another complete apartment building without giving a single discussion. Our feet and backs ached, and we had no appointments that evening, so all we had to look forward to was four more hours of knocking. Instead of our moving on to the next apartment building, however, I followed Quamme into a small grocery store.

Quamme asked the lady behind the counter for two Samarski Desserts and two Cokes, and after he paid for them, we walked outside and sat on a bench. He handed me a Samarski Dessert, and I opened up the yogurt-like container to find a rich chocolate pudding. As we dipped our fingers into the pudding and then licked them clean, Quamme started to tell me a story in English about the time when he was a greenie in Novokuibyshevsk over a year ago and he and his companion were having a miserable time of it. No investigators, no appointments, no members but the usual stalwarts coming to the meeting, and no money – they had already spent most of their monthly stipend and were living off cheap bread and grechka. One day, after knocking in this same area, his senior companion had snapped. He came to this very store, spent the last of their money on two Samarski Desserts, laughed maniacally, and told Quamme that they were done for the day and that they were going home to eat their pudding.

I was hoping that Quamme would also call off work for the day, but he just leaned back, licked his long fingers, and said:

"You know, sometimes I wish I was back cruising the streets of Idaho Falls with my friends in my El Camino."

"You had an El Camino?!" I asked, stunned. How was it possible that I had spent every second of the past two months with this guy and had not known that we shared this peculiarity? "Seriously?! No way! Me too! I loved that car! What color was yours?"

After that we started talking in English more and more. As we sat waiting for the bus we talked about marriage and what qualities we would look for in a wife when we got home. I told him about competing in quiz bowl competitions in high school, and so, walking between appointments we started quizzing each other on language and gospel trivia. I told him about working on a sod farm, and we spent our lunch hours plotting out how we would start our own when we got back home. We bought toy guns that shot little plastic pellets and used them to play a game in the evenings after work that we called Pain. We placed the lid from a plastic Coke bottle in the middle of the floor and took turns shooting at it – the one who hit it the least number of times had to "walk the plank," or remove his shirt and stand up against the wall and get shot and take the pain. When our backs got tired of getting stung, we turned to target practice. We hung up our signboarding pictures on the wall and delighted in the sacrilege of shooting Adam in the face.

This all helped with the loneliness and drudgery. Even the proselytizing seemed to take on a lighter air. But part of me was still looking forward to a companion change, though, mainly because I was looking for some reassurance that we were doing the right thing.

Alienated and peculiar, I think most missionaries needed the occasional reassurance that we were doing the right thing by being there, that we weren't the brainwashed agents of a kooky religious imperialism that so many viewed us to be. I think the need was particularly strong for those of us serving in places like Russia. In certain Latin American missions, for example, cultural attitudes and behaviors and conceptions of politeness generally caused people to act more deferentially and sympathetically to the missionaries, or to be what missionaries called more "humble." Russians were not particularly "humble." They had grown up proud Soviets, cold warriors for a superpower, and the fall from going toe-to-toe with America for world domination to toeing the World Bank's line at America's insistence was painful. They took our presence there as an insult, like America was rubbing salt in their wounds by sending them missionaries now, like they were some third world colonial backwater full of primitives who needed to be converted to Christianity. And Russians were brash and blunt. If a missionary was going to travel all the way from America to knock on their door and ask to speak with them in mangled Russian about an American prophet who had seen God, Russians were going to take a few seconds and let him know how they really felt about it. And how they really felt was not exactly reassuring.

Quamme had helped. The matter-of-factness and quiet diligence with which he had gone about being a missionary had helped to normalize it for me. If the stares and the taunts and the condescension and the rejection and the alienation had meant nothing to him, then they meant nothing.

But most of the time I felt fairly assured that we were supposed to be there preaching the Gospel in Russia, anyways; I was looking more for reassurance that not only were we doing the right thing by being there, but that we were also going about it in the right way. Everything I knew about being a missionary in Russia had come from Quamme's guidance. So while I was sad to see my mentor leave, I was also excited to get a new perspective on missionary work. Maybe my growing uneasiness with the salesman-like way we tried to convert people came solely because of Quamme's style, I thought at times. Maybe with a new senior companion missionary work would be something different – something more holy and less manipulative, something less corporate and rote. Maybe stats wouldn't matter anymore. Maybe we would have more success touching people's hearts. Maybe I'd feel the Spirit more.

As it turned out, the essence of missionary work with my new companion, Elder Enders, was no different than it was with Quamme. But there were some noticeable differences in personal style.

For one thing, he prayed less. We missionaries kept God busy listening to all our prayers; we prayed upwards of twenty times a day some days. Every time we left the apartment – a please-let-us-be-safe-and-have-some-success-today prayer. Every time we ate – a please-bless-this-food-that-it-might-strengthen-and-nourish-us prayer. Every time we met with an investigator – a please-let-the-Spirit-be-here-today-so-that-we-will-know-the-truth-of-what-is-being-taught prayer. Every time we met with a member – a please-let-us-know-Thy-will-so-that-we-may-better-serve-Thee prayer. Every time we left a member or investigator's apartment – a we're-so-grateful-to-have-had-the-opportunity-to-meet-in-Thy-name-and-feel-of-Thy-love-for-us prayer. Every time things got rough out knocking doors or after getting dogged by an investigator – a Lord-guide-us-to-those-who-are-seeking-Thy-truth prayer.

Enders never suggested that we perform any of the latter spontaneous pleas for help, and we never did the leaving-the-apartment prayers either, and he spent only a few minutes on his knees at night before I heard his mattress squeak with recumbence.

He also studied less. The only studying he'd do in the morning was to read Tolkien in Russian, calling it Russian language practice. And for companionship study we always just played chess for an hour.

And he cared about stats less. Bad statistical reports were like cockroaches. You get a couple and next thing you know all their nasty little friends are swarming all over: visits from the concerned district leader, phone calls from the upset zone leader, uncomfortable interviews with President Hatcher, demotions to junior companion, and assignments to the worst cities in the mission. Best to keep the pests away with a good report. And since there was plenty of subjectivity in how to count things like Ds, percentage of the time Russian was spoken, and hours of companionship study, there was room for creative accounting. Quamme had fudged a little on occasion, it had seemed to me, but Enders took it to a different level. The rule was that we had to say every word of the first D for it to count, but Enders counted any D in which we covered the gist of all the principles. "Did you mention the Book of Mormon to him?" he'd ask me after the man I had been talking to had walked off right before the last two principles about the Book of Mormon and Holy Ghost. "Yeah, I told him I wanted to tell him about the record of Christ's visit to America." "Ok, good. Did you say anything about the Holy Ghost?" "Yeah, I think I mentioned it in my testimony." "All right, good enough. Good work."

Still, Enders was known in the mission as a good, obedient missionary. Members loved him and he worked well with them. He baptized well. He spoke Russian wonderfully. He knew how to teach and read people. He kept most of the rules, and all of the big ones.

He just had a different way of going about being a missionary. He cheerfully punched the clock at 10:00 when we left the apartment and went back to Tolkien at 9:00 when we got back home half an hour earlier than we should have. He spent hours chatting with members, and rarely, if ever, knocked. When people on the street rejected his approaches he wished them a good day with the same automatic jolliness of a cheerful grocery clerk at the checkout counter.

I knew this different way of going about being a missionary was acceptable not only because Hatcher had made Enders branch president, but because I was starting to pick up on the mission gossip enough to know who was a "good" missionary, and who was not so good. Quamme's reputation was excellent, and Enders' was good, too.

This second look at how one could go about being a good, righteous missionary, when combined with my slowly growing absurdist bent, helped me to relax a bit. To not be so concerned about every little rule. To start to understand deep down that missionaries were just trying to do the best we could. To realize that it was ok to lapse into a little English at night to ward off the loneliness and still claim that we spoke Russian 95% of the time on the stats. To quit beating myself up so much over the fact that I couldn't eliminate sexual thoughts from cropping up every now and again. And it was getting harder to eliminate them.

Spring was turning to summer, this time for good. The days were getting lighter for longer, and clothes were coming off. My suit and raincoat gave way to short-sleeved shirts and a tan pair of Dockers. Awkwardness around the members melted into the conviviality of picnics, the friendly banter of early-morning soccer games, and the warm clasps of hands and the genuine joy of reunion when I greeted them in the fresh air outside our meetinghouse on Sunday mornings. Helplessness and frustration with the language were being replaced by a growing confidence in my ability to get and give the gist of most communications. The dark guilt was being faded by a sunny optimism.

Part of my optimism came, perversely, from the apocalyptic rumors swirling around the mission ever since Hatcher had given us the lowdown at zone conference about how we might soon have to leave the country because of the registration problems. Every night Enders would take out the list with all the missionaries' phone numbers and call his connections among the APs, zone leaders, and office Elders to get the latest news. And if there was no news there was always speculation.

After Enders would hang up and recount the latest rumor of our imminent deportation, he would regale me with stories of the proselytizing-free week he'd spent in Moscow to receive dental treatment, eating home-cooked meals at the mission president's home, walking around Red Square and the Kremlin as a tourist, finding root beer at the Starlite diner and peanut butter in the GUM, and wearing civilian clothes.

We'd then sit quietly by the telephone for a while and savor the hope, which neither of us dared speak aloud but which we both obviously shared, that a break from proselytizing was just a phone call away. But the phone call never came and Enders would head off to the bedroom to read Tolkien and I'd study the phone list Enders used to shake the gossip grapevine, dreaming about where and what and with whom I'd be next.

The phone numbers of the two AP companionships headlined the list, which was organized into zones and districts. Each missionary came with a label: AP, zone leader, district leader, or branch president. If the missionary was an Elder with no leadership position or a Sister, then he or she was tagged simply as senior companion, junior companion, or, in rare cases, co-companion. I was Elder Young – Junior Companion, and it was reassuring to look up all the Elders from my MTC group and see that they were all still junior companions as well.

Just like within most hierarchical organizations I suppose, your place in the mission's leadership hierarchy went a long way towards determining your identity. Only on a mission your place in the hierarchy always spoke completely and honestly about your worth and merits, for you couldn't get there illegitimately by luck or by currying favor with the boss; you got there by currying favor with *the* Boss, and He knew all. And on a mission your place in the hierarchy meant your complete identity – there was no family or life outside of work, no hobbies or associations, no clubs or church groups to provide an alternate sense of identity. I was no longer Jacob Young, or even Elder Young. I was greenie Young or Alpha Young, zone leader Young or Omega Young.

This corny little anonymous bit of a joke that was printed one month in the mission newsletter actually gives a pretty good sense of the whole who's who of the hierarchy and the respect they were accorded, including the possibly patronizing but nevertheless well-deserved praise of the Sisters.

THE MISSION PRESIDENT:
Leaps tall buildings in a single bound,
Is more powerful than a locomotive,
Is faster than a speeding bullet,
Walks on water,
Associates with God.

THE ASSISTANT TO THE PRESIDENT:
Leaps short buildings in a single bound,
Is more powerful than a switch engine,
Is just as fast as a speeding bullet,
Walks on water if the sea is calm,
Talks with God.

THE ZONE LEADER:
Leaps short buildings with a running start and favorable winds,
Is almost as powerful as a switch engine,
Is faster than a decelerating bullet,
Walks on water in an indoor swimming pool,
Talks with God if special request is approved.

THE DISTRICT LEADER:
Barely clears a mud hut,
Loses tug-of-war with locomotives,
Can fire a speeding bullet,
Swims well,
Is occasionally addressed by God.

THE SENIOR COMPANION:
Makes high marks on the wall when trying to leap tall buildings,
Is run over by locomotives,
Can sometimes handle a gun without inflicting self-injury,
Dog paddles,
Talks to animals.

THE JUNIOR COMPANION:
Runs into buildings,
Recognizes locomotives 2 out of 3 times,
Is not issued ammunition,
Can stay afloat with a life jacket,
Talks to walls.

THE GREENIE:
Falls over doorsteps when trying to enter buildings.
Says, "Look at the choo-choo!"
Wets himself with a water pistol,
Plays in mud puddles,
Mumbles to himself.

THE SISTER MISSIONARY:
Lifts buildings and walks under them,
Kicks locomotives off the tracks,
Catches speeding bullets with her teeth and eats them,
Freezes water in a single glance,
Knows God.

I could feel that I was moving out of mud puddles and into the pool with my life jacket on and that the day was not far ahead when I would start to dog paddle. Although all my MTC mates were still junior companions, some of them had already been transferred, and I knew that my time in Novokuibyshevsk was coming to an end. I figured that I'd probably be there just long enough to introduce our beat and investigators to Enders.

And sure enough, a few short weeks after Enders had arrived, the zone leader called our apartment and asked to speak with me: I was getting transferred to the Zavodskoy district in Saratov, a city of about a million people downstream the Volga from Samara. My new companion, Elder Vandeburg, had been out about a year.

I was sad to part with Enders. He had been cheerful, intelligent, and relaxed, and an exemplary missionary in a lot of ways. And he had been a good influence. But, just as with Quamme, I was left without a clue as to how he really felt about the whole mission experience.

21

Story Time

Companion-swapping time, or transfers, could be a bit knotty sometimes due to the rule that a missionary may never be alone. Illustration: Suppose Elder A in Penza needs to join his new companion Elder B in Samara. Elder A can't just hop on the train from Penza to Samara by himself. Instead, he must travel from Penza with his old companion Elder C. Elder C, however, is now stuck in Samara and needs to go back to Penza. Meanwhile, Elder D, Elder C's new companion, must also travel to Penza, but is currently in Saratov after escorting his old companion Elder E there from Engels. And the fox is eyeing the goose, and the goose the grain. Sometimes the APs who made the transportation arrangements would make an exception to the togetherness rule and simply send Elder A to Samara and Elder D to Penza. Whether this was done because of budgetary and time constraints, a peculiar dislike of logical puzzles, or an epiphanic burst of common sense was unclear. The APs' level of trust in the solitarily traveling Elder was certainly a relevant factor. Could he be trusted to refrain from sharing his empty sleeper berth with the girl who wandered up from platskartny class looking for a place to sleep?

My transfer out to Saratov to meet up with Elder Vandeburg, though, was pretty smooth, as the Church simply hired a driver to take several of us in a van the eight or so hours from Samara to Saratov.

Vandeburg and I got along well. I let him be him and he let me be me. It was summer and he liked to street contact in a shady park near a water fountain where people would splash and swim. There were always lots of girls our age walking by licking ice cream cones. Quamme and Enders would never have contacted single girls, but Vandeburg sought them out. In the evenings he liked to call up the girls he'd met on the street and chat. This was an egregious violation of the *White Bible* rule to "not communicate via phone or letter with anyone of the opposite sex living within or near mission boundaries," and so I was a little bit concerned, but only a surprisingly little bit. Mostly, I just didn't see much harm in it. He wasn't going to commit any kind of sin – I was with him 24/7. If he wanted to flirt by phone, let him do what he had to do to pass the time.

Besides, we worked hard, and we even ended up baptizing five people in the month that we were together, a stat which even the zone leader, who seemed to visibly dislike Vandeburg for some reason, had to admit was impressive. And although I wouldn't have admitted it to myself, I of course secretly liked talking to the girls in tight shorts those warm summer evenings and then observing Vandeburg talk with them by phone later that night with a lovesick smile and a hungry look in his eyes, as I would half-fantasize, half-fear that Vandeburg would invite them over to our apartment where we would watch the sun go down from our balcony and eat fresh raspberries with vanilla ice cream.

While Vandeburg submersed himself in fantasies of Russian girls, I delved into fantasies of elves, wizards, and hobbits. Enders had given me a Russian copy of the *Fellowship of the Ring* as a parting gift, and I slowly savored the story in every spare moment I had, borrowing Ender's justification for reading an unauthorized book by calling it Russian language study. And it was indeed good language study, even though I rarely had the chance to use words like dwarf, troll, ranger, wraith, and elf in my proselytizing.

As Frodo made his way to Rivendell, Vandeburg and I made the trek to a village in the countryside to visit a family in the branch that lived out there. Every Tuesday we caught the 5:00 A.M. bus to Balashov. As the bus rumbled along the pocked road I read Tolkien by the pastel light of early dawn until we finally got off the bus a few hours later at a dirt road diverging from the highway into the middle of a vast nothingness. The old red bus vanished into the horizon and the throaty chugging of its diesel engine died out, leaving Vandeburg and I alone in the cool morning air of the Russian steppe. Nary a high-rise concrete apartment building to be found. For as far as the eye could see there was nothing except the rolling fields and shaggy grasses and the cornrow-straight line of windbreak trees which rose stiffly from the grassy sea to parallel the road off into the distance. Wide-openness to all horizons.

For several minutes we would stand and stretch in the fresh glow of the young sun, breathing in deep the early summer smells of morning dew, fertile earth, pubescent flora, and nitrification. The honest smell of the elemental. Then we set off to amble along the sandy chestnut loam of the dirt road. It took two hours walking to reach the village. We rarely talked, preferring instead to meditate to the music of the chirping birds, the soft swish of the undulating grass, and the rasp of our shoes against the rough soil. I watched a steppe eagle swoop down through the clear blue sky to snatch a small rabbit, and my heart soared. I was thoroughly happy and spiritually full. I looked over at Vandeburg, who was from North Dakota, and without a word being exchanged I knew he was feeling the same way. We remained tranquilly immersed in nature, where there was no one to proselytize to, until we were pulled back into the world-that-must-be-saved by the emergence of an abandoned nuclear silo in the distance, a signal that the road would soon bend into the village.

To enter the village was to step back in time. There was no electricity, running water, or heat, just a dozen or so wooden homes loosely clustered around an old hand-drawn water well. A small dilapidated church sat crumbling on the hillside, and a small pond below was ringed by a few blackened bathhouses. Next to each family's home teetered small wooden shacks with rusty corrugated iron roofs which housed pregnant sows, milking cows, egg-laying hens, hay, and sacks of feed. Abutting the sheds were gardens of garlic, potatoes, beets, onions, carrots, corn, cabbage, and sunflowers. Extending out from the gardens were pastures marked by rickety wooden fences where goats, cows, and horses grazed. Rolling out from the pastures were tidy fields of alfalfa and wheat. Here and there sat an old tractor or station wagon and here and there sat horse-drawn wagons, carts, and plows.

Story Time

Stepping into the village also made me feel like I was disturbing some ecological balance, like I was an invasive plant, a noxious weed, an exotic. First the dogs started to bark and yap, then the turkeys, geese, and chickens started to flap and strut, angry and territorial. Then came the impenetrable stares of the old men and women as they retreated into their izbas. Finally, the kids caught wind of our arrival in time to tail us at a safe, curious distance until we arrived at the home of Kolya Stepanovich and his family.

Vandeburg had baptized Kolya and his family by working with Kolya's father, a grizzled member of the Zavodskoy branch who had long since moved from the village to Saratov. Vandeburg rationalized our trips out there as being a combination of service, new member discussions, and proselytizing since Kolya would sometimes bring over a neighbor to hear a discussion. In reality, though, we spent most of our time just working on Kolya's farm. We mowed hay with scythes, and gathered it into big mounds with long-handled rakes. We felled trees by two-man saw in his stand of birches down in the swale, sheared off their branches, and carried them on our shoulders to the house to build a pen for his pigs. We weeded his large garden and mended his fences. We would work hard all morning, pausing to sit down with his wife Sveta and two young children for a hearty meal of chicken soup with fresh cream, goat tripe, young rabbit meat, hard-boiled eggs, whole cloves of raw garlic, black bread smeared with hand-churned butter, homemade goat cheese, and rich milk straight from the cow. After lunch we all would go to the cooler back room of his house, lie down on the big family bed and take a nap, which we followed up with hard work until the late afternoon.

Kolya would then go clean up at the bathhouse while Vandeburg and I would decline his invitation to join him and go instead to the village well to rinse off. We'd then all change into our white shirts and ties and pile into his station wagon along with his young son and go into Saratov to visit the members as home teachers. Kolya was on fire with passion for the Gospel and his enthusiasm was contagious among the members. It was one thing for the foreign bumblers to share their testimonies, and another thing altogether for Kolya, the clean-shaven, well-spoken Russian peasant who loved the Lord, to do the same. He was marvelous.

One evening after home teaching, Kolya and his son came up to our apartment with us to fetch some cinnamon. Vandeburg had brought cinnamon rolls that he had made into the village that day, and Sveta, who had never tried them before, had fallen in love and wanted to make them but had no cinnamon at home. So, youthful Kolya, who looked every bit the part of a missionary in his white shirt and tie, drove us to our apartment, got out with his son, and followed us past the babushka sentinels on the bench and up into our apartment, where we gave him the cinnamon and chatted for a bit before they left.

That night, I was jarred from sleep by angry shouts and the sound of boots stomping on the bare wooden floor of our apartment. I opened my eyes to see masked and camouflaged men storming through the dark hallway. A few carried submachine guns, the rest held flashlights with guns slung around their shoulder:

"Where's the boy!? Give us the boy you Yankee bastards! We know you have him," they yelled as they rushed into the bathroom and kitchen.

Vandeburg stumbled groggily out into the kitchen. "What? What's going on?"

"The boy. We know he's here."

"What boy? What are you talking about?" Vandeburg asked while I lay in bed confused and a little frightened, not sure if I was dreaming or if this was really happening.

"The boy that you brought up here last night."

A couple of the men entered the bedroom and I got up as they came over and shined their lights on my face.

"Where is the third one? Your other friend? Where is he?"

"I don't know, I don't know what you're talking about," I said, completely frightened now that I was face to ski-masked face.

They muttered something disgustedly and went into the kitchen. I followed them.

Vandeburg was talking calmly with what looked to be the leader.

"The babushkas said that the three of you came up here with a little boy," the leader said.

Story Time

Although I had absolutely no idea what was going on, Vandeburg had figured it out and he explained to the men about Kolya and his son and hometeaching in white shirts and ties and cinnamon rolls, and that, no, Kolya was not an American missionary, and that, no, despite what the babushkas had said we had not kidnapped Kolya's son. Having swept through our apartment without finding a trace of the boy, they must have been inclined to believe him because they left as abruptly as they'd come.

"Whoa," I said simply, unsure if this was a commonplace occurrence or something that I should be freaked out about. Vandeburg seemed pretty nonchalant about the whole thing.

"Fricking babushkas!" he said. "Can't mind their own damn business. Oh well, it makes for a good story at least," he said with a smile as we headed back to bed.

And there were plenty of such stories, some more serious than our brief little scare. I once asked Vandeburg if he'd known the two missionaries who had been kidnapped in Saratov right before I'd received my call to Russia. I'd read about it in the paper, but I wanted the inside scoop. Vandeburg smiled, nodded his head, and proceeded to tell me the tale he'd obviously told before, about how the two missionaries were known in the mission as disobedient and immature, how they'd taken some "gangster" pictures with branch members in which they flashed fistfuls of "Benjamins" around, how a friend of one of the members had seen this and thought that the missionaries and the Church must be really wealthy and that they would therefore fetch a healthy ransom, how they had been kidnapped at gunpoint and taken to a cabin in a snowy village somewhere while the kidnappers demanded a $300,000 ransom from the Church, how the Church had refused to pay or negotiate, and finally, how they had been released in a field outside Saratov after five days of being handcuffed to their chairs. I talked to other missionaries who knew the kidnapped Elders, and although the details of their stories differed, each version seemed to place the blame for the kidnapping on the missionaries themselves, as if the missionaries had brought what must have been a harrowing experience upon themselves by their minor acts of disobedience to mission rules.

Then there was the tragic story that no one ever talked about and that I cared not to ask anyone about: the story of the missionary who had been stabbed to death in a stairwell while knocking doors in Ufa, a city not far from Saratov, right before I had entered the MTC. I had read an article about it in the *Arizona Republic* as I was reading up on my future mission on the Internet. The article was about the slain missionary's companion, who had also been stabbed, but who had survived the knife wounds to his upper intestine, liver, and pancreas. The father of this surviving missionary spoke about his family's reaction to getting the phone call with the news. How, upon hearing that there had been a problem with their son, they were at first "worried that he'd done something unworthy," because "You see, we'd rather have him come home in a pine box than do something unworthy." This "death before dishonor" sentiment was not an uncommon one within the Church:

> Loss of virtue is too great a price to pay even for the preservation of one's life - better dead clean, than alive unclean. Many is the faithful Latter-day Saint parent who has sent a son or a daughter on a mission or otherwise out into the world with the direction: 'I would rather have you come back in a pine box with your virtue than return alive without it.' (Apostle Bruce R. McConkie, *Mormon Doctrine p. 124*)

Finally, there were the less serious stories, my favorite ones, the run-ins with the law kind. Like the story of the two missionaries who had been kicked out of the country for taking pictures of nuclear power plants. Or the stories tied together by the strange coincidence that in three different cities, Samara, Pskov, and Kransnoyarsk, missionaries had been arrested, detained, and expelled for trespassing on military bases, even though in one case they had allegedly entered at the invitation of an officer at the base, and in another case, they allegedly had no idea that they were even on a military base as there were no fences to mark the boundary. The most recent of such stories had taken place just that month in Samara, when a group of Sister missionaries had been pepper sprayed at the railway station for insubordination after being arrested and detained by police there. I, like Vandeburg, was happy that we had just gotten a missionary story of this sort under our belt, and I hoped for more such experiences.

Story Time

Vandeburg was all about making the most out of the Russian experience in general, getting fodder for stories, and being with him was making me that way, too, or rather, making the mission me more like the pre-mission me. So we got out and saw the country.

On P-Days, as the Nine Walkers tried to cross the Misty Mountains, we rode in a taxi out to the village of Smelovka, home of a memorial complex commemorating the site where Yuri Gagarin, the first man in space, had landed in April of 1961 after his groundbreaking (literally) 108 minutes in space aboard the spherical Vostok I.

Or, as the company of nine entered the mines of Moria, we climbed in a taxi up to Victory Park, where we made our way through innumerable tanks, boats, planes, trains, guns and sundry other weapons, and rows and rows of marble slabs honoring the more than 175,000 Saratovites who had died in World War II. We stopped when we reached the 120 foot tall monument depicting cranes in flight emblazoned with the red star and we sat and gazed on the panorama of Saratov, following the city up from the banks of the Volga to the willowy tendrils of homes creeping up into the foothills.

And as the Gandalf-less company entered the enchanted Elven forest of Lothlorien, we ascended into those foothills to visit investigators, members, friends, and strangers, where we would sit in the shade of cherry trees and eat fresh raspberries and sip hot tea, herbal of course. I was loving the summer, enjoying my time with Vandeburg, starting to speak the language pretty well, and, following Vandeburg's lead, ignoring the pressure to put up big numbers and climb the leadership ladder. Slacking but baptizing. Life was good.

Elder Thornton, our district leader in Saratov, however, was not slacking and not baptizing. He had only been in the country for a few months longer than me and he was wound up tight and clearly intent on working his way up the hierarchy. He knew that the surest way to do that was to pump up the stats, which meant more baptisms and stricter obedience.

Thornton was obsessed with the dangers of Russian girls. Every district meeting we had to read *Lock Your Heart* in its entirety. Back in Novokuibyshevsk we had been aware of the danger presented by *devchonki*, and we had read *Lock Your Heart* every month or so, but it was always in a lighthearted, this-doesn't-really-apply-to-us kind of way. But Thornton preached *Lock Your Heart* each week like it was the Gospel itself. It was, after all, a speech purportedly given by Spencer W. Kimball, the twelfth President of the Church, to some missionaries in Latin America.

The speech has become a cult classic among missionaries. It opens with an anecdote: in one mission which President Kimball visited, the missionaries had started to go over to a certain member's house for Sunday dinner. This soon became a regular thing and the missionaries started to stay and play cards and then to dance in the dark with the Saints' girls, and then, one pet led to another, and a missionary was excommunicated. After blaming the other missionaries for the excommunication, relating some more stories about toenail painting and craters, and identifying the heart as the only organ with the ability to fall in love, President Kimball hits his stride:

Just keep your hearts locked. Your whole thought should be missionary work. How can I make it more plain and more important than that? I'd like to because there is no reason whatever for any missionary to ever become involved, not even in a decent way, with any girl in the mission field. It isn't the place! You guaranteed, you promised! You went through the Temple! You remember what you did in the Temple? Remember you promised you'd do all the things the brethren request of you, to live the commandments. That's one of the commandments when you go into the mission field: "Thou shalt not flirt! Thou shalt not associate with young women in the mission field - or anyone else for that matter - on any other basis than the proselyting basis."

Sometimes we find a young man who has not been popular at home; he has been very, very backward at home and he hasn't had many dates. So when he gets out into the mission field and somebody flatters him a little- some girl shows a lot of interest in him - why he's flattered. He thinks all at once, "Well, that's whom I should marry. Well, I say this once more by repetition and for emphasis, you LOCK YOUR HEARTS and if you haven't done so, do it now and send the key back! You will not permit any impression, no romantic thought or impression in your mind. For two years you have given yourself to the Lord, totally, to teach the Gospel to the world.

This talk had become a fundamental part of the missionary mindset, and any time a missionary happened to talk to a girl for a couple of minutes after Sacrament meeting, he was sure to get a friendly reminder from a couple of Elders to lock his heart.

Thornton had good reason to preach *Lock Your Heart* hellfire and brimstone. Vandeburg clearly was breaking the commandment *"Thou shalt not flirt."* And we were all breaking the commandment *"Thou shalt not associate with . . . anyone . . . on any other basis other than the proselyting basis."*

But despite Thornton's and others' valiant readings of *Lock Your Heart*, we all knew of a few missionaries who had married a girl from their mission. It had even happened in our mission. In fact, Thornton himself returned to Russia after his mission to marry a member.

Ours was a motley district heading in to that month's zone conference. Vandeburg's heart was unlocked, and he was just trying to enjoy the best that Russia had to offer. Thornton's heart was under strict public quarantine, and he was trying hard to be the company man. Thornton's greenie's heart was split – half back at home and half back in the warm womb of the MTC – and he was just trying to appear as if his heart was in it. My heart was starting to follow its own beat, and I was starting to let it.

That month's zone conference was held out on an uninhabited island in the middle of the Volga. Instead of testimony meeting there was capture the flag, and instead of soggy pizza there were shish kebabs. After an exhausting round of capture the flag, I sat down next to a big oak tree, leaned back into its thick trunk and closed my eyes. I must have been daydreaming about something, about something non-proselytizing I'm sure, when I heard Elder Olsen, my MTC mate who had given a Book of Mormon to the guy on the plane so many Ds ago, talking to Quamme about how he needed to set up an appointment with him to take the Omega test next month. I was stunned. Omega? I hadn't even got my Beta. Most missionaries didn't get their Omega until they'd been in the country for at least a year. Most didn't get it at all.

I continued leaning against the tree, hoping that Quamme, who had presided at the conference as AP to my great pride at having been his son, would come over to acknowledge me, too, even though I wasn't on track for prodigious Omega achievement. He finally did.

"Young, how are you my son?"

"Really good, Quamme. And you?"

"Good, I've really learned a lot in the last couple of months."

"Yeah? Me too. I learned from Dave that the big roll machines are definitely the sod cutters of the future. One roll of 350 square feet. But the best part is that people have to pay you to lay it out cuz it takes special equipment. 30,000 feet a day. Three cents a foot, you do the math. We definitely gotta get us a big roll machine when we get back."

"No, I'm serious Young. I mean, my mission is almost over, and I've learned that I've got to make every minute count. You should do the same. How are you coming with your Beta?"

"Not that good I guess. I haven't been working on it too hard," I said, deflated, as I stared at Quamme's giant hand which held a shiny leather briefcase.

22

The Strain of Twain

Upon returning from zone conference I stashed Tolkien at the bottom of my luggage, took out a legal pad, and drew up a detailed plan for the discussions, scriptures, and language concepts which I needed to master in order to get my Omega at the next zone conference. Vandeburg had gotten transferred, and I was working with a new companion, Elder Everett. A week and a half later, thanks to some early mornings and the utilization of every spare moment, I passed my Beta test, and two weeks later, when I called Quamme to set up my Omega test for the next zone conference, he informed me that I would be attending the zone conference in Togliatti, as I was going to be made senior companion in the Old City district there.

I stopped in at the office to take my Omega test on the way to Togliatti, and so it came to pass that I arrived in Togliatti in early September eager and zealous, chomping at the bit to use the proselytizing skills of an early Omega and the executive-decision-making authority of a senior companion to thrust in my sickle and harvest, harvest, harvest.

My co-harvester's name was Elder Goddard, and only Elder Goddard, as he saw no need to share personal details like his first name with me. It wasn't until I spied his name stenciled in golden letters on the outside of his Book of Mormon as he sat cross-legged and straight-backed in bed reading it as he did every night after work, that I learned that his first name was Richard.

Rich liked to hum, and Rich liked to sing. He hummed as I studied the language in the morning, he hummed as I wrote in my journal in the evening. He sang as I made grechka for breakfast, he sang as he made sandwiches for lunch, he sang when I was on the toilet, he sang when he was on the toilet. He hummed and sang mostly hymns, with the occasional nameless viral ditty mixed in. It drove me batty, his self-contented little merry humming and his self-righteous strained falsetto. How I missed Vandeburg and our peaceful walks through the steppe.

We were living in a foursome with the district leader, Elder Lindsay, and his greenie. They'd just been kicked out of their apartment and were searching for a new one. They slept on our floor and didn't wash the dishes they used, apparently operating under the assumption that since they were our "guests" and the dishes were ours, that we could wash them. Lindsay didn't seem to be bothered by Goddard's warbling. He was a singer and often joined Goddard in a hymn with his nice melodic voice. The greenie was clearly too shell-shocked to notice or care who sang or hummed what.

Goddard was like the old seminary teacher who walks around at church youth dances and sticks a twelve-inch ruler between slow-dancing couples to make sure they weren't getting too close to each other. Only Goddard had it backwards: he felt it his sacred, inviolable duty, yea, his very raison d' être, to be within a foot of me at all times. Enter the investigator's home. If I sat down on the couch, Goddard would grab the spot next to me, scooting close until our thighs and knees were touching. If I sat in the chair instead, he would shoot me a dirty look and go sit in the nearest seat. And unlike my other companions, he would never get up to use the bathroom while we were at an apartment with a female present, but would instead wait valiantly until we got home. For to use the investigator's pot would be to leave me alone with temptation – for thirty whole seconds! And if I happened to be audacious enough to avail myself of the bathroom, he would shoot me another dirty look, follow me to the door, and wait impatiently outside, periodically shuffling his feet or clearing his throat to alert me to the fact that, yes, he was still standing right outside the door and not off boinking the investigator.

The worst were the buses. They had become my sanctuary of sorts, my solitude in a crowd, anonymity among the masses, places where I could take a break from proselytizing and pretend that I was just another teenager checking out the girls. But Goddard insisted on ruining this by breathing his garlicky breath down my neck. Like a soldier taking a bullet for his comrade, Goddard would throw his body in front of any female in the vicinity to shield me from sin. If anyone was going to be jammed up next to me, it was Goddard, golldarn-it. His persistence and perspicacity at maintaining proximity were nothing short of astounding. When we were boarding the bus in a big crowd I would wait until the last possible moment to commit to a bus door, in the hope that Goddard would get swept up in a people current that would take him to another door, providing me with some separation, but he sniffed out this trick pretty easily and would not commit until I did. And even on the couple of times when it did work and I entered in the middle and he in the back, he simply gave me the dirty look, lowered his pit bull head, and doggedly shoved his way through the crowd to stand right next to me.

One chilly morning, however, we went to board the bus that took us to the city's central park where we frequently contacted. The bus was jam-packed with people, and it was clear that only about half of the crowd would be able to push their way onto it. I recognized the opportunity immediately and pounced. With great finesse I worked my way near the front of the line, leaving Goddard a couple babushkas back. When I got to the entrance, the only available space was on the bottom step, room for about three. I stepped up and squeezed in with a couple non-Goddard others, but I was not out of the clear yet. Those trying to get in would push us bottom-steppers, meaning that we'd push the middle-steppers, who'd push the upper-steppers, and so on, until sometimes a bit more space would open up. Sure enough, the chain of pushes came, initiated by a frantic Goddard. I pushed my part and then held my breath. *Yes!* The pack was as solid as wet sand. We bottom-steppers weren't going anywhere. Goddard made one last desperate effort: he found a foothold on the bottom step, grabbed a hold of the stair railing, and tried to ride the bus San Francisco cable car style, with his body leaning out of the open doorway. I'd seen it done before. It all depended on whether the driver would allow it by not closing the doors. *Score!* The driver was having none of it. He closed the doors on Goddard, and he was forced to let go of the railing. I turned around and made a show as if I had just realized he wasn't going to make it in, and acted as if I was trying to fight my way out of the closed door. I looked at the panic tinged with spite in Goddard's eyes, and I hid my triumph with a look of concerned helplessness as the bus drove off.

I was free! As free as a missionary wedged on the bottom step of an old Russian bus at 10:00 in the morning can get. I took the bus all the way to the park. Goddard knew where we were going, and would surely meet me there since we began nearly every morning by waylaying the unsuspecting for a couple of hours at the arched gates that marked the entrance to the park. I didn't dare use my freedom to do something really crazy like hit up the nearby casino, but I wanted to do something to relish the moment, so I mustered up my courage and crossed the street where I bought a hotdog and sat on a bench to savor it while I waited for Goddard to catch up. He showed up fifteen minutes later, furious. I made the requisite insincere apology, and he looked at me suspiciously for the rest of the day, as if trying to determine whether I'd fornicated in our time apart.

Mark Twain, by any definition a very successful man, once said that the only two things it takes to succeed in life are ignorance and confidence. Goddard had plenty of both. He'd only been out for a couple of months and could barely speak the language, but he was cocksure that the Gospel was true and that, out of the two of us, he knew best how we should go about helping everyone else come to see that.

He insisted that we street contact together. I resisted the idea. Most companions contacted separately, but within hearing distance of each other, in order to get the 30 Ds out of the way as quickly as possible. Efficiency reasons aside, I simply liked contacting on my own: as my language skills progressed I was starting to enjoy freewheeling discussions about God, religion, and life philosophy with people, something I couldn't do with a companion by my side, particular one who was a stickler for the rules like Goddard. However, Goddard did have the recently-clarified interpretation of the rules that said that we must teach together on his side, so I caved in, although this didn't prevent me from slinking off every now and then once he'd started a conversation with someone. What was he going to do? Ditch the person he was talking to and come running over just because I was talking to some old man ten feet away?

The Strain of Twain

As a newly commissioned senior companion, I had some firm ideas about proselytizing that I was eager to put into practice. Nothing innovative – just my observations of what seemed to work and what didn't.

What didn't was street contacting. We stopped people in parks and on corners for hours each day in order to get our 30Ds, but we rarely saw any of those who did stop ever again. I blamed this on suboptimal conditions for the Spirit. First, we started the discussion off on the wrong foot by interrupting people who were trying to get somewhere: to work, to the market, to their family at home, to their own church, to get laid. And then we were constantly fending off their attempts to leave before the discussion was up: "Just a few more minutes, Sergei. Please! . . . You can go as soon as I tell you about this book. . . . Don't you want to hear about this book? … Don't' you want to get the book? It's free!" And so on until the discussion which was supposed to be spiritually moving became simply moving as we were reduced to chasing after Sergei as he sped away.

And then there were the people who felt it their duty as good Russians to let their compatriots know how disgusted they were with them for talking with the American propagandists. They shot them icy looks, clucked and sighed demonstratively, shook their heads in disapproval and pity, and outright warned them not to talk with the dangerous cultists. Not to mention distractions like the roar of traffic, the beautiful girls walking by, and the cold and rain and wind. And besides, even when we were able to push through the distractions and give Sergei a mobile D and by some miracle get his address, the address would often turn out to be fake, especially if Sergei had not been drunk. Then we'd have to waste a whole hour tracking it down.

No, the Spirit preferred the quiet and warmth of people's apartments, and there was no danger of fake addresses with knocking. Sure, it annoyed people just as much, and we got fewer discussions, but the ones we did get were usually quality ones which sometimes led to continuing investigators and baptisms. We could sit down across from them in their living rooms, look into their eyes with our trademark earnest sincerity, comment on their bowling trophies, ask them searching questions, take our time presenting the message, and take as long as we wanted.

So more knocking was one item on my agenda. The other two were more work with the members and more English lessons, which had recently been reauthorized. Work with the members was always being emphasized as the most effective proselytizing method, the holy grail of converting methods, and when we could get the members to set up a discussion with their friends it usually worked pretty well. The problem was getting members to approach their friends about the Gospel. Even the most enthusiastic of them were hesitant to jeopardize friendship for the possibility of a conversion. But I thought that we should try to get them to do more somehow, although I wasn't exactly sure how. And English lessons were a great way to attract the non-xenophobic types and help them get to know us not as weirdos in white shirts and ties but as fairly normal kids who just happened to be really devoted to a religion. Once established, that personal connection was like the spoonful of sugar that helped the message go down.

So we started pasting advertisements for English lessons, reminding members of their duty to share the gospel, and embarking on some marathon knocking sessions. We began knocking out a huge apartment building every day, sometimes without giving a single discussion. On those occasions, after having offered a hundred or so homes the chance to hear the good news, and having been rejected by every single one of them, I thought of the words which the Lord had given to missionaries in these the latter days:

> And in whatsoever house ye enter, and they receive you not, ye shall depart speedily from that house, and shake off the dust of your feet as a testimony against them. D&C 75:20

> And in whatsoever place ye shall enter, and they receive you not in my name, ye shall leave a cursing instead of a blessing, by casting off the dust of your feet against them as a testimony, and cleansing your feet by the wayside. D&C 24:15

> And shake off the dust of thy feet against those who receive thee not, not in their presence, lest thou provoke them, but in secret; and wash thy feet, as a testimony against them in the day of judgment. D&C 60:15

Despite the fact that the Lord had repeated these clear and simple instructions to missionaries on three different occasions, no one seemed to take them seriously, and I'd never seen a missionary actually dust off his feet as a testimony against those who'd rejected our message. The whole idea that we'd just sent an entire apartment building to hell was just too depressing to think about. But think about it I did, between nearly every door we knocked.

Goddard hated knocking and was confident that it was a waste of time. So between doors, between all the no's and hell no's, we had our little passive-aggressive exchanges: "Don't you think that there's a more effective way to work?" "Yeah, probably." "We could have had four or five discussions in the park by now." "Yeah, probably." "I've never seen a baptism come from knocking." "Yeah, well I've seen more from knocking than from street contacting." ""We should be out working with the members." "Yeah, agreed, but how should we do that?" "I don't know, you're the senior companion."

He also disagreed with my classification of English lessons as proselytizing hours, and argued that we should count them as service hours. I refused. I told him of all the baptisms I'd seen as a direct result of English lessons, and told him flatly that they *would* count towards our proselytizing hours. Let him write a letter to President Hatcher about it, see if he or I cared. I wanted to save our service hours for volunteering in hospitals and orphanages to do maintenance, winterizing the windows by stuffing the cracks with rags, mopping the floors, scrubbing toilets and the like, anything to get my mind off proselytizing for a few hours.

Although I'd only been on my mission for four months longer than Goddard, I felt entitled to the immediate respect of *the decider*. Sure, I would ask for Goddard's opinion, and I would consider it, but in the event of a difference of opinion I was to be the one who would ultimately decide if we were going to knock or street contact that day, if the English lessons counted as service or proselytizing, if we were going to visit this member or that, if we'd write off an investigator as hopelessly eternal or keep on visiting her. I also felt entitled to be the clear leader: I'd start and dominate the BRT, I'd ask someone to give the opening and closing prayers, I'd dictate the pace and direction of the discussion, I'd decide what commitments to ask them to make, I'd set up our next appointment. In short, I'd be the only one with the authority to say at the end of every visit: "Well, we should probably get going, it was nice to talk to you."

Someone had to be in charge. The *Missionary Guide* made clear our roles:

> The senior companion should ask for his companion's counsel and consider it carefully. The junior companion, after offering his counsel, must be willing to accept his companion's righteous decisions. He should accept them with his whole heart, without doubtful feelings. The senior companion must make sure that his junior companion feels like a full partner. He must include his junior companion in the planning process and show sincere trust in him.

Even though the *Missionary Guide* clearly assigned final decision making authority to senior companions, however, in actual proselytizing practice one's role and authority turned out to be more a function of ability and personality than of diktat. The most determinative factors were proselytizing skills, time in area and country, relationship with the investigators, and language ability, particularly and especially language ability. Of course, in the case of a dispute, the senior companion always had the trump card of having been formally assigned authority.

I initially deferred to Goddard as he introduced me to our investigators and members, since he already had a relationship with them. However, my deference didn't last long. As Goddard would stumble through the unscripted portions of our visits like BRT, finding out, and resolving concerns, I began to step in and control the conversation, and once that happened, Goddard with his language skills just couldn't keep up, and the visit was in my hands. I did this partly because of impatience: I knew what he was trying to say and I could say it so much more quickly and clearly. Partly it was pride and insufficient faith in the Spirit: I thought that the more clearly, precisely, elegantly, and logically the thing was said the stronger its impact would be on people. And partly it was jealousy and the selfish desire for attention and glory: I wanted our investigators and members to care about *me*, to ask *me* questions about myself, to look to *me* for help and answers, to come up to *me* during Sunday meetings to chat, to thank *me* for converting them to the Gospel, to ask *me* to be the one to baptize them.

My selfish and ignoble motives notwithstanding, I tried not to be too overt in my gradual power grab. I never would interrupt Goddard and would only step in once he'd looked to me for help. And I was only doing what I'd seen done before. I had been a suitably submissive junior companion and had let my senior companion do the work his way, accepting his decisions with my "whole heart, without doubtful feelings." Now it was my turn to expect the same, and I felt that I had not only the *Missionary Guide*, but also the historic, unwritten code of proper companionship dynamics to back me up.

Goddard, though, apparently didn't see it that way, and we butted heads in our passive-aggression fashion. I lacked the maturity to initiate an honest and open dialogue about our silent and stubborn competition for control, and I lacked the wisdom to see that in order for Goddard to respect my leadership I needed to show more respect for his desires and opinions. Now that I was a new Omega senior companion, however, I, like Goddard, lacked not those two prerequisites for life success: confidence and ignorance. But what may be good for the one was bad for the twain. Two confident and ignorant Elders, each competing for the right to dominate the companionship, each believing himself to be entitled to that right, each coming to resent and dislike the other, each required to be within garlic breath's distance of the other at all times – it was a recipe for constant stress and strain. But we were obedient and strove for harmony in the companionship by burying all of this nastiness beneath a fragile veneer of exaggerated politeness and niceness.

23

Doubt

All the knocking did slowly build up our teaching pool, however, until we had a few solid continuing investigators, an improvement on the single one we had when I had first arrived – a thin, middle-aged Georgian woman named Bedisa.

Bedisa was my first real project, my first real test, my first potential baptism. Sure, my companions and I had baptized about ten people by now, but I had been junior companion, so those didn't really count as "my" baptisms. My senior companions had called all the shots, asked all the important questions, done most of the talking, built the relationship of trust, and done the actual immersing.

At the beginning, when Bedisa was still our only investigator and we were desperate for appointments to avoid long dark evenings of knocking, we visited her frequently. She had been through the first three discussions by the time I arrived and had already committed to baptism, so initially it seemed that a baptism was ripe for the plucking. We ran into a snag in the fourth discussion when we came to the Word of Wisdom, however, when she told us that she smoked and didn't know if she could quit.

So we worked with her. We met and prayed with her almost every night for weeks. We told her to read the Book of Mormon every time she had the urge to smoke. We brought her bags of sunflower seeds as a substitute for tobacco. We prepared inspiring little lessons from the Scriptures to motivate her. And it seemed to be working. She sat in the loose, silky robe that she always wore and told us that she read the Book of Mormon every night and believed it to be the word of God. She spoke wistfully of her desire to be become clean again through baptism and to lead a virtuous, godly life. Eventually, she told us that she had quit smoking and was ready to be baptized. She was golden, she was cherubic, her countenance was brightening, and the joy of cleanliness was evident in her face. And so, finally, she passed her baptismal interview with district leader Lindsay and was scheduled to be baptized the following Saturday. I was elated.

That Friday evening before her baptism, we went to her apartment to make sure that she was ready for the big day. We knocked and knocked without an answer. We could see a crack of light under the door, however, and since we presumed that Bedisa lived alone, we figured that she had to be there and so we kept knocking. Finally, the door opened to reveal Bedisa in her slippers and silk robe, loosely bound. She looked terrible. She had dark sunken bags under her eyes, which had a starry faraway look in them: the warm pools of her once lively pupils had shriveled into pinpoints. And she looked droopy, like a marionette whose strings had suddenly gone slack.

We followed her into the apartment, where she lay down languidly on the bed. She immediately started to nod off, like I did when I was trying to fight off sleep sitting in church on a hot summer day.

"Is everything okay, Bedisa?" I asked.

She simply looked at me, disoriented, as if asking who we were and what we were doing there, not just Goddard and I, but all of us, what were we all doing there.

"Are you everything right?" Goddard repeated the inquiry to which I had received no response.

She drifted into what seemed to be a more aware state and answered: "Everything is wonderful."

I was relieved. Everything was wonderful. "Are you ready for your baptism tomorrow?" I said excitedly.

"I don't think I'll be getting baptized, boys."

"What? Why? Why would you say that?"

"I'm not the type of woman who gets baptized."

"What does that mean?"

"I'm a very dirty woman, Young. God does not want a woman like me."

"No, that is not true. God loves you and wants you to get baptized. It will give you a fresh start and you will become clean as new snow."

"You do not know the things I have done, Young. You don't know the things that I now do."

"That's not important, Bedisa. That is why we have baptism, for the remission of sins. God will remember your sins no more." Then the thought struck me. "Did you start smoking again?"

"Tobacco? No, not yet."

"Then you are ready to be baptized. Don't worry, it's normal to be a little nervous about it. But I can promise you that it will be the best day of your life. The love and peace and joy you will feel at being completely, perfectly clean in God's eyes – it is indescribable how wonderful a feeling that is."

She was drifting back into a sleepy, drugged-like state. "No, boys, I won't be getting baptized tomorrow."

"Have you prayed about this and asked God what he wants? Whether He wants you to get baptized tomorrow?"

"No."

"Can we pray with you now about it?"

"Okay."

"Who would you like to say the prayer?"

"I don't care, you choose."

"Elder Goddard, would you like to say it?"

"Yes, of course," Goddard said solemnly.

After the prayer, a sincere pleading on the part of Goddard for God to touch Bedisa's heart and let her know of His love for her and His desire for her to be baptized, Bedisa looked at us with a look of absolute bliss on her face. I felt a surge of joy thinking that she must have felt the Spirit during Goddard's prayer.

"How do you feel now, Bedisa?"

"Wonderful," she said. "Incredible."

"So will we see you tomorrow at your baptism?"

Doubt

"No, boys. No."

We went back and forth like this for a while, but to no avail. Something drastic had happened since the day before, when Bedisa was near tears describing how happy she was to be getting baptized. We finally left with a promise that we could come see her the following night.

The next night, Bedisa was more awake, but she looked just as miserable. In short order she came clean with us. She hung out with "bad people," her boyfriend and some other guys. They had arrived yesterday from Georgia with a load of heroin. She had shot up again. She was so sorry, but that was who she was. She couldn't deny herself. She talked some more about the situation, but the long and short of it, as I understood it, was that she was choosing heroin and a bad crowd over the joy of the Gospel. It was a tough blow to take. I knew that she had felt the Spirit. I knew that she had a testimony. How could she deny that? How could she not even want to try to do the right thing?

We kept visiting her, despite her warnings that the guys were dangerous sorts and weren't happy about our visits and the attention which they attracted among the neighbors. One evening I came prepared with a special lesson about how God was a God of miracles. I told stories from the Scriptures about all the miraculous things that God had done through the power of faith: the healing of lepers, the casting out of demons, the woman who touched Christ's robe and was made whole. I was filled with a spiritual fire, and testified to her with a burning born more of hope than conviction that God would perform a miracle and help her change if she only had the faith. But what could I and my hopeful faith do against the fearsome power of heroin? She returned my fire with a tired smile. Finally, she asked us to stop coming.

The failure with Bedisa hurt. I craved success. Partly to parry the subtle jabs from Goddard about the way I was doing things. Partly to reassure myself that I was a good missionary with enough faith who had the Spirit. But mainly, I simply and sincerely wanted people to be saved and I was afraid that if they didn't accept my message they would miss out on their chance for salvation.

The essence of the message was straightforward. The purpose of our existence was to progress and become like God. We could not progress in the premortal Spirit world where we had lived with our Heavenly Father because we lacked physical bodies. So our elder brother Jesus proposed a plan of salvation wherein we would receive physical bodies by being born on Earth. But in order to be saved and return to God and receive a fullness of glory, we had to obey God's commandments and receive certain ordinances in The Church of Jesus Christ of Latter-day Saints, including baptism.

I remember well the first time my mind every seriously entertained the sliver of a thought that this plan of salvation was fundamentally flawed and that the Church might not be true. Yes, I had questioned it all before, as a hypothetical or intellectual exercise, but there had never been any real intent or urgency behind it. This was the first time that I had ever thought about it without knowing going into it what the answer was; in essence, this was my first doubt that struck at that paradigm, that foundation, that premise of all premises.

It was a Saturday. We had no appointments with investigators that day, no English lessons to teach, no service to do, no member visits scheduled. It was a cold, rainy day, which meant that neither of us felt like street contacting. Knocking was our only option left. A whole day of nothing but knocking. We took the bus to a part of the city where our area book said that no missionaries had ever knocked, and we chose a block where three high-rise apartment buildings towered over the rest of the neighborhood. Twenty floors each, four apartments to a floor. Two hundred and forty apartments total between the three buildings.

By the end of the first building, I was on the verge of tears with frustration. Out of eighty apartments, not one single person had cared to listen to what we had to say. My back and feet hurt, and I wanted nothing more than to sit down. I was severely depressed by the thought of seven more hours of knocking. Seven more hours of spitting out the same old spiel over and over again with some minor variation that I hoped would strike some kind of chord. Seven more hours of trying to ignore the looks of anger, pity, disgust, and indifference before we shuffled on to the next door. After a quick lunch at the local store of bread, cheese, raw garlic, and Coke, though, I felt better, and we moved on to the second building. Three and a half hours later, we crawled out of the cold dark stairwell of the second building into the biting rain of the darkening day. I was tired of screwing my face up into that damned pasted-on missionary look supposed to broadcast the joy of the Gospel, and I was tired of pleading over and over again to share a wonderful message about God's plan with people. There was nothing to do, however, but move on to the third and final building.

I was on auto-pilot now. Goddard was upset at me that we didn't have something else on the schedule besides knocking and wasn't talking to me. Not that we talked much anyways since he refused to speak English. So, since I could say the spiel without thinking and since I didn't expect any kind of response but a slammed door, I was completely alone with my thoughts. They started out the same way these thoughts had started so many times before on the doors, but they ended up in a new place. *What are we doing wrong? Why isn't anyone's heart softened enough to let us in? Why isn't the Spirit softening their hearts? People need to hear this message! Maybe we aren't worthy to have the Spirit with us. Whatever! That's bull crap. I've been a lot less obedient than this, and we still had success. I haven't masturbated since the days in Saratov when I was with Vandeburg, and we had five baptisms there. We're working our butts off here for the Lord. Well, if it's not us, then what's wrong?*

If it's not us, then what's wrong? It was the first time I had asked myself that question, and I couldn't answer it. I couldn't answer it. Part of me wanted to follow the Lord's instructions as revealed to Joseph Smith and dust off my feet as a damning testimony against every last one of the hard-hearted, stiff-necked Russians living in those two hundred and forty apartments. But I knew that that wasn't fair.

I had grown up believing that everyone would get the chance to receive the Gospel and accept baptism in the Church, if not in this life, then in the next. An egalitarian idea, one that had always provided me great comfort. Only now that I was actually out giving people their chance to accept the Gospel in this life, and person after person after endless person was rejecting it, it didn't seem so egalitarian. It seemed downright unfair, discriminatory even. I had been born into the Church, it was easy for me to accept it. But what if roles were reversed and some Russian sect called Borgomilism was the one true church into which all must be assimilated by baptism? My family and I would be doomed. If two nineteen-year old Russian kids had knocked at our farmhouse back in Idaho and told us that we had to be baptized in a church founded in the 19th century by a Russian prophet named Josef Smitsky, we would have given them a drink of water and two copies of the Book of Mormon and sent them on their merry way. Just how, exactly, was this plan of salvation just *or* merciful?

I was still pondering that question on the bus back to our apartment as I stared glumly through the dark, rainy night at the myriad lights glowing inside the apartments of the three buildings we had just knocked. I pictured each light shining warmly on a family, a family that was together, together around a table full of food, drink, conversation, and love, love for each other, love for country, love for their own religion. Each light was warmth, shelter, joy, human touch, family, togetherness. These were the lights we'd seen shining through under the cracks of doors. These were the lights that had flooded out hot and bright for a few seconds before the door slammed. Each one of these lights had rejected us. Each one of these lights had wanted nothing to do with us. Through the tears and rain these lights began to blur and run together, until I was gazing on a trinity of candles, getting fainter and fainter as the cold dark bus rolled away. What could I possibly offer these people, these people of the lights, these people who already possessed the very things that my heart desired more than anything? Why would they want what I had?

That night, after a quick supper of fried eggs, I took out a sheet of paper from my legal pad, lay down in bed, looked over to make sure Goddard could not see what I was doing, and wrote <u>Against</u> at the top of the page. I stared hard at that word for a while before beginning to write. It befits the Russia Samara mission that I began with statistics:

1. {Only Mormons will live with God after this life. Baptism in this Church is the <u>only key</u> to the Celestial Kingdom.} At 10 million members we're only one sixth of a percent of the world's population, and half of those members aren't even active, let alone worthy. The true church wasn't on this earth for almost 1800 years, so all those people are gone who lived in that time. At any given time in history, the percentage of church members has

probably been less than one percent (remember Noah). This means that God is only saving about a half of a percent of all his children (a very generous estimate). Not a very successful plan he prepared for us.

2. {Okay, you say, all these people will have a chance to accept the gospel in the Spirit World.} Then why did God even make the plan for us to come to earth if we could all accept the gospel as spirits? How can we make a choice between good and evil in the Spirit World? We don't have bodies, and therefore we can't be tempted. All temptation is from the flesh (lust, greed, pride, etc.). That isn't a true test. We're here on the earth to prove ourselves by accepting the gospel and living by its principles. We can't do that in the Spirit World!

All of these musings about the plan of salvation may not have been particularly novel or profound and probably could have been overcome on a certain detached intellectual level by those inclined to do so. But there was nothing detached and intellectual about being rejected over and over again in my attempts to offer the LDS Gospel™ to people who already had their own set of good, moral beliefs and therefore only naturally rejected my foreign ones. It was on a gut level that these doubts about the justice and mercy of the plan of salvation started to gnaw on me. Despite the best attempts of my intellect to use theory about the Spirit World and the ultimate wisdom of God, with each rejection the whole plan of salvation felt more and more wrong deep inside.

The hull of invincibility had been breached. I was now willing, for the first time, to honestly consider the possibility that the Church had no monopoly on the truth, and I began to reexamine some issues which had previously bothered me, but which I had approached not as a sincere investigator of truth, but as an apologetic seeking to reinforce a conviction. I began adding items under the heading Against:

3. {Blacks and the Priesthood.} For the first 148 years of this Church's existence blacks were denied the blessings of the priesthood based solely on their race. This is totally incomprehensible to me. Whatever happened to "God loves all his children the same?" Germans, Japanese, English, Koreans, Indians, Spanish can all receive the priesthood, but if your skin is

black, if you have even a drop of blood in you from black ancestors, no way. How could "God's one true church" have been so obviously, sickeningly racist? I could maybe understand if the Church had apologized and called it an erroneous doctrine of man or something, but no, God just changed his mind. What kind of God would stigmatize and humiliate an entire race like that for 148 years?

The list grew over the following days as some new experience would cause me to seriously ponder questions that before the hull breach I would have quickly pushed from my mind or resolved in some barely satisfactory manner in order to avoid the sinking discomfort of cognitive dissonance.

One such experience came about when Goddard and I started meeting with a man named Alyosha whom we met knocking. Alyosha was as golden as they got. He had bright, deep gray eyes, thoughtful and serene, and a kind, intelligent face. He was a listener. He appeared humble and eager to learn from us. He testified that he knew from experience that God talks with us personally through prayer if we are meek enough to listen. We often prayed together, and his simple, anxious prayers, spoken straight from his heart, lifted my soul like beautiful music. When we introduced the Book of Mormon to him, he became visibly excited by the idea that there was an additional testament of Jesus Christ that he had not known about. He enthusiastically committed to read the book and take Moroni up on his challenge to pray and ask God if what he had read was true. We kept meeting with Alyosha and giving him the discussions, but each time when we asked him if he had received an answer to his prayer, he replied that he wanted to read the whole book before asking God about it. We told him that he needn't read the whole book to find out whether it was true, and that as soon as he asked with a sincere heart, real intent, and faith in Christ that God would make the truth of it known unto him, but he quietly yet firmly insisted on reading the whole book first. Finally, he told us that he had finished the book and prayed carefully about it. He looked at us tenderly, regretfully, and said:

"I am sorry Elders. I know how much this book means to you, and I really admire your dedication in trying to bring people into your religion. I think that this book has some good teachings. It is a good book. But, I am sorry, I do not believe that it contains the words of God."

"God told you that when you prayed about it?" I asked in a quivering voice, completely shaken by this unexpected response.

"Yes. I am sorry."

"Are you sure?" I felt silly for questioning this man whose sincerity and honesty I had no reason to doubt, but I did not know what else to say.

"I feel it strongly, Elder Young. I cannot deny what I feel."

That night I added a fourth item to the list.

4. {How can two people pray to the same God and get different answers about what is the truth?} Who am I to say that my answer is any better than Alyosha's answer? How can I say that what I believe is superior to what others sincerely believe? How can I just dismiss the fact that billions of people pray to a God who tells them that what they believe is true?

The next P-Day I insisted that we visit a Russian Orthodox church, as I was curious to witness one of their services. Ever since coming to Russia I had been mesmerized by the outward appearance of Russian churches. I loved the brightly painted onion domes, which, depending on my mood and the ambient light, would mystically morph in my mind's eye. They were giant upside-down blood-stained teardrops sitting atop an edifice built up by the blood, sweat, and tears of Russian peasants of centuries past. They were puffy dollops of golden whipped cream crowning a fairy-tale gingerbread castle that had magically sprung into existence by some archaic incantation. They were flickering candle lights placed on a windowsill by a solitary monk before he knelt in his ascetic room to pray. The churches seemed so full of history and mystery, so unlike the franchised office-building-with-a-steeple LDS churches of Idaho and Utah.

We entered through the church's massive wooden doors to a single large room illuminated by the baroque glow of gold and candle light. There were no pews or folding chairs, just open space where people were standing, slowly swaying, crossing themselves, and bowing. The blackened stone walls and domed ceilings were covered in icons depicting saints and scenes from the Bible. From somewhere above our heads came floating the haunting deep basses and ethereal angelic sopranos of the choir. The sweet, lavender smell of incense filled the air. From the inner nave the priest emerged through the iconostasis, perfuming the air with a censer and chanting in a rich low voice which the choir echoed in swells and crests. It was beautiful. I stood just taking it in for half an hour, the art, the music, the smells, the mystic priest, the women with covered heads lighting candles and placing them on the votive candle stands. Finally, Goddard tapped my shoulder, and nodded impatiently towards the exit.

I just wanted to meditate on the reverent beauty of the experience, but as soon as we had left the church Goddard started right in, apparently deciding that what he had to say was important enough to break the rules and switch to English.

"That was disgusting! How can they believe in something like that? Everything covered in gold. Give that gold to people that need it. And people were buying candles and books right in the church! It's like the moneychangers at the temple. If Jesus was here, he'd drive them out. And all the icons?! Hello!! 'Thou shalt not make unto thee any graven images!' A little thing called the Ten Commandments, people! Ever heard of them? And the 'priest!' He was just creepy. Get a shave. That was just plain evil. Maybe it's not just Catholics that are the great and abominable church."

"Yeah," I said simply, hoping he'd just shut up or at least switch back to Russian.

On the way back to the apartment I thought about how there were thousands and thousands of these churches across the vast expanse of Russia. I knew nothing about their beliefs yet I was supposed to believe that they were wrong, or, to speak euphemistically, "incomplete." When we got back to the apartment I added another item under Against.

5. Is it really true that the billions of people who believe in their own religion are wrong, and that the small sect of Mormons holds the only complete truth? How can I say that my Idaho experiences, acquaintances, and studies that gave rise to my feelings and produced my testimony are any more legitimate than those of the Russians?

24

We All Want to Change the World

I couldn't resolve these questions, and they wouldn't go away. They were making it hard to get to sleep at night, hard to get off the mattress and study in the mornings, hard to don the suit and nametag and leave the apartment on time, hard to think about anything else, hard to be happy. If I hadn't been on a mission, these questions probably would've just faded in intensity and importance. I would've just gone to my job five days a week processing loan applications at a bank, met my buddies for a round of golf on Saturday, and taken my usual place among family and friends in the pew on Sunday, and these thoughts would have been nothing more than a slight uneasiness that crept into the back of my mind when someone bore her testimony about the "one true Church" or when a nonmember friend mentioned how happy his religion made him. As it was, though, I was spending one hundred hours a week doing everything I could to better convince people that they should, nay, *must* at their eternal peril, join my religion and abandon their own. These questions were unavoidable.

Still, I could try my best to avoid them. Enders, Vandeburg, and Everett had all done their escapist best. Enders had immersed himself in reading books and studying Russian. Vandeburg had worked out in the village once a week and flirted with Russian girls the rest of the week. Everett had slept a lot. And, to varying degrees of magnitude and levels of conscious intentionality, they had all tried to avoid proselytizing – the street contacting, door knocking stuff – as much as they conscientiously could by creative accounting of the 30 Ds, ineffective scheduling of appointments that left long bus rides between each one, lengthy visits with their favorite members, frequent illnesses for which we were allowed to stay at home, superfluous attendance of branch activities, et cetera.

Only Quamme had steered clear of the escapist route, had avoided those "pitfalls that limit missionary effectiveness" and approached the model missionary with the square jaw and briefcase, that missionary who knew that the sole reason he was on a mission was to harvest, the missionary who committed himself to doing whatever it took to maximize the yield. But even Quamme had seemed rather numbly committed: he'd gone through all the right motions but hadn't seemed too emotionally invested one way or the other in the results.

Perhaps numbness was the secret, but it wasn't a secret that gave me a whole lot of comfort. I had another fifteen months to go. Fifteen months of rejection, boredom, and doubts. Fifteen months of feigning complete confidence in something I wasn't sure about, of hypocrisy, of hard work for a cause I was no longer sure was worth working for. And even if that was the secret, that numbness wasn't something you could just one day wake up and decide to have, it seemed to me. It was the result of months and months of hard work and rejection. Such an attitude hardly befitted a newly minted senior companion.

Or perhaps I could try to avoid these thoughts by giving myself over to the heathenry of the "lazy" and "problem" missionaries. The Samara mission only had a very few of those, but most everyone knew who they were. They ignored the rules, watched movies, went to concerts and hockey games where they might even have a beer, and invited girls over to their apartment. They generally only had a few months left and didn't give a fig about baptisms; they were just trying to physically make it to where they'd been mentally for months – home. A sense of duty prevented me from this. Not just duty to the Lord and to the truth, but duty to my parents who were supporting me, duty to my companion, and duty to the abstract idea of hard work and obedience.

Finally, what seemed like a sure way to avoid these thoughts was to go home, to go back to the safety of the non-missionary life where such thoughts weren't so pressing and didn't make your head pound. I could hit the road as a long haul trucker and see the country roll by from high up in my cab, roll the windows down, crank the radio up, and let out a howl just because I felt like it. Live life instead of just thinking about it. An intriguing idea, but scary. Certainly a last resort, desperation kind of thing. And besides, what would be my reason for leaving? I couldn't just pack up and leave nine months into it because I was pestered into unhappiness by some prickly thoughts. And I was past eating raw pork or some other such nonsense again. This mental torment was different, more defined, than the one that had driven me to the pig. Before, I had known only that I was unhappy, that the mission was somehow making me unhappy, and that I wanted it to end. There had been no way to address such an amorphous unhappiness save with a silly, flailing act like eating rotting pig. Now, however, the unhappiness fit neatly into a category: cognitive dissonance caused by my recent doubts and troubling thoughts. So, unlike before, at least I could now clearly point to the cause of my unhappiness. Knowing the cause gave me something to work with. And I couldn't go home until I had finished this work.

So it seemed to me that, for the time being, anyways, these doubts and thoughts were unavoidable. Unavoidable and un-addressable, save by one or two means – cocksureness or faith. I knew the prescription. Fast, pray, read the Scriptures, keep the commandments, pray some more. Rinse, lather, repeat until I got my faith back. Until I could be one of those missionaries like Goddard. The ones who stood up at every testimony meeting to testify that this is the one true Church on the face of the Earth today, and whose defiant faces told you that they meant every word. The ones who could shake their head in condescending pity at people like Alyosha who prayed and received different answers. The ones who could attend a beautiful religious ceremony and call it creepy and evil. The ones, perhaps the only ones, who seemed to have no problem with the fact that being a model missionary indelibly meant that you saw every last individual you met as just another someone who must be converted to your, Mormon, way of thinking.

Despite my fears that the cure might be worse than the disease, I decided to take the medicine. If I couldn't avoid these questions, I would immunize myself against them with faith. Then, even if some of these questions still nagged at my mind, unresolved and unresolvable, my hypertrophic faith would flood my mind with its antibodies and render them impotent.

I hoped that such a hypertrophic faith would not result in a Goddard-like cocksureness. I wanted to somehow overcome what seemed to me to be the contradiction between, on the one hand, believing that I must labor diligently to bring everyone into the LDS Church because it was God's One True Church, and, on the other hand, believing that other people's beliefs were equally valid.

It was an elusive mix which I was seeking, one of certitude and open-mindedness, of conclusiveness and curiosity, of allegiance and tolerance, of faith and reason, of serenity and inquisitiveness, of confidence and humility, of boldness and unobtrusiveness.

I wanted peace of mind, that sweet balm of assurance that the Church was true and that I was doing the right thing, without shutting down parts of my mind to achieve it. And I simply hoped that, once I had achieved that peace of mind, it somehow wouldn't bother me as much to push my beliefs so aggressively on other people.

So I wrote my own prescription. I took out a sheet from my legal pad and wrote at the top in big, bold, capital Russian letters:

REVOLUTION

Strictly translated, the rest of the page read as follows:

Preamble: I, a person of this mission, being of sound mind, create this declaration on the 1st of October, 1999. Recognizing that the time of my mission is limited and precious, I consciously create this declaration in order to build up my faith, to use my time more effectively and not waste it, and also in order that we may achieve our goals relating to BAPTISM.

1. I will wake up at 6:00 every morning.
2. I will exercise for 20 minutes.
3. Goddard and I will speak Russian 100% of the time, not even one word of English (except for the "how do you say" rule).

4. I will carefully study the gospel for a good full hour.
5. I will learn 10 new words every day.
6. I will study one chapter in the *Modern Russian* grammar book and do all the exercises.
7. 100% Obedience!!

I took out another sheet and drew a giant red star on it with the red pencil I used to mark my Scriptures, and then I pinned these two pages to the middle of the wall. This was my October Revolution. A new day was dawning, and I was recommitting myself to the mission with everything I had, with all my heart, might, mind, and strength. I was going to try to get that peace of mind back, to reassure myself once and for all that this was the Lord's Church and that I was doing His work.

Beyond fulfilling the 7 goals of my revolution, there were two more things to be done which I felt uncomfortable about posting publicly: fasting twice a week and intensifying my personal prayers. I didn't feel the need to broadcast these to the world, even if that world consisted solely of Goddard and district leader Lindsay.

So I dug in my luggage and pulled out the jump-rope and push-up bars that I hadn't used since Novokuibyshevsk with Quamme, and I started exercising in the early mornings in the courtyard in front of our apartment building. I kicked my study of the Old Testament and Russian Book of Mormon into high gear, concentrating and pondering over each verse and looking up all the cross-references at the bottom of the page. I commenced fasting twice a week. Each morning after gospel study and each evening before bed I stayed on my knees until I felt like I had exhausted all that was on my mind and in my heart. And I tried my best to keep each and every little mission rule, with partial but decent success.

I felt like I had a plan, a real solution: I was going to change my head. Everything was going to be all right.

25

The Reprieve of Simply Living

And everything was all right for a spell. The revolution bought me some time. I had a clear purpose to drive myself towards again, like when I was at the MTC, like in the first days with Quamme struggling to learn the language, like when I was studying for the Omega in Saratov with Everett. The questions and doubts didn't go away, but I was able to hold them at bay with the thought that I was doing something concrete to resolve them, and that soon I would have peace of mind.

It also helped that I could keep my mind distracted from these doubts for hours at a time. For there was day-to-day life to be lived. In Russia. With Goddard. And that was something in and of itself.

Goddard and I had been together for about a month at this point. Lindsay and his greenie had finally found their own apartment and moved out, leaving me alone with the nasally and whining one-man MoTab. The sun was going down earlier and earlier each day, and the darkness was becoming less mellow and more menacing. The air began to nip and bite, the leaves to lose their green. Persimmons and pumpkins replaced the berries and tomatoes at the market stalls. The smell of roasting chestnuts and sap skated through the cool air. The women's nylons got darker, and the men started wearing their hats: sheepskin flat caps, leather and felt Lenin's caps, ushankas, Cossack hats, and Persian ram fur hats.

The Reprieve of Simply Living

I knew the infamous Russian cold was coming on. The kind of cold that tore up your lungs to breathe. The kind of cold that I'd just gotten a taste of when I'd arrived in March.

So come sweet precious P-Day we went shopping for winter clothes. I didn't have to deal with thoughts about the injustice of the plan of salvation as I was buying things, feeling a small rush of power as I improved my lot in life with a few swift purchases. I bought a cheap synthetic parka, a felt Lenin cap, some leather gloves lined with wool, and some thick socks. Then we headed across town to the main department store and I bought a Sony Discman and some classical music CDs. I missed music and I needed something to drown out Goddard. I also bought a good spatula and a non-stick frying pan that I intended to carry with me come transfers. I made hash browns almost every night and was tired of scraping off the grated potatoes and onions welded to the bottom of the old iron skillets that came with the apartment.

We dropped everything off at home and met Lindsay and his greenie so that we could share a taxi to New City, home of the big Lada car factory and probably the richest area in our mission with its American-style shopping mall, cans of Dr. Pepper, and bottles of Heinz 57 sauce. There we met up with the New City district at the fanciest banya where all the Mafiosis and New Russians hung out. Goddard was none too happy about the trip, and I could tell he thought that the banya was against the rules, but since the zone leader and two district leaders were all going, he couldn't really argue. The banya's pool was enormous, big enough to swim laps in, and the water was lukewarm, the kind of water that Satan had dominion over, the kind of water that had drowned disobedient missionaries of yore. We were all used to small basins filled with freezing water and this banya's big pool made us all nervous. So we all made a point of showing how far away from breaking the rule against swimming we were by gingerly entering the shallow water feet-first and then simply standing around, talking only about missionary work. All the talk of obedience, baptisms, and discussions started to vex my mind a bit, but I ducked my head underneath the water, held my breath, and it was gone by the time I came back up.

In the evening after the banya, our bodies rejuvenated and tingling, Goddard and I went and watched Tennessee William's play, "The Rose

Tattoo," in the theater in Old City. This was our monthly cultural evening: each month we were allowed to take an evening off and attend cultural events like plays, symphonies, circuses, hockey games, etc. We were the only mission that I knew of where missionaries were allowed to take a cultural evening, and with every play and hockey game I attended I was grateful once again for my good fortune at having President Hatcher as my mission president. Not having watched even a flickering television screen for several months, my attention was riveted, and there was no mind meandering, no dangerous freethinking, during the play. Another good P-Day.

The next morning, still hung over from the relatively bacchanal P-Day the day before, we looked out our window to a cold gray and an icy rain and we sighed. It was going to be one of those miserable days again. We had an appointment for a second discussion first thing in the morning with an investigator we had met street contacting, so we put on our long-john garments, sweaters, suits, and long black trench raincoats. I put on my new Lenin cap, and we set out to find the address we had been given. It was raining hard, a freezing, spiteful rain. We approached the right side of the apartment building where our investigator had told us he lived. I figured it was probably a fake address as usual, but we had to go and verify anyways. I checked my blue sheet – apartment number 79; I quickly counted the floors – five; at four apartments to a floor, that meant twenty apartments per stairwell, so our investigator must live on the top floor in the fourth stairwell from the left. So we started walking right to left along the road parallel to the front of the building, heading for the fourth stairwell. As we drew closer, I spied the dirty black plastic numbers over the fourth stairwell: 46-60. Блын! Dang it! This building must have been one of those with three apartments to a floor, which meant that he lived in the sixth stairwell.

We were walking quickly since we were cold and wet and getting wetter and we wanted to get inside and out of the freezing rain as quickly as possible. So as soon as I recognized that we needed the sixth stairwell and that we had gone too far, I made an abrupt about face and sprinted back to the sixth stairwell, Goddard at my heels. As we entered the sixth stairwell on the run, I heard a police siren and looked over my shoulder to see a police car, lights a-blazing, heading towards us on the road in front of the building. I paid it no mind and we started to climb the stairs. But before we could make it to the second floor we were frozen by the barks of authority: "Stop! Put your hands in the air!" The police had followed us into the stairwell, guns in hand. We spun around and they stuck the guns in our faces.

"Руки вверх! Hands up!" they repeated. I couldn't help but think of the popular Russian band from Samara called "Руки Вверх" that we would always hear blasting away in taxis. I understood this meaning of the group's name for the first time, and I was amused.

We put our hands in the air, turned around and stood up against the wall with our backs to them. They asked to see our passports. We told them that we had left them at home, so they handcuffed us and shoved us into their patrol car. I looked at Goddard and smiled – now this was what a mission was all about. He looked back, scared and confused.

On the way to jail I tried to make sense of it all. I'd seen the parked police car at the end of the road from underneath the brim of my Lenin cap bowed to the rain. They'd seen two dark, foreign-looking figures clad in long black trench coats walking towards them who had suddenly turned around and fled into the last stairwell of the closest building once they'd gotten close enough to notice the police car. Must have looked suspicious, I supposed.

They brought us to the police station to interrogate us.

"What are you doing here in Russia?"

"We're missionaries; we came to teach people about God." I said defiantly, relishing the moment.

"Missionaries, huh? Maybe you are spies! Where are your passports?"

"At home, we just didn't bring them with us today. Take us home and we'll show them to you." I knew of some missions where the mission office confiscated all the missionaries' passports and locked them away, ostensibly for security reasons, but our mission did not, could not, do this, since we were supposed to carry our passports around for occasions just like this.

"Why did you run from us?" They seemed to be enjoying the interrogation as much as I was, and they tried to hide their smiles.

"We didn't even see you! We were just walking to meet with someone, and it was raining, and we ran to the apartment."

"Mmmm-hmmm. Give me your bag."

I handed them my Church-approved handbag.

"Why do you have a camera?"

"To take pictures."

"Of what?"

"Of anything I see. Of friends, of anything."

"Hey Ivan! Check out this map! Why do you have such a map of the city?"

"Because spies need good maps! How else can I spy on your super-secret apartment buildings?" I retorted, pleased with my cheekiness.

"Don't get smart with me!" He feigned anger.

"Take us home and we'll show you our passport and visa. We are here as missionaries!" I half hoped that they wouldn't take us home, that they would keep us there. It would beat a day of proselytizing.

"Missionaries! Do you think that we are so primitive that we do not know about God?"

"No, we know you know about God, but we have a message about God's plan for us."

"God's plan? And what is this plan? Join an American church and give it all our money?"

"No, just ten percent," I felt like saying. I said instead: "No. God wants you to return to Him in heaven, and this plan shows you how."

"And we can't return to Him if we are members of a Russian church?"

"Look, we are not here to try and convert you. We are just sharing a message about God and His plan for those who are looking for the truth. Obviously that is not you." I was getting tired of this exchange.

"The truth! And how do you know that you have the truth and that we Russians don't?" The police officer asked the question with an aggressive sincerity that had not been there in the other questions.

"Well, you might have some of the truth, but not all of it."

"And you have it all, huh?" He asked testily.

"Can we please just go? We were on our way to a meeting with someone who wanted to find out the truth." I was starting to feel frustrated.

"No. Not until we find out who you are and what you are doing here."

"We're missionaries! We spend our entire day trying to speak with people about God!" I said, exasperated.

"Yeah, and if you were spies pretending to be missionaries, that is exactly what you would say."

I was now utterly frustrated and it showed. They put us in a jail cell. Behind bars. With cracked blue paint on the wooden floor. With a plastic two liter bottle with the top cut off in the corner, filled halfway with urine. Nothing more. We sat on the dirty floor for an hour, silent. No one came to talk to us. It was just us, the smell of urine and feces, the dirty wooden floor, and the iron bars. We were both a little shell-shocked, subdued, wondering where we would end up, how this would turn out. I started to replay the conversation with the police officers about truth over in my head, thinking about how they seemed to have gotten the better of it. And just like that the doubt started creeping in again. But the revolutionary spirit pushed it back. I grabbed the bars and began chanting, "Freedom! Freedom! Freedom!" and Goddard joined in. Delighting in the absurdity of our situation, we begin singing the Star-Spangled Banner as loudly and proudly as we could, over and over again, until the policemen came and told us to shut up or else.

After a few hours they had to release us from the cell to make way for some crazy drunk woman. We went out into an office and sat in swivel chairs and talked America with the police officers there. They told us they had to do some routine processing and then they would take us to our apartment and verify that our passports and visas were all in order. We sat and waited for hours, joking about being CIA agents. They said they had to wait for the interpreter to formally interview us. I acted offended and told them that I didn't need an interpreter, but they said that it was protocol. Once the interviewer arrived they asked some questions for the record and then they took our fingerprints. I asked the policeman to use my camera and take a picture of us as we were getting fingerprinted. Goddard and I had never looked happier together than in that photo. Big cheesy absurdist grins. Finally, they took us back to our messy apartment, looked at our passports and visas, and wished us well. The day was nearly over; another day had passed without proselytizing, without feeling the doubts creeping up after every slammed door and spiritless mobile street D.

HARVEST

A couple of days after getting out of jail, the evening before zone conference, Goddard and I began to chop all the ingredients for a huge pasta salad. The zone leader had put me in charge of providing lunch for thirty at zone conference, and I saw it as the first test of my leadership ability, my ability to get things done. My funds had just been drained by my shopping spree, so the lunch de rigueur of zone conference, the soggy pizza, was out of the question, and I didn't know where to buy pizza anyways. So pasta salad it was. As the chopped onions and peppers and roasted chicken began to pile up, I realized that we had nothing to put the salad in. The one pot we had wouldn't come close to fitting it all. It was past 9:30 and therefore too late to leave the apartment to try to buy some cheap containers at the store. I looked around the apartment for a solution, but all I could find was two rusted out mop buckets in the bathroom. Absurd idea, I suppose, but I cleaned them out good with soap and water, and we put the salad in them. When I grabbed the old tin buckets by the handles it looked like I was going out to feed the hogs their slop, so we laughed and Goddard took a picture.

I took some razzing for the rusty buckets, and I got some weird looks from President, but everybody except Goddard and Sister Hatcher partook. Zone conference was as motivational and inspiring as always, and it made me glad I was fighting the revolutionary fight. I was, however, disappointed to learn that there would be no transfers for our companionship, which meant that I'd be with Goddard for at least another month. The disappointment was mitigated somewhat by a foreboding sort of excitement, however, when Hatcher enigmatically told me in our interview that:

"God has a plan for you, Elder Young. I have a feeling about you. I think that you have a big role to play in this mission. I don't know what it is that you're going to do, but I'll find out. Something special."

Maybe my revolution was working, I thought. Maybe.

26

What I Am and What I Do

Goddard and I kept setting our modest baptismal goals every Sunday during companionship inventory. And each subsequent Sunday we had to discuss the reasons for our failure and brainstorm ideas for how we'd do better the next week. We were working hard and had built up our teaching pool so that it now contained some strong investigators, but none had taken the plunge yet. A few had gotten close. Bedisa had seemed like a sure thing until the heroin. Alyosha had seemed golden and heaven-sent until he had prayed to find out if the Book of Mormon was true. Babushka Rita had come to sacrament meeting and said that she believed we were sent from God, but once her son found out that she was meeting with us, he'd put the kibosh on our visits. Dima, a friendly sort about our age, had seemed genuinely interested until he researched the Church on the Internet. Far from encouraging me, all these near misses only served to accentuate the sting of failure.

As did Lindsay and his district meetings. He'd only been out for a couple of months longer than I, and this was his first stint in a leadership position. Apparently he and his greenie were starting to have phenomenal success, at least according to the gushing he would do over the phone whenever he called to ask for my stats. Loads of investigators lining up for baptism as a result of the Lord's blessing them for keeping some covenant they'd made. Lindsay could be a bit over the top, but I respected him for his sincerity and quiet obedience and liked him for his friendliness.

His excitement was nascent and irrepressible, and so at the next district meeting his lesson was on how our district would have twenty baptisms by next zone conference by following the covenant he had drawn up. It involved some formula: x number of hours spent proselytizing and studying the gospel, x number of doors knocked, etc., and, of course, perfect obedience. I played along, keeping my mouth shut about my doubts that we could get twenty baptisms this month when last month we hadn't gotten a single one. But I felt the pressure: If they could do it then why couldn't we? The look Goddard gave me asked the same question, slightly rephrased: "If Lindsay can do it then why can't you?"

Lindsay was in high gear talking up his covenant, channeling the MTC teachers. He had his greenie read us a classic passage from the *Missionary Guide* that I had memorized by now:

> Your purpose as a missionary is to help people come to Christ through the ordinances of baptism and confirmation. As the people you teach open their hearts, listen to your message, and obey the Lord's commandments, they will feel the Spirit of the Lord. They will be converted when they feel the Spirit and act on the promptings they receive. . . .
>
> Your ability to help people become converted depends primarily upon what you are (your attributes) and what you do (your skills). You will need to develop Christlike attributes and effective proselyting skills.

"It's that simple, Elders. Baptism's our purpose. We'll have baptisms when people feel the Spirit. People will feel the Spirit if we have It. We'll have It when we develop Christlike attributes and effective proselyting skills."

Lindsay stopped and looked professorially at us to make sure that we understood this logical principle before continuing: "So what are some of the obstacles that can keep us from developing these traits and achieving these baptisms? What are the things we must avoid in order to have success? Elder Irving, could you read the next passage please?"

Irving obediently read from the *Missionary Guide*:

> You have received your call from a prophet. But you are free to make choices that will keep you from bringing souls unto Christ. Disobeying

the commandments and mission rules, for example, will hinder your work.

Lindsay looked at us with humbled awe, like a Mormon child who had just shook the hand of an actor playing Joseph Smith in a Mormon Disneyland.

"Just think about that for a moment," he said and paused, giving us several seconds to ponder the statement. "A prophet of God was inspired to personally call each and every one of us to serve here in Samara!" He seemed genuinely wonderstruck by the thought.

He paused for another moment to let this sink in, then continued: "But it's up to us to live up to that inspired calling. Like the *Missionary Guide* said, we all have free agency, but if we use this free agency to disobey or break mission rules, then what good does this calling from a prophet of God do for us?"

"Actually, I'm not so sure our calling was from the Prophet," said Elder Irving, surprising us all by daring to question such a widely accepted and officially endorsed notion. Such freethinking was especially unusual for a greenie fresh from the MTC. I liked Irving for it, and also pitied him, fearing that his mission was going to be a long, difficult, one.

"What do you mean, Elder Irving?" Lindsay couldn't conceal his annoyance at being interrupted from the masterful lesson he had prepared. His question, like all others, had obviously been rhetorical.

"Well, one time in the MTC my companion and I were looking at each other's mission calls, and we noticed that President Hinckley's signature on his was exactly the same as the signature on mine. Every little blue loop had exactly the same curve to it, the same amount of ink, the same width, everything. So we rounded up all the calls from the other Elders in our district, and they were all *exactly* the same as well. The Prophet didn't sign them; they were just signed with an autopen made to look like a real signature."

"Well, I seriously doubt that. But even if it's true, just because the Prophet didn't sign the call, that doesn't mean he didn't make the call," Lindsay said with exaggerated patience.

"There's like over 60,000 missionaries serving right now. If the Prophet actually called us all, he wouldn't have time to do anything else. It's just farmed out to some committee and signed with an autopen." Irving had obviously done a lot of thinking about this and was eager to get it out.

"There is no reason that the Prophet can't delegate his authority to others, Elder Irving," Lindsay reminded him.

"Yeah, I know. Of course. But it just bugs me that we treat it like the Prophet himself received our missionary applications, knelt in prayer over them, and decided to send us here. Let's be real about it."

I couldn't believe that I was hearing a missionary speak so bluntly.

"Ok, Elder Irving, we'll be *real* about it. The *Missionary Guide* says that we received our calls from a prophet. That is enough for me to have faith that my call is from a prophet. I don't need to know the exact procedure – it doesn't matter to me. I suggest that you show a little more faith as well." Lindsay's voice now had an edge to it.

Irving knew he had been beat with the faith card. "Yeah, I know. You're right. I wasn't trying to say that our calls weren't from the Prophet, I was just trying to say that they were signed with an autopen, that's all." He looked like he regretted having spoken up.

I searched for something to back Irving up, to let him know that I appreciated his critical thinking. "Yeah, it's like with our assigned companions in the MTC," I began. "You know how they kept telling us that the Lord had given us our specific companion for some important purpose, like it was this huge spiritual deal? Only, did you guys realize that they just paired us up alphabetically? I mean, I was only with Viska because he was the closest alphabetically to Young."

"Yeah, that bugged me, too," Irving sympathized, but then wisely stopped there.

Lindsay stepped in. "Let's get back to our covenant, guys. So, as the passage that Elder Irving read states, and as we all agree – right? – we have received our call from a prophet, but we are free to make choices that will prevent us from bringing souls to Christ. That is where this covenant comes in. We pledge not only to make the right choices, but we spell out in detail what those choices are. We state specifically what we are going to study, how we will spend each hour of the day, how many doors we will knock and how many contacts we will make, and we make specific pledges of obedience.

What I Am and What I Do

I'd like to read a well-known scripture, and I'd like you to ponder it in connection with this covenant: It's in Doctrine and Covenants 82:10, and it reads: 'I, the Lord, am bound when ye do as I say; but when you do not as I say, ye have no promise."

Elders, I testify to you in the name of Jesus Christ that if we will bind ourselves by following this covenant, the Lord will be bound, and the Spirit will be with us, and we will have baptisms.

Elder Young, Elder Goddard, and Elder Irving, will you covenant with the Lord this very moment to do the things we discussed in order to have the Spirit with you?"

I, like all missionaries, hated it when another missionary tried to use the commitment pattern with its direct "will you" questions on me – "Hey, that's my trick!" I wanted to say. But there was not really anything to do but make the covenant. Goddard had jumped all over the covenant: "I do so solemnly covenant," he'd said overeagerly, shooting me a sidelong significant look. Even though Irving and Lindsay had already made the covenant, they did it again for our and thoroughness's sake. It was down to me. Part of me wanted to just say, "Are you guys crazy?", but I went along and showed my faith and covenanted myself to follow the program in exchange for baptisms.

Lindsay finished up by reminding us that this covenant was only as good as our faith: that if we performed the covenant without sufficient faith that God would do His part, then the covenant would have no binding force and God would be under no obligation to provide us with baptisms. In support of this, he ended the lesson with a quote from that favorite book of district and zone leaders everywhere, Grant Von Harrison's *Drawing on the Powers of Heaven.*

> When you set goals that cannot be attained or realized without the Lord's help, you should consistently remind yourself of the process of faith that is required to call down the powers of heaven. You will become frustrated if you set goals that require assistance from the powers of heaven to be realized and then fail to exercise the necessary faith that will allow your Father in Heaven the opportunity to assist you in attaining your particular goal. It is extremely important that you are conscious of the role of faith as a principle of power in the attainment of some goals. The faith that motivates you to have

determination will make it possible to realize some goals, but faith as a principle of power is the key to achieving many other goals. (p. 24).

So, in the ensuing weeks, we followed the covenant: we knocked our doors, met our benchmarks of obedience, did our extra hours of proselytizing and gospel study, and tried hard to exercise the necessary faith. But still we had no baptismal commitments. I had been senior companion for a month and a half now, and I had not had a single baptism or baptismal commitment besides Bedisa, who wasn't even really my investigator to begin with. I was starting to fear getting busted back down to junior companion for failure to prove myself as a missionary.

The myopic focus on baptisms, the constant pressure to put up numbers, it was getting to me. I hated that it affected me so much and made me feel so badly. I looked to the *Missionary Guide* for some words of advice on how to deal with the lack of baptisms:

> Despite your best efforts to teach and baptize, people may exercise their free agency and reject your invitations. For missionaries who truly seek to bring souls unto Christ, this will be a painful experience.
>
> There is a temptation in such circumstances for missionaries to try to deny their disappointment. They might stop talking about baptism, for example, and feel threatened when baptism is mentioned as a goal. Or they might rationalize that other missionaries are letting numbers become more important than people. They may feel that their hard work is unnoticed. "Besides," they may think, "I can't help it if the Browns decide not to be baptized."
>
> Do not yield to this temptation. One of the attributes of a true disciple of Christ is that he allows himself to feel sorrow for the sins of the world. He is developing the Christlike attribute of loving people even though their actions cause him grief.

So I told myself that I was *supposed* to feel so badly about it.

Our best baptismal prospects were a woman named Polina, her twelve-year old son Pasha, her seventeen-year old daughter Dasha, and Dasha's friend Nadya. We had found them through knocking, and they were always very excited to see us whenever we visited them. Polina would shake our hands with the smile of an eccentric, usher us into the kitchen, and feed us some organic hash of fried sprouts and legumes that she had made for us, lecturing us all the while about the importance of proper nutrition for the organism. Pasha would jump around, show us some lizard he'd found, and beg us to play checkers with him. Dasha and Nadya would smile and blush and giggle and whisper to each other, periodically disappearing into Dasha's room only to emerge with the cool faces of coconspirators. We visited them a few times a week, and I always looked forward to those visits. It made me so happy to have friends to spend an hour or two with in the cold dark evenings.

Nadya clearly had, in the words of Goddard, a "puppy love" for me. She was always the last to greet me when we arrived: after I'd greeted all the others she would extend her warm little hand oh so coyly and we would shake with just the slightest extra squeeze and she would tell me in her adorably serious, too thin to hide the girlishness, voice, "Good evening, Elder Young." As I taught she would rest her doe eyes on me and gaze dreamily until I would turn and look at her and she would look at me nakedly for just that extra second before she blushed and lowered her eyes. And she was always the first to say goodbye: she would stand close to me in the narrow vestibule as I bent over to tie my shoes, and when I stood we would shake our hands just so again, and she would ceremoniously wish me a good night and speedy return before she would retreat to the back of the vestibule to watch us make our goodbyes with the others.

We became comfortable there, the home away from home sort of thing. I would talk vegetables with Polya, and Goddard would play checkers with Pasha. They had lots of questions about us and we'd tell them about our families and previous lives back in America, and they'd tell us about school and about Pasha's and Dasha's older brother serving in the military down in Chechnya. We showed them all our pictures, and they showed us theirs. I gave in to their persistence and told them my first name, while Goddard held out. Dasha, who studied English, and who may have been starting to develop her own puppy love for Goddard, began to sit next to him, and Goddard was suddenly full of questions about how to say this or that in Russian, questions with which Dasha was eager to assist him.

HARVEST

Polya's family was faithfully reading the Book of Mormon, and their knowledge of and commitment to the Gospel was coming steadily along. We asked them about baptism each time, but each time they would hesitate and turn us down. I didn't want to rush it or force it. I figured that we would get them involved with the branch activities, let Polina make friends with the women in the branch, let Pasha, Dasha, and Nadya come to the picnics, the English lessons, the district Halloween party in Samara, the weekly soccer games, meet the youth, and see what the branch was like. So, since they had listened to all the discussions by now, we kept meeting a few times a week and would just chat for the first half an hour or so before we would share a message about the Gospel and ask about baptism again.

It was just a matter of time, I thought, before they joined, just a matter of exposure to the Lord's Church. I was starting to feel good about myself, good about my attributes and skills, good about my abilities as a missionary, about my ability to have the Spirit and bring people to Christ. I could do this. And what happiness it gave me to be able to visit people who seemed to love and care about me.

One cold evening, Goddard and I were headed out to an appointment with Polina's family. We were huddled at the bus stop waiting for our bus and I was watching the pack of wild dogs that roamed free in the area. There were several of them, all male, and we saw them nearly every day, mangy mutts without a home. One of the bigger dogs was mounting a smaller dog from behind. This wasn't the first time I'd seen this, they were always going at it, whether it was just a display of dominance or whether it was sexual I don't know. But I started thinking about homosexuality, how it seemed to have a biological basis. Then I started to wonder why God would make someone that way only to call them an abomination to Him. Then I started to think about my <u>Against</u> list buried at home. Then I started to think about some other things that could go on the list if I were to pull it out again.

Despite my best efforts at suppressing them, these kind of thoughts were still worming their way into my mind, eating holes in the serenity I had left, and hollowing out the faith I needed, that revolutionary faith I needed to not only make the baptismal covenant work, but, more importantly, to immunize me against these thoughts and make me whole again. An apparent catch-22. I needed faith to immunize myself against these thoughts, but I couldn't get that faith because I kept having these thoughts. Regardless, I tried hard to push these thoughts aside by thinking about how nice it would be to see Polina and everyone that evening. Everyone, including Nadya. Nadya and her doe eyes and upturned face and warm little hand and coy little smile. Eek! Dangerous thoughts everywhere. To the Book of Mormon, quick! Horses, elephants, oxen, cows, goats, wheat, barley, plows, chariots, iron, brass, steel, silk, swords, scimitars, sheep, and swine in ancient America, oh my! Eek! Must think about baptisms and the covenant, that always works. Count up what I'd been doing wrong today. Wallow in guilt where there was no room for doubt.

I was interrupted from my thoughts by Goddard. He turned to me and began speaking in a halting but firm voice that told me that this was something important that he'd been thinking about for a while but was afraid to bring up:

"Elder Young, I really think that tonight we must speak with Polina and her family more about the Gospel and God and less about ourselves and America," he said in his agonizingly slow Russian. The grammar was perfect and the line sounded memorized, like he'd spent a good twenty minutes on it this morning.

I stared him down for a moment before the words rushed out my mouth. "Do you think that I don't know that!? What the hell do you think we are going to talk to them about?! What the hell do you think that I'm trying to do here?!" I hadn't felt such anger since long before my mission, nor had I used profanity. And for a moment the anger and profanity felt so good, so gratifying. But for just a second, and then I immediately regretted it. Now I had sworn twice and gotten angry. In English no less. I was as far from a Christ-like missionary as one could get. And on top of that, I had lost any moral high ground that I might have had. From here on out, Goddard had one up on me, a moral superiority which I knew he would subtly wield in the constant power struggle that our companionship was turning into.

"I'm sorry, Goddard. I really am." I said a few moments later, as he looked away. "It's just that, I mean, you know I want baptisms just as much as you do, and for you to say that…. You make it sound like I just want to hang out with them. And that's so not true. I'm really trying my best here."

"That's okay," he said, still not looking at me. "I understand, and I know that you is trying. I wanted for to say only that I think that they must know that we are not here for to be cool friends, but that we are here for to teach them about God and plan of God." He finished slowly and patronizingly.

He was starting to grate on me again. Why wouldn't he follow my lead and speak about this in English so we could have a normal conversation? What, he needed even more moral superiority, I thought cynically, forgetting about my earlier persistence in speaking Russian with Quamme, my desperate desire to just learn the language, and the very real fear that if I broke the rules and spoke English the Lord wouldn't help me – a desperation and fear that Goddard probably was feeling even more than I ever had.

"Yeah, I agree with that," I said as patiently as I could, continuing in English. "But, I also think that having a good relationship with them can only help them to trust what we have to say about God."

"Yes, that is true, but I do not want for them that they do get baptized since the incorrect reasons."

"I don't either, Goddard," I said, my voice edged with annoyance again. "But I don't see that happening. They're reading the Book of Mormon every day. They can answer all our questions about the Gospel that we give them. They pray about it and say that they feel good about it. What more do you want?"

"Let us simply be careful," Goddard said, with his oh-so-wise tone.

"Yeah, sure."

While Goddard had a way of making everything more annoying to me than it needed to be, I knew this was a case of "truth hurts." Goddard's words had stung me deeply. I knew he was right. I *did* like to just hang out with Polina's family too much, and our conversations were not as Gospel-focused as they should have been. Every branch was full of inactive members who had gotten baptized simply because they were friends with some missionaries. Inactive members who, once those missionaries had left, had never come to church again. And maybe I did want baptisms so badly that I was in danger of "flirt to convert" with Nadya.

What I Am and What I Do

So, beginning with that evening's visit, Goddard and I made our visits shorter and we avoided the friendly chats as much as possible. It was achingly clear that they were hurt, and a big part of me wished that I could just quit being a missionary, move into their apartment, eat Polina's organic hash for dinner, go on strolls through the park with Nadya and hold her hand, play checkers with Pasha on Saturday mornings, and attend church for three hours on Sunday.

But Goddard's words had also stung me for another reason. I felt like he had seen right through my mask to the ugly hypocrite inside. Who was I kidding? Yes, on the outside I was a good missionary, working hard, and obeying most of the rules. But, inside, I was still torn up by those same doubts about whether or not I was doing the right thing, whether or not this was even God's one true church. So, of course, my heart was not in the right place – it couldn't be, and, of course, Goddard could see that play itself out with Polina, Nadya, and the family.

I was starting to wonder who I was. Who was the real me, the true me? Was it the missionary who kept all the rules, worked hard, tried to exercise his faith and do his best to bury the doubts? Or what if the true me was the part of me that kept questioning all these things, the part of me that had made the Against list, the part of me that wanted to hold Nadya's hand, the part of me that felt uncomfortable shamelessly using every sales tactic in the book to try to convert everyone to Mormonism, the part of me that wanted to respect others' beliefs and not force myself on them, the part of me that despised obsessing and lying about statistics and worthiness, the part of me that thought that a racist God or a homophobic God was simply inexcusable, the part of me that wanted to ponder the big questions of life without knowing their simplistic answers beforehand, the part of me that wanted to think freely and rationally and discover my own path in life, the part of me that could not believe that only Mormons go to heaven, the part of me who wasn't even sure if there *was* a heaven and who didn't want to *have* to be sure? What if that part of me was me? What if that part of me was my true identity that was trying to break out? What if the pain was coming from trying to bury that part of me? What if the pain would stop if I let that part of me breathe freely? Why should I bury that part of me? Why shouldn't I think these thoughts? What if a good question was every bit as valuable as a good answer? Why shouldn't I see where a little freethinking might take me? Why shouldn't I follow the unknown path? Why should I live out of fear?

What if I hadn't been born Mormon? Who would I have been? Who would I be if I stopped being Mormon?

I was getting pretty good at asking tough questions, but I still had no answers. Except for those I'd been given and relied upon my whole life. So I kept on following them, kept praying and exercising faith, hoping that this would work, that it would take away the pain and give me peace of mind.

One thing seemed clear to me, though. This couldn't go on forever. I couldn't keep on testifying over and over again to the truth of things I doubted until the end of my mission, I couldn't keep on working more out of duty than conviction for fourteen more months. I couldn't keep burying a part of me, I couldn't keep stifling that voice inside me forever, I couldn't keep just telling myself that, of course, this is all true and right. I wanted to *feel* the truth and rightness of what I was doing and saying again, like back in the MTC. I wanted to be *whole* again. I needed some help, I needed some answers, I needed some inspiration.

To that end, I was really looking forward to that Saturday when we would travel to Samara for a special mission-wide conference with Elder Wolfgang H. Paul, Second Counselor in the Europe East Area Presidency and a native German. He was the first General Authority to visit our mission, the first General Authority I would lay my eyes upon since those who had so inspired me in the MTC. This man was one of the Seventy, just one step away from being one of the Twelve Apostles. In fact, according to D&C, his authority was equal to that of the Twelve Apostles. Perhaps at this conference I would find those answers which I had been seeking in fasting and prayer for weeks now. I felt I was approaching some critical juncture, some crossroad, and the timing of this conference seemed to me to be a sign. I pled with the Lord at night in my prayers, asking him to use this conference to give me some kind of answer, some kind of comfort to my mind.

I guess what I probably needed was for Elder Paul to get up there and give us some praise. Tell us that no matter how many baptisms we were getting, we were doing a good job just by being there and working hard. Tell us that the Lord and the Prophet and the Apostles appreciated the work we were doing. Maybe tell us one of those hokey little stories like the one in which the master tells his servant to go and push on a big boulder, and so the servant pushes and pushes and pushes, but the boulder won't budge, but he keeps on pushing until he becomes super strong and muscled, but the boulder still won't budge, so he finally goes to the master and says, "I'm sorry, Master, but I couldn't move the boulder," and the master laughs his patient wise laugh and says, "I didn't ask you to move the rock, I asked you to push on it. I will move it for you my dear and faithful servant, but in the meantime, look how strong you've become." I'm not sure if this would have quieted the doubts and questions in my mind, but it would have certainly cheered me up, invigorated me, made me more capable of dealing with them.

As it was, I was only further depressed by Elder Paul and his talk. It was all about what we were doing wrong, one thing after another. Right jab then left hook. Not enough baptisms, not enough priesthood holders, too many inactive members, too many members who weren't paying their tithing. And who was to blame? The missionaries, of course. We needed to be more obedient. We needed to open our mouths and tell the good news to everyone at the bus stops, in the buses, in the grocery stores. We needed to work more with the inactive members. We needed to work more with the members. We needed to stop thinking about home and writing so many letters. All that would have been okay, I'd heard it plenty of times before, but it was his main theme that he kept hammering home over and over in that Teutonic accent of his that really got to me: "Your motives as missionaries must be pure. If your motives are not pure your work is not counted unto you as righteousness. If you are serving the Lord with impure motives, you might as well go home."

27

What Profit Hath a Man of All His Labour Which He Taketh Under the Sun?

I could feel myself getting low, lower than when I'd eaten the raw pig. All the work, all the striving to be obedient, all the sacrifice of my books, music, family, and flyfishing, it was all for naught. It was not counted unto me as righteousness. My motives weren't pure. They couldn't be. I didn't have a testimony. I didn't *know* whether the Church was true. I thought that it probably was, that it had to be, but I wasn't sure. I'd been struggling with these doubts and questions for over a month now, and all my fasting, prayers, and gospel study hadn't helped. I was as confused and conflicted as ever. The optimistic feeling which I'd had in the wake of my October Revolution had vanished. My faith hadn't gotten any stronger, it had weakened.

The thoughts would not go away. I was starting to crack. All throughout the long days of proselytizing my mind was fixated on the same tedious thoughts. You know the Church is true. You know it! There's no way Joseph Smith could have written the Book of Mormon. Or could have he? How can you ignore all the spiritual experiences that you have had? But people in other religions have had these experiences as well.

I think that I had the barely conscious hope, maybe even the barely conscious expectation, that these doubts would go away once we started having some success, once we tasted the sweet fruit of our labors and witnessed the beautiful transformation that took place in people as they

212

accepted baptism. Perhaps I just needed some success to balance out all the rejection. Perhaps I just needed to see that my labors were not in vain, and that if I helped but one person draw nearer to God, it was all worth it. Perhaps then these thoughts would go away. Dusty abstractions swept from the mind by the gusty, fresh dynamism of personal experience.

And the winds of fortune did begin to blow our way. Polina's family and Nadya all decided that they wanted to be baptized. Unfortunately, Lindsay's baptismal interview of Polina uncovered that the man who would shyly greet us each time we visited before slinking off to the kitchen was not actually her husband as we'd assumed, but rather a cohabiting boyfriend of several years. Lindsay told her that she was therefore not worthy to be baptized. Polina took some offense to that, arguing that marriage was just a piece of paper from a godless state, but, in the end, despite being told she wasn't good enough for the Church, she was fine with her children being baptized.

And then a wonderful babushka, Valentina, whom we had found knocking, also accepted baptism. She had read the Book of Mormon from cover to cover and had even borne her testimony at Church, and already fit the profile of a solid member.

So, that Saturday, I took my clean white baptismal clothes from my luggage for the first time, took hold of Nadya's tiny wrist with my left hand, raised my right arm to the square, said the magic words, put my right hand on the small of her delicate back, and lowered her into the warm water of a local indoor swimming pool. Pasha, Dasha, and Valentina followed. It was another nice feeling for me, and they all looked as if it had been a nice feeling for them, too.

Four baptisms was a good number, a really good number. Lindsay's loads of investigators had all dropped out somewhere along the way, so these were the first baptisms in our district for a while. The zone leader called to congratulate me; this bumped his zone up to nine baptisms for the month, second only to the central Saratov zone. Goddard seemed to relax, and I felt relieved, like I had proven myself as senior companion.

But the success did not push out the doubts, and the doubts made the joy of bringing souls unto Christ an empty, hollow kind of joy. Elder Paul's words kept running through my mind. "If your motives are not pure your work is not counted unto you as righteousness. If you are serving the Lord with impure motives, you may as well go home." All that the success of baptisms did was to add a new stanza to my thoughts. "I'm working hard, I'm even baptizing, but I'm doing it for the wrong motives because I still don't know if this Church is true."

So, since none of it was counting for me as righteousness anyways, the following P-Day I bought some CDs: Bob Dylan, The Beatles, Simon and Garfunkel, Neil Young. They were pirate-cheap, less than two dollars each, and I told Goddard that I was buying them just so that I could send them home. He, of course, gave me the self-righteous look, and I knew that I'd just lost some more moral high ground, but I didn't care anymore. I then went to the library and tried to check out an English-language book of Hemingway's, *Islands in the Stream*, but the librarian wouldn't let me because I wasn't a citizen. I argued with her to no avail. Goddard was fidgeting uneasily, and I knew I was making a scene, creating a bad impression of the Church, but I didn't care. Finally, I walked out in disgust with Goddard trailing a few steps back. I'd been rude, and I knew it, and I felt badly for treating another person, another functionary of an institution, like that.

I should have also felt badly, felt guilty, for being a bad poster boy, but I didn't. We were in plainclothes without nametags, but even had we been wearing the uniform, I probably wouldn't have cared. I was starting to snap. I was sick of constantly being gawked at – a freakish thing to behold – the eternal center of unwanted attention – a thing to be pitied. I was sick of always being the face of the Church. Always putting on that best face that said: "Look how wholesome, clean, and happy we are – you, too, can be clean and happy and professional-successful." Walking billboards. PR tools for an appearance-obsessed culture.

Later that day, I told the story of not being able to check out the book to Vlad, a rather mysterious member our age who looked Japanese, spoke flawless English, was rumored to have a fabulously wealthy father, and whom no missionary or member had ever visited at home. He showed up at our apartment the next evening with an English copy of Hemingway's *Fiesta*, which, as I found out when I got back to the States, was the title under which *The Sun Also Rises* had been first published in the UK.

In the evenings after work I started to listen to the music and slowly read the book, savoring every word. Goddard gave me the usual look, a little sharper than usual perhaps, but he said nothing about my clear violation of the rules: after our four baptisms he wasn't pushing quite so hard anymore. I would take off my suit and put on my robe, prepare myself a plate of artificial crab meat, olives, mozzarella cheese, and gherkin dill pickles, pour myself a glass of apricot nectar, lay in my bed, put on my headphones, and I was off flyfishing with Jake Barnes in the mountains of Spain. Sometimes I would put the book down for a song, close my eyes, and I was riding a Greyhound with Kathy looking for America and counting the cars on the New Jersey turnpike, or working as a cook for a spell in the great north woods, or finding things to do in stormy weather with my El Camino. Maybe it was escapism, but I felt like I was escaping into a world more real than the one whose air I breathed and earth I trod and inhabitants I proselytized to.

I found myself relating deeply to Jake Barnes: the pervasive sense of a loss of innocence and optimism – his from the war, mine from the battle for souls; the impotence – his apparently physiological, mine mandatory; the relentless pull of a woman – his a Katherine Hepburn-like Brett, mine nearly every woman I met; the temporary refuge and happiness in earthy pleasures like fishing – his real, mine vicarious except for the weekly treks to the village outside of Saratov; "the feeling that all your life is going by and you're not taking advantage of it," and the desire to "[find] out what it's all about."

The book reminded me that there was a life to be had outside of the mission, and my pickled gherkins and crab meat became Barnes' sliced cucumbers and pickled herring and my glass of apricot nectar became his brandies and sodas, bottles of champagne, steins of cold beer, and liters of wine tipped at arm's length from leather bags.

I began to fantasize about sneaking out of the apartment at night while Goddard was sleeping. My fantasies never got very far. I would just imagine myself taking a taxi downtown, where I knew that *something* interesting would happen. Something that would tell me what life was all about.

I was diving headfirst into the shallow pool of escapism. But the water was so warm and inviting. I wrote home for the first time in three weeks and asked my mom to send me some books for Christmas: *Les Misérables* and *War and Peace*. I stayed up late into the night reading Hemingway and listening to music and woke up late the next morning. I started to dream about the next CDs that I would buy. I started to look into the shop windows at all the clothes and electronic gadgets. I started to look for souvenirs like old Soviet medals, pins, and banners. I started to spend more time planning and cooking more elaborate meals.

I finished *The Sun Also Rises* greatly dissatisfied. The whole book I had been waiting for Barnes to fill the emptiness with something meaningful, to find a purpose and direction in life, to commit heart and soul to something of value, to pull himself out of the suffocating ennui and seize the day, to live for something rather than just live. But he and Brett never passionately embraced, realized that they were meant for each other, and walked off into the Parisian sunset hand in hand as happy, contented lovers. Alternatively, he never threw her off to embrace independence and a new path in life. No, instead, after the fiesta was over, he interrupted the obvious happiness of his solitary holiday in San Sebastian to come running to Brett in Madrid as soon as she but telegraphed the word. And for what? Just to tell her, when she told him that they "could have had such a damned good time together," "*Isn't it pretty to think so?*" Apparently Barnes never did have the desire to "find out what it is all about," I thought. Apparently he just didn't care anymore. Apparently he would remain floundering in his escapist pool of alcohol.

I really wanted Barnes to be happy. And it seemed to me like there had to be an answer to his happiness, if he would just embrace it. And he seemed to know the answer, whatever it was, I knew he did. And for a moment there at San Sebastian I thought that he had embraced it, and that the book would end happily. I couldn't understand why he came running to Madrid for Brett because of one little lousy telegram. After everything he had been through, he must have known what would await him. He must have known he'd soon be back to alcohol, aimlessness, relativism, and escapism. So why did he go back?

28

Fork in the Road

I didn't want to be lost like Barnes. I wanted to find out what it was all about. I wanted to be able to fully commit to my mission, and if I couldn't do that, I wanted to go home, and I would find out what it's all about there. Elder Paul was right: if my motives weren't pure, I might as well go home. I didn't want to spend the rest of my mission escaping.

I needed advice from someone who knew what it was all about. So I went and gave a painful birth to my internal struggle by talking about it with President Hatcher at the next zone conference. I was now the proud new owner of an official crisis of testimony rather than just the incubator of some tormenting thoughts.

President Hatcher gave me a priesthood blessing in his ancient soothing voice. A man called of God who had it all figured out. A holy, confident man speaking for God. His words and counsel inspired me to continue to fast, pray, and devote myself to getting my testimony back. I came out of my meeting with him with a calm sense of optimism. A renewed vigor. Yet again. I gave the book back to Vlad and put away my CDs.

A week later, my optimism already worn down by the daily grind of proselytizing and the doubts raging as strongly as ever, I received a call from the zone leader informing me that Goddard was being transferred, and that I would be getting a greenie straight from the MTC.

HARVEST

The night before Goddard left, I watched him pack his suitcase, expecting to feel great relief. Instead, I felt mainly guilt and regret at how badly things had gone between us, and I wanted to apologize.

"Elder Goddard," I said hesitantly. "I know I haven't been the best companion to you. I'm sorry for being so short with you lately. It's just that . . . well . . . I'm going through a hard time right now." This sounded weak to me. We all went through hard times. That was just part of being a missionary. I felt the urge to explain myself more, to let him know that it wasn't just a typical hard time that I was going through. That there might have been a deeper, less personal, reason for why our relationship had failed. So I continued, "I'm really struggling with my testimony right now. In fact, I'm not even sure if the Church is true. I've talked to President Hatcher about this, and I'm even thinking of going home if I can't figure it out." I hadn't planned on telling him all this, and it was painful to admit. A missionary without a testimony was like a soldier without courage. It felt so good to let it out, though. To confide in someone down in the trenches. Maybe he had similar feelings. Maybe he had some advice for me – he seemed to have such a strong testimony.

He looked less surprised than I thought he would. "I am sorry to hear that, Elder Young. I don't know what to tell you. I know that this Church is true."

Goodbye Goddard, hello Sanderson.

I was surprised that Hatcher was making me a trainer after I had just confessed to him that I had no testimony. Trainers were held in high esteem for the obvious reason that their influence played a large role in how the young missionary developed. To make me a trainer was a sign of trust on Hatcher's part. In retrospect, it was also a shrewd management decision to give me a son, especially one like Sanderson who was so easygoing, friendly, and teachable – one of the genuinely nicest people I have ever met. I couldn't ruin his mission right out of the gate by sliding into apathy or laziness, so I continued to work hard, largely for his sake, despite my mental turmoil.

I wanted to help him as much as Quamme had helped me. To mean as much to him. So I made little language exams for him. I tried to ward off any signs of loneliness by switching into English to chat around a little. I tried to give him just the right amount of responsibility in proselytizing to make him grow but not enough to overwhelm him. But my heart wasn't in it at all, and I knew that I was a poor trainer. I was too wrapped up in my own problems. I was aloof for long periods of time. Right next to him, but miles away. We had good success, though, and I added a couple more baptisms to my résumé, including one whose circumstances had all the makings of one of those great faith-inspiring missionary stories, if told right.

One day, we knocked out a building near Polina's without success. The first door we had knocked, an apartment on the top floor of the leftmost stairwell, was answered by an old babushka, a Jehovah's Witness, who was full of verve and vituperation. She argued the Bible for a bit with us, then called us the devil and chased us off the landing.

A week later, we went to knock in the same area after finishing a new member discussion with Nadya and Polina's family entitled "Proclaiming the Gospel," which was all about how they needed to start being missionaries themselves. There were two identical buildings next to each other in that area. I knew we had knocked one of them the week before, but I couldn't remember which one it was. So we picked a building and knocked on the first door, and lo and behold, it was the old babushka again. I expected the venom again and I started to apologize for re-knocking, but her face lit up with joy and she invited us inside. She told us she had felt badly for chasing us off, and that she wanted to hear what we had to say. She hung on every word, was baptized two weeks later, and, the last time I saw her, she was one of the most faithful and enthusiastic members I have ever met.

I was surprised by how little this incident moved me. This was the kind of story I'd heard growing up that had made me so eager to serve a mission, the kind of experience I'd dreamed about one day having. Maybe it had somehow been God's answer to my prayers, but it didn't feel like it to me. It felt like a fortunate coincidence, nothing more. I was too far gone.

In my journal, this story is just a blip in a torrent of desperate scrawling about how paralyzing and debilitating it was to not have a testimony, about how frustrating and confusing it was that God was not answering my prayers.

I knew the story well. I told it 30 times a week. Joseph Smith was struggling to decide which church to join and he wanted to know which of all the many churches was the most correct. One day, while reading the Bible, he came across a verse, James 1:5, which struck him powerfully: "If any of you lack wisdom, let him ask of God, who giveth to all men liberally, and upbraideth not; and it shall be given him." Joseph kept repeating these words over and over in his mind as he worked in the fields. He thought about how if anyone had ever lacked wisdom, he certainly did, and so he decided to ask God which church he should join. He went to a grove of trees, prayed, and God the Father and Jesus Christ appeared to him as two glorified personages and told him that none of the churches were correct, and that he should not join any of them.

We'd usually end the retelling of this story by testifying to investigators that if they wanted to know which church was true that they, too, could ask of God, and, although He might not personally appear to them, He would answer their prayers.

Every night before sleep and every morning as soon as I woke up I would kneel next to my bed and pray. I always began right away by asking God to tell me if the Church was true.

"Please, my dear Heavenly Father, please help me to know if this Church is true! Help me to know Thy will! Help me to have faith and not doubt!" I stayed on my knees repeating some variation of these lines over and over, waiting for an answer, then repeating them again. I knew not what else to ask. So I simply begged for Him to give me wisdom, to tell me the truth. I begged with as much real intent as I could summon, bringing myself to tears sometimes with the strain.

But I felt nothing. God was not answering. I was beginning to think that His failure to provide that reassurance *was* His answer. Maybe His silence in response to all my pleas meant that the Church wasn't true. I wasn't looking for a visit in a grove of trees, I just needed to feel whole, to not feel so split and torn up inside, to just simply go back to having calm in my mind. To just simply *feel* that it was true.

I needed to talk to someone who I knew would respond. I needed to tell those who knew me the best and loved me the most. It was time to go to my parents and let them know about my crisis of faith. It was time to test the waters of a possible return trip home.

Fork in the Road

So the following P-Day, I wrote them a long, painful letter. I photocopied it, sent a copy to Hatcher, kept a copy for myself, and placed the original in an envelope on which I had written, above the home address:

FOR MOM AND DAD ONLY!!!!

The letter read as follows:

Dear Mom and Dad,

I've been thinking for some time about writing you this letter. I hesitate, not wanting to worry you, and dreading to disappoint you. However, I've finally decided that my situation is such that I need help and advice from you, even at the risk of hurting you. Please don't tell Westin and Mandy about this. This is what pains me more than anything – that I am supposed to be an example to them, as well as to others.

So, what is the problem? To speak bluntly, I've lost my testimony, and I no longer know if this church is true. I won't even attempt in this letter to explain how this happened, but it was a gradual process, and being here in Russia, my testimony has weakened and waned to the point where I am absolutely clueless. I have no idea if the Church is true or not. I could list all my reasons for this uncertainty, I could spell out all my doubts and concerns to you, but they're, in essence, not important. Suffice it to say, I can't work out anything in my mind. I've pondered and meditated about all of this until my head hurts, and I can't come to any conclusion. I'll start to convince myself that the Church is true, and then the other half of my mind will almost succeed in convincing me that the Church isn't true.

Now, I know that this is no way to find out the truth. Like I always tell our investigators, "you need to pray and ask God, and He will tell you the truth." So, the past month, that is what I have been doing. Every night and morning I asked God to help me find out the truth, to help me to regain a testimony. But, nothing happened, and I was just as confused as before. I thought that I had had faith in James 1:5.

This last zone conference, I told all of this to President Hatcher. I told him that, "I'm still working hard, I'm even baptizing, but I'm doing it for the wrong motives, and it isn't counted unto me for righteousness. Elder Paul told us that if we were serving the Lord for impure motives we might as well go home. My motives aren't pure, they can't be, because I have no testimony. I am working now out of a sense of duty, and out of a love for my family. Therefore, if I can't gain a testimony, I see no other choice than to go home. I can't continue like this. It is getting harder and harder to testify to investigators, I feel like I'm lying, especially when I promise them that God will answer their prayers."

President Hatcher is awesome. He gave me some scriptures to read, and encouraged me to fast. He gave me a priesthood blessing in which he blessed me with the assurance that I would find out that this church is true. He told me that the Holy Ghost would make it known unto me, that I'd feel a burning throughout my whole body, but especially in my heart.

So, the past few days, all that I have been doing is fasting, praying, and reading the scriptures. I've been sincerely, desperately seeking the truth, seeking a confirmation from the Holy Ghost. But, nothing has happened. I'm just as confused as before. I feel so frustrated. Why can't I get an answer? I really believe that God answers prayers, but why isn't he answering mine? I don't know what I'm doing wrong. I honestly feel that I'm doing all I can to find out. I'm obeying all the commandments, I'm reading the scriptures, I'm serving a mission, I'm fasting, and I'm imploring the Lord in prayer for an answer.

I also really want that answer to be in the affirmative. I simply want to receive the confirmation that this church is true so that I can continue to serve the Lord with all my heart by fulfilling an honorable, full-time mission. Things would be so simple and wonderful again if I had that sweet assurance that the church is true. It would be so much easier for everyone. But, the frustrating thing is, I don't have that assurance. I can't go on just ignoring that fact, my mind won't allow that. If I could receive that assurance, that testimony, that confirmation, everything would be wonderful again. But, it hasn't come.

So, in the meantime, I'll continue to fast and pray for that confirmation. But, this can't go on forever. I can't go on praying the rest of my mission, the rest of my life, to find out that the Church is true. There comes a point that I have to realize that the Lord has answered my prayer by <u>not</u> confirming the truth of this Church. But, when is that point? If God doesn't answer my prayers after a week, does that mean that the Church isn't true? Or do I need to pray for a month? A year? Five years? It's so simple in the scriptures. It's written everywhere – Ask God in faith, and He'll tell you. It doesn't say – Fast 3 times a week, pray 10 times a day for a month, and constantly read the scriptures to find out the truth. If God wants me to know the truth, why doesn't He tell me? I'm pleading with Him, with a sincere heart and real intent to tell me, but He isn't. All this just serves to further weaken my testimony.

I'm fully prepared to do whatever God tells me. If He tells me the church is true, I'll gratefully, joyfully finish this mission. If I don't receive this confirmation of truth, I see no option but to go home. I think that it's obvious that I can't continue my mission without a *testimony. No one, especially God, would want that. I <u>don't</u> want to go home, I don't even know if I have the courage to do so, but I have no other choice, if it happens that this Church is not true.*

I can clearly see the road of life ahead of me. I'm at a fork, the biggest and most important fork I've ever been at. One road, marked by the sign "Yes" is clear and inviting. It includes along its path an honorable full-time mission, a warm loving reception after that mission by a proud family and community, an active life in the service of the Church, a wonderful family of my own, and a good, secure occupation. The other road, marked by the signpost "No" includes along its path a mission cut in half, a reception by a disappointed family and a misunderstanding judgmental community. The rest of this road is not clear. It may contain all the wonderful things of the other road, a family, good work; it may contain a miserable life of sin. But, I am prepared to take either fork. It's all in God's hands.

Mom, Dad, I want more than anything to set off along the road marked "Yes", but I can't do that if I don't receive the confirmation from the Holy Ghost. I don't want to go down the other road, but I will if I have to. I can't go on being a hypocrite, deceiving people, deceiving myself, my conscience won't allow it. So, I'll do what is right, I'll act in accordance with what I know, what I feel. More than anything I don't want to hurt you, but I'll do what I know I must.

I hope this letter does some justice to my feelings and that I have presented an accurate picture of what I am thinking and the problem I am facing. I realize that I am coming up on a life-altering decision of the utmost importance. I have been, and fully intend to continue to include God in that decision. In fact, He is, in effect, the author of this decision. I also wanted to include you in helping me to make this decision. Any advice and all prayers would be greatly appreciated.

I apologize for all the hurt and grief that I know this letter will cause. I <u>love</u> you more than I have words to express. But, as strong as that love is, it isn't a strong enough motive, nor a proper, clean, pure motive to continue serving this mission without a testimony. I pray that God will give me the confirmation I need so that I can continue to serve Him for the right motives. I love you so much, and I am so sorry for all of this.

Love,

Your loving, confused son,

Jacob

29

Moving Right Along

I was in a cold and brackish sort of limbo waiting for my parents' response. The red of October had given way to a hardboiled white. Winter was all the rage and Russia had become the Mother Russia of cartoons: bearish men in furs and frosty perma-scowls trudging head-down through the blizzardy tundra, snow princesses and ice queens, Tchaikovsky and Father Frost, Siberia and taigas, ice sculptures and sledding, kiosks of vodka, statues of Lenin, soldiers in Red-army-esque attire, menacing grays and blacks staining the sky, hoarfrost, rime and snowflakes trellising everything below. Something essential about Russia only comes out with that first snowfall, something eccentric to elsewhere, something that makes Russia another world, glittery, exotic, and exhilarating.

I had written *the letter* on the twelfth of November, but I knew that I wouldn't get a response until mid-December. I found it tragically comic: I'd just sent my parents the most important and painful letter of my life, threatening action of the direst nature, and the letters I was getting back from them were telling me the results of my sister's volleyball games from an Idahoan Indian summer in October.

I was still praying for an answer, but my prayers had lost their urgency and I was just going through the motions. I had despaired of God's answering me by now, and I was basically biding my time, waiting to see what my parents' letters would bring. I had convinced myself that I was still trying hard to find answers, a bit of convenient self-delusion to prevent me from feeling too low, perhaps. In moments of what I considered honesty, however, or maybe it was depression – the two were becoming indistinguishable for me – I would admit that I knew why I hadn't received an answer yet. I wasn't doing everything I should be, everything I could be to get an answer. I wasn't worthy. Not even close, actually.

I had been masturbating.

Not with reckless abandon or anything, but every few weeks the temptation would become so unbearable that I couldn't resist tampering with my little factory's release valve. It always followed the same pattern. I'd give in once and then the following few days would be filled with self-loathing episodes until I quit again.

I'd had one series of episodes since the revolution: shortly after the conference with Elder Paul when I was stressed out, feeling low, and looking for escape.

After masturbation came the guilt. I would go into hyper-obedient-and-resolved-never-to-sin-again mode, and I would pray hard for forgiveness until I felt better enough to assume that I had been forgiven. I hadn't confessed any of these factory tamperings to Hatcher, as I had interpreted, perhaps mistakenly, his soft response to my initial confession to mean that this was something for which I could receive forgiveness on my own. Perhaps intentionally mistakenly. It was so shameful to talk about that I wanted desperately to be able to deal with it on my own.

So in those starkest moments, when I wrenched my brain trying to understand why I hadn't received an answer, I felt compelled to admit to myself that my failings, my sins, my desires to sin, were what was preventing me from getting my answer, that I was too unworthy for God to speak to me. Sometimes I even accused myself of secretly not wanting the Church to be true so that I could sin without guilt, and that this was the reason why I could not get an affirmative answer.

Not long after Hatcher received his copy of the letter to my parents, he called me to tell me that I was getting transferred. "You've been doing some excellent work there in Togliatti, and I hate to pull you out when you've been having so much success with baptisms, but I need a real champion to be my district leader here in Samara," he had said, but it was clear to me that he just wanted me close to his office so he that could keep a helpful eye on me.

The frequent transfers and companionship changes were hard. It was the whole adjustment period all over again: no friends in the branch, no investigators, a new companion with different quirks, a new zone leader with different demands and goals, new maps and bus routes to memorize, stress, stress, and more stress.

But a lot of Samara was just more of the same. The big blocks of Soviet apartments where I would spend hours knocking were the same as the big blocks in Togliatti, the people streaming by on the street whom I would spend hours stopping were the same as the people in Togliatti. For all I knew I could have been knocking and street contacting in Togliatti, if it weren't for an intangible big city feel to Samara, as if something worldly and tempting and sinful was lurking there, waiting to ensnare me.

The only serious investigator my new companion, Elder Richardson, and I had when I first arrived was an Azerbaijani man named Ramiz. I found it remarkable how people from the minority groups, like those from the Caucasus and the "Stan" republics, were so much more willing to talk to us, and seemed so much more humble and open to our message than the proud Russians. The funny thing was that my friend serving in Germany wrote me that the Russians there were so much more humble and willing to listen than the haughty know-it-all Germans. Perhaps the explanation for the apparently disparate psyches of the Russians in Russia and the Russians in Germany lay in the basic principle underlying the Church's instructions in the new version of the *Missionary Guide*, entitled *Preach My Gospel*:

-   Visit people who are experiencing changes in their lives, such as marriages, births, or deaths.

-   Visit and help people who are moving into the neighborhood.

The given rationale for these instructions:

People who are experiencing significant changes in their lives – such as births, deaths, or moving into new homes – are often open to learn more about the gospel and to make new friendships. For example, when meeting someone who has experienced a death of a little child, the missionaries could relate the teachings of Mormon and give comfort to the family. They could affirm to the investigators that they can be reunited with a deceased child. (Statement on Missionary Work from the First Presidency and the Quorum of the Twelve Apostles, 11 Dec. 2002, reissued 6 Feb. 2008).

Whatever the reason, these immigrants made for easier Ds and quicker investigators, but not necessarily for good baptisms. The majority of them were stubbornly Muslim, albeit the secular, pork-eating, alcohol-drinking type, at least most of the ones I met, although I had met several times with a devout and tremendously kind and friendly Muslim back in Togliatti. He was Chechen, and having a rough time of it. Many Russians openly detested the groups they considered not to be ethnically Russian, especially the darker skinned Caucasians and Central Asians. But the most vicious hate was reserved for Chechens, and this man had no chance of employment and he took plenty of abuse whenever he left his tiny, sparsely furnished apartment, so he spent most of the time inside with his young son while his ethnically Russian wife supported them by working at the market. He had no real interest in converting to Mormonism, and on the occasion of our last meeting he insisted on giving me his sole, well-worn copy of the Koran in Russian as a parting gift, writing on the inside cover what to me was a very poignant inscription:

Bilalov Umar Husseinovich.
Chechen.
To Young:
For the good of everyone and everything.

Ramiz, too, was Muslim, but he wanted to convert to Christianity. He had the entrepreneurial spirit, and he was always in the thick of some deal involving trucks of watermelons, cartons of cigarettes, or loads of leather coats. He was an effusive, extroverted guy by nature, and he seemed to believe everything we taught him with such enthusiasm and excitement that I thought for the first time that I really understood why we called our best investigators golden. As we taught him his face would shine and glow like the face of a young child seeing snow for the first time.

He really wanted to get baptized, but he couldn't quit smoking, and there were complications with marrying his longtime live-in girlfriend. So we kept visiting him a couple of times a week to push and prod him into getting married and quitting smoking.

In the meantime, the 30 Ds weren't going to get themselves, so we hit the streets and the doors. I thought the Ds would be harder to come by in the winter, but the Russians truly impressed me with their utter indifference to the cold – if they felt anything at all for it, it was a cool contempt. These were the same people who kept the outdoor ice cream stands doing brisk winter business, queuing up at the countless portable kiosks full of nothing but icy confections. I'd inquired about this seeming anomaly and heard different explanations: that they eat ice cream in winter because it's warmer than the weather, that the organism needs the extra fat to make it through the cold months, that it was a matter of economics – production and storage costs were cheaper because no artificial refrigeration was required. Whatever the reason, outdoor ice cream kiosks were just an accepted part of winter, and winter was just an accepted part of Russian life.

Our Russian life consisted mainly of ice fishing for Ds. Every morning we slipped and skated on the icy sidewalks from our apartment to our favorite spot near the confluence of the people flows from a metro stop and an outdoor market. Richardson would take a position near one metro exit, and I would stake out the other. The metro kept spitting out a good supply of D material, and as soon as people would emerge from the dark belly of the underground we were there to accost them. If there was a lull in the metro supply, then there was always a good stream of people on the other side of the sidewalk trying to get their shopping done.

We usually pulled in two or three Ds an hour, comparable to summer rates. I thought there was no way that someone would stand for twenty minutes in temperatures approaching thirty below, but people did. Granted, half of the ones who stopped were probably too drunk to care about the cold or the message, but I had garnered some quality investigators from drunken 1st Ds on the street, so that didn't bother me.

It helped, too, that I was becoming an old seasoned angler, adept at all the little tricks that kept people on the line. It was all about being able to quickly identify and read people and tailor the approach accordingly: for the ones who liked to hear themselves talk that meant asking them lots of questions while deftly weaving in a quick rote recitation of the principles needed to constitute a D; for the polite-but-in-a-hurry crowd it meant relaying the script as rapidly as possible and not slowing down for questions or testimony; for the drunk or the timid it meant being a bit forceful and gently ordering them to stay a wee bit longer to finish the discussion; for the ones who exhibited an interest in getting a free book it meant using the prospect of giving them a Book of Mormon as a carrot to entice them to stay; for the kind-hearted and empathetic it meant looking cold, pathetic, and desperate; for the rare ones who were genuinely interested in hearing our message about God and His plan it meant straying from the script enough to make the first D truly a discussion rather than a monologue while simultaneously sticking to the script enough to be able to count it as a D without a guilty conscience.

One thing I liked about contacting in the same spot every day was that the city became more familiar, a place to which I belonged, a place where if I didn't show up one day people would notice that I was missing, a place where a few regulars knew my name.

One of them was a friendly, well-spoken Jehovah's Witness. He would often be hanging around the stop doing the same thing that we were doing: proselytizing and handing out pamphlets. We talked for a few minutes nearly every day. He lived in Samara and worked nights as a taxi driver; proselytizing was just something that he enjoyed doing on the side. He'd met with the missionaries many times, and knew a lot about the Church and its doctrine and history – certainly more than I knew about his religion.

I often met Jehovah's Witnesses on the street, my brothers and sisters in proselytizing. They were polite, neatly groomed, and cleanly dressed, but I disliked discussing religion with them. Earlier in my mission, I had avoided them because of how futile it was to talk to them: they were just too cocksure that their religion was right, too narrow-minded, too focused on their own dogma to really open their ears and hearts and listen to our message. Now I tried to avoid them for a different reason: it was like looking in a mirror and being reminded of how I appeared to others.

Besides the JW man so uncommonly pleasant that I made no attempt to avoid him, I also got to know the women who worked in the tent-like stalls of the outdoor market behind their tables full of teas, cigarettes, soaps, fruits, vegetables, candies.

"How's the work going today, Youngich?" They would ask whenever they saw me.

"Ah, you know. Same old, same old. People seem really busy today. No one has time for God. How's your selling coming?"

"Oi, God help me, not too good. It's too cold today. Yesterday! Now yesterday, that was a good day."

"How cold do you think it is?"

"Cold enough to freeze my tits off, I'll tell you that," she said and laughed her rough phlegmy laugh.

I would laugh too. "Yeah, and my feet."

"You need to get yourself a pair of these," she said and pointed to her heavy felt boots called valenki. "How can you go around all day in nothing but shoes, like some kind of manager?"

"It's okay, I have thick socks." I rarely wore my big Sorel Bear boots. They clashed with my suit and seemed very un-missionary-like, and my socks really were quite thick.

These rather crude middle-aged women bundled roundly in their muskrat shapkas, heavy felt boots, and multiple layers of old, dirty synthetic coats never failed to arouse me. As they would crack their vulgar jokes I would look at their twinkling eyes buried in the creases of their ruddy, sunburned faces and I could feel that underneath all the bulky winter clothing simmered a lusty heat, a red-blooded vitality, and I ached with desire.

One day Richardson and I descended down into the metro as we were following up on an address we'd gotten street contacting. As we passed the magazine stall located in the underground hallway, I kept my face pointed straight ahead as usual in order to avoid accidentally catching a glimpse of the small pictures of topless girls that dotted the magazine and newspaper covers. Out of the corner of my eye, however, I thought that I saw the word Penthouse and a flash of exposed flesh. I'd never seen such a magazine in Russia, and I was wildly curious to verify if it was indeed a Penthouse. I'd never inspected Russian magazines enough to even know if any of them were pornographic – newsstands were like red-light districts for missionaries, and we avoided them whenever we could. News was forbidden, and the chance glimpses of skin were just too tempting and corrosive for a young missionary working hard to be chaste, so we just never looked. But a Penthouse – I knew that it had pictures of naked women – there was no need for verification there. If it was real. I had to know. So, on the return trip I turned my head ever so nonchalantly towards the newsstand. The flurry of ecstasy and sickening desire confirmed to me that it was indeed a Penthouse.

As we continued street contacting at that metro stop over the next few days, I was consumed by the obsessive thought that beneath my very feet were beautiful women who for a hundred rubles would shamelessly show me every inch of their beautiful naked bodies. I could feel them down there, provocatively posing. Looking over their bare shoulders with a smoldering look inviting me to follow them down into the dark abyss, where for a hundred rubles they would make me breathe fast and hard, make my heart pump furiously, my legs go weak, my stomach rise into my throat, and my head spin.

Barely conscious of what I was doing, I began laying the groundwork. Instead of standing ten or fifteen feet away from the entrance of the metro so that I could stop people before they descended the staircase, I began to stand closer to the entrance so that I'd often follow somebody a few steps down the stairway as I tried to get them to stop and talk to me. Then I began giving discussions on the stairway, still visible to Richardson as he stood at the other entrance. Then I began following them a couple of steps lower until I was invisible to Richardson. Richardson, like any good missionary would, reacted by maintaining his line of sight by going down his staircase until he could see across the hallway to my staircase and observe me giving a discussion. Sometimes, however, he'd be in the midst of giving a discussion when I went down the staircase, and he couldn't descend for a few minutes until he'd finished.

In this way I had effectively trained Richardson not to panic if he looked over his shoulder while giving a D and saw me missing. I estimated that it took him anywhere from fifteen to twenty-five minutes to give a D, and I observed that about half of the time that he got somebody to talk to him for over ten minutes he was able to finish the D. Which gave me at least a 50/50 chance to make it down to the magazine stall unobserved. Everything was now in place for me to make my move, and I was waiting only for him to began talking to someone for ten minutes with his back turned to me. It took a couple of excruciatingly long contacting sessions, but finally a big burly drunk man turned to face Richardson as Richardson was walking away from me trying to stop him. After several minutes I figured that it was now or never and that I would take my 50/50 chance that he was going to talk for at least ten more minutes.

I vaulted down the steps, yanking off my nametag and jamming it into my pocket as I went. I speed-walked down the hallway, approached the magazine stall, and breathlessly croaked, my voice cracking like a pubescent teenager's, "Can I have a Penthouse please?" I grabbed the rubles which I had ready in my pocket and shoved them into his hand, telling him to keep the change. I then crammed the magazine into the front pocket of my handbag which I'd prepared beforehand so that all the proselytizing materials that I'd need for the day would be in the main compartment and I'd have no need to open the front one. I then turned around with dread, fearing to see Richardson's tall figure behind me. But the coast was clear, and I ran back up to my staircase, fumbling to pin my nametag back on as I went. I resumed street contacting with nary a look askance from Richardson.

I realized I was moving out of limbo and into hell, taking the road marked "No" to get there, the stairway down to the abyss. There had been no resoluteness on my part or anything, though, to take that first step. It was as if I had just shut off any conscious decision-making about that step and given myself over completely to a diabolical drive, obediently enacting its devious scheme to get what it wanted. I was still racked by uncertainty, doubt, guilt, self-loathing, and all the other typical mission emotions, and I couldn't answer the question that gnawed at my mind: How could I tell if I had bought the Penthouse because God hadn't answered my prayers and I didn't know whether the Church was true, or if God hadn't answered my prayers and I didn't know whether the Church was true because all along all I had wanted to do was to buy the Penthouse? It was a version of the same old question I'd always had of how to tell the influence of the Spirit from my own emotions and the temptations of Satan from my own desires to sin, and a version of the even older question of the chicken and the egg: what was of God and what was of myself and what was of the devil? Could it really be that everything good was of God and everything bad was of the devil ? What was of myself, the natural man, then? Anything? Or did I merely choose between the bad and good of the agitator on each shoulder? And if there was really something of myself, was it good, or bad, or neither? And why did the bad feel so of myself and also so good? All these were intractable questions to my mind, even though I knew, or thought I knew, what answers the Church would give. But I didn't want the answers to be just the Church's. I wanted them to be mine.

30

Men Are That We Might Have Joy

Inside I was all mixed up, like a jigsaw puzzle that somebody had thrown against the wall in frustration at not being able to figure the damned thing out. I knew what the picture was supposed to look like, it was there on the front of the box after all, but no matter how I kept jamming the pieces together, they just wouldn't fit. But I kept on jamming them together because I knew that joy was the reward for a perfected puzzle. "Adam fell that men might be, and men are that they might have joy." (2nd Nephi 2:25). Joy. Three little letters that comprise the entire reason for our existence, the telos of life.

"And if it so be that you should labor all your days in crying repentance unto this people, and bring, save it be one soul unto me, how great shall be your joy with him in the kingdom of my Father.

And now, if your joy will be great with one soul that you have brought unto me into the kingdom of my Father, how great will be your joy if you should bring many souls unto me!" (D&C 18:15-16).

I'd brought several souls unto Christ by that point, but I'd never been more depressed. But it did say that the joy came in the kingdom of Christ's Father, which meant after death.

"Wherefore, fear not unto death; for in this world your joy is not full, but in me your joy is full.

Therefore care not for the body, neither the life of the body; but care for the soul, even the life of the soul." (D&C 101:36).

234

So that was indeed the rub. My joy would not be full in this world, but fear not, for death would bring joy. Fear not unto death. Care not for the life of the body, care for the soul. The reward is eternal, not earthly. Lilies of the field. All fine and dandy, in theory. After all, life after death was eternal and eternal joy certainly trumped the transient joy of earthly existence. But I lived in this world, and not just theoretically. I couldn't help but want joy now, in this world. I couldn't help but care for my body and the life of my body. To do otherwise required more radicalness than I possessed.

I knew that long suffering saints and martyrs and other spiritual geniuses who had cared for the soul and not for the body and had devoted themselves so wholly to God had undoubtedly experienced moments of ecstatic joy, when the soul opened up and poured out into the deep and embraced the infinite, and God became real, present, tangible. Moments when their identity was temporarily obliterated and they became one with God and eternity and knew immortality. I had experienced small tastes of such religious joy myself, and believed the accounts of those who were spiritually superior enough to experience this joy more deeply and frequently. But now I was starting to wonder if this religious joy was anything more than the temporary deliverance from despair. The more faith one had, the more one felt despair at one's weakness and smallness, and thus the greater one's joy upon being delivered from such despair. The less faith, the less despair, and thus the less need for a religious joy. And I was trapped in the middle – I had enough faith to feel despair, but not enough to let go of my identity and give myself wholly over to God and the infinite like the saints and spiritual geniuses.

"The best two years of my life" – the nearly universal declaration of missionaries upon returning home, a declaration so mimetic and memetic that it was hard to know if it retained any meaning. I never once heard this from a currently serving missionary.

I knew the two years of my mission would be the hardest thing I'd ever done. I had looked forward to the hard work. I thought it would be like a long hard day of stacking sod. My muscles would ache, my mouth would be dusty and dry, my body and mind fatigued. But ice water from the sweaty plastic milk jug underneath the sodcutter's seat would course through my body with a mountain brook's delight. The sun would set and the high valley air would cool and condense the smell of freshly cut grass and my fatigue would drift off as I felt the joy of an honest day's work.

So, although I'd known that they'd be the hardest two years, I'd also expected that they'd be the best two years as I experienced the joy of an honest day's work doing the most important work there was. But now I was starting to feel like it was all a sham. That the emperor had no clothes. That we missionaries weren't filled with joy. That we weren't even as happy as normal people. We knocked on doors that opened up to parties with music and laughter and dancing and girls and after we had smiled and asked to share a message about God and the door had closed we'd drop the smile and move on to the next door and look at each other and wordlessly tell each other that these wicked people only *looked* happy but that they lacked the Gospel and that *we* were the ones with the *true* joy, all the while knowing inside that we were lying to ourselves.

But all this murmuring, complaining, joy-deriding, was going on inside. On the outside I had assembled my pieces well enough to at least resemble the picture on the box. To Richardson I was a good enough missionary, a bit jaded perhaps, and one that slept more than he should, but otherwise good enough. As far as he could see I was keeping the major rules and acting like I felt guilty for breaking the minor ones, so I was obedient enough. And I worked hard. Wearily, but it was enough. And that was the main thing.

Hard work. President Ezra Taft Benson, in a quote we recited at every district meeting, said: "I have often said that one of the greatest secrets of missionary work is work! If a missionary works, he will get the Spirit; if he gets the Spirit, he will teach by the Spirit; and if he teaches by the Spirit, he will touch the hearts of the people and he will be happy. Work, work, work—there is no satisfactory substitute, especially in missionary work."

So all I could see to do was to put away all the stuff going on inside and continue to work, work, work. Perhaps President Benson's promise would come true and I'd touch the hearts of the people and I'd be happy. So we left our apartment on time every morning to go out into the cold Russian winter and hit the streets and doors.

For some reason we were encountering a lot more anger on the doors than I ever had before. A few times we were threatened with violence if we kept on knocking. Maybe I *had* reached the point where I cared not for the body and feared not unto death, because I was courting danger. Maybe I just wanted excitement, maybe I wanted an excuse to start to wail on someone and let out all my frustrations, maybe I wanted some physical pain to match the emotional, or maybe I was looking for another easy way home, but I found myself hoping that someone would try to attack me. So I started reacting to all these threats by amplifying with sarcastic retorts and smirks the typical missionary arrogance that came from believing that you're on the Lord's errand.

One day my secret hopes materialized in the form of a drunk bear of a man whom we must have awoken from hibernation. He opened the door, took one look at us, and became instantly apoplectic.

"You! You foreign swine either get the hell out of my building or I'll fucking *throw* you out!" He screamed.

I was more than a little surprised by his sudden vehemence, but then something snapped inside, and I smirked and shot back: "We are special witnesses of the greatest organization in the world with the most important message in the world and we aren't going to leave until you and all your neighbors have heard that message."

That did the trick. The man let out a contorted roar and came barreling at us. Richardson, six foot three and well built, stepped forward to meet him. But he grabbed Richardson by his leather coat and threw him up against the chalky wall. Richardson twisted out of his grip, gave him a shove, and took off running down the hall. I was nailed to the spot, buzzed on adrenalin, in flight or fight mode, when the man grabbed my neck with his big bear paw and started to bulldoze me out of the building. He was frighteningly strong, and I didn't resist as he escorted me down the stairs and out the building. He went back inside and I stood in front of the building waiting for Richardson, who must have had gotten disoriented on his way out. After Richardson came running out, we stood there for a while, trying to gather ourselves and stop the shaking. While we were discussing whether we should go back in or not, the bear-man came barreling out the door again, this time with a couple of friends close behind. "I thought I told you to get the hell out of here!" he shouted. It was shameful to run now that we were standing outside in the bright sun and open air, and so we stood our ground. He came at me first this time, trying to grab me by the neck again, and I wrestled back his arms as he attempted some ridiculous Karate Kid sweep with his leg and slipped on the ice. He let loose with a barrage of infuriated profanity and it looked like it was about to get bloody. But as bear-man got up off the ice and charged me again his two friends grabbed him by the arms. "He's drunk," they apologized.

I was happy to add another notch to my sickle: I'd now been physically attacked for spreading my beliefs; I'd been truly persecuted. Richardson appeared to view matters the same way.

Knocking wasn't all anger and rejection, however. One day the door was opened by a beautiful young woman with long black hair and green eyes. I stammered out my usual pitch: "Hello, we are representatives of Jesus Christ and His Church. My name is Elder Young and this is my friend Elder Richardson. We would like to talk to you about God's plan for us if you have a minute." I could see Richardson laughing silently out of the corner of my eye. To pass the time we were always trying playfully to throw each other off at the doors, to get each other to muff the usual pitch, to forget a line, to stammer, blush, or fidget nervously. A cute girl was always the best way to get to me, and I knew I was going to take some ribbing from Richardson for this one because I had obviously been rattled by her age and beauty and I could feel the blood rushing to my face.

"Sure, come on inside," she said freely.

This was totally unexpected. This almost never happened. What should I do? "Umm, we can't come inside. That is, we are not supposed to be alone with a woman. So, umm, is there someone else with you in your apartment? Because if not, umm, we can't come in." My face got even hotter with embarrassment for how childish and inept I sounded.

"Oh, my friends are here, so we won't be alone," she laughed and replied brightly.

We stepped inside the doorway, removed our shoes, put on the slippers she handed us, and followed her tall slender frame as she led us down the hallway to the single room of her apartment. Sitting on her couch were two other girls who looked to be about our age.

Richardson and I exchanged looks. Being alone in an apartment with three girls our age was just as much against the rules as being with one was. But we had agreed to come in, and we had taken off our shoes and coats, and it would be rude and embarrassing to put them back on and leave. What harm could it do just to give a quick D and then leave? I knew I wanted to stay and chat with three beautiful girls, and I was pretty sure Richardson felt the same way. He shrugged his shoulders to signal his deference, and I signaled back by taking a seat on the chair offered me.

As soon as we had exchanged greetings and I'd explained that we had come from America to share the Gospel with people, one of the girls spoke up:

"How much do you get paid?" It was a very common question; everyone always assumed that we wouldn't be doing this unless we were making good money.

I let Richardson handle this one. He had just learned the idiom to explain that this was all on our dime, and he loved to talk about how we could be back in America right now going to college, going on dates, and earning money, but that instead we had come to this country from literally halfway across the world, had left our friends and family for two years, learned a language with little formal training, and received no pay for all of this, in fact, we paid our own way. And would we do this if we didn't absolutely know that this message was true and important? As he finished delivering what had become his favorite and most fluent speech, he looked exultantly at the girls, as if he expected them to be so awed by our devotion that they would commit to baptism right then and there. It reminded me of Goddard and how he carried around a foldout from the Church's magazine *The Ensign* that had thumbnail pictures of the First Presidency and the Twelve Apostles and the Quorums of the Seventy, all laid out in hierarchical order. Whenever we taught people about prophets and the importance of modern-day revelation he would bring out that foldout like a poker player throwing down a royal flush. He would then point to the prophet and look at the people with that expectant triumphal look that said *read 'em and weep*, as if tiny pictures of a bunch of old white guys were irrefutable evidence that we had the truth.

"So you're not earning money here, you're not going to school either. And you can't go on dates?"

Not without some pride, we shook our heads. "Nope."

"What do you do for fun then?"

"Bring people to Christ. Help people change their lives," I said easily, glibly, almost flippantly.

"That's it?" They teased.

"Well, we also have one day a week called preparation day when we can do other stuff."

"Like what?" They leaned forward with interest.

"Sleep mostly. Go to McDonalds. Write letters. Read letters. Play monopoly or chess. Go to the banya."

"You go to the banya?" They seemed surprised.

"Oh yeah, I love it. Especially to beat myself with the venik," I said enthusiastically.

The hostess, whose name we had learned was Zhenya, laughed a sweet musical laugh.

"Are you two always together?"

We nodded in unison. "Yeah, at least we can never get lonely, right?" I joked.

Zhenya laughed again. She was lovely.

"How about you, what do you like to do?" I asked, looking directly into her eyes, green with flecks of gold. I then pulled away to glance at Richardson, fearing that he might be giving me the look Goddard always gave when he'd judged that we had *BRT'd* enough and that it was time to start talking about the Gospel, but Richardson seemed to be enjoying the conversation as much as I was.

Zhenya had just arrived from Penza to Samara to study literature at the university, she told us, and she liked to cook, read, and listen to music. I wanted to ask her what kind of books she liked to read, and what kind of music she liked to listen to, and how many brothers and sisters she had, and what were they like, and how about her parents, and did she like Samara, and did she speak English, and had she traveled outside of the country, but to do so would have been to cross a line I wasn't ready to cross, at least with Richardson sitting right next to me.

So finally, and somewhat reluctantly, I started the discussion. The girls asked thoughtful questions and seemed genuinely interested. We gave them a copy of the Book of Mormon and they committed to read Chapter Eleven of Third Nephi. The next step was to set up a return appointment, but in this case, we obviously couldn't come back.

"We also have female missionaries here in Samara. Would it be okay if they come to visit you and talk with you some more about this?" I asked. The correct commitment pattern question would have been: "Would this weekend or early next week be a better time for you to meet with them to discuss any questions that you might have from your reading of Chapter Eleven of Third Nephi?" but that question now seemed to me impossibly phony and presumptuous.

"Why can't you two come back?" Zhenya asked.

"Well, we have a rule that says that missionaries of the same sex should teach single investigators like yourselves when possible."

"Why?" She probed.

"To avoid problems, I guess."

"What kind of problems?" She was teasing me now.

"Well, you know, problems of a sexual nature, I guess" I said.

"Because you Elders can't control yourselves around women?" she smiled.

"Yeah, something like that." I smiled back. "But also to avoid even the appearance of evil."

"Sex is evil?"

"No, I didn't mean it like that. Sex is sacred, but sex outside of marriage is a sin."

"I see," she nodded. "Well, I don't mind them coming over, although I'd rather have Young and Richardson come back."

"We'd love to come back too, but the rules are the rules," I said, rather pleased with myself for dealing with temptation so resolutely, even though I knew that I was doing it mainly for Richardson's benefit. "The Sisters are great, though, and I'm sure that you'll have a good time meeting with them. I'll pass your address along to them, and they should be by within the next week or so."

"Okay. I look forward to meeting with them."

"Well, we should get going I guess. Right Elder Richardson?"

He nodded his head. "It was really nice to meet you, and I hope you enjoy the Book of Mormon. I love that book." He offered the last bit of informal testimony.

We got up to go and I couldn't help but ask the question that had been on my mind all discussion. "Where do you all sleep? There's only one bed here."

They laughed. "Oh, only Zhenya lives here, we're just visiting."

I couldn't believe it. How could she afford to have her own apartment? In the thousands and thousands of doors I'd knocked I'd never yet met a student living alone in her own apartment, and a fairly nice, well-furnished apartment at that.

We said our goodbyes and left. We were running late for an appointment with Ramiz, so we quit knocking and exited the building. But my thoughts stayed with the beautiful green-eyed girl. Alone in her own apartment! Such a nice smile, and it seemed like she liked me. I thought that I should have asked for her phone number so that the sisters could call and set up an appointment with her.

We found Ramiz waiting for us on the bench outside the stairwell to his apartment, excited and anxious to see us. We were never late. He was still smoking so we gave him a little lesson about the Brother of Jared from the Book of Mormon. Four thousand years ago he had built these unique barges that were like watertight footballs so that he could sail from the Middle East over to America. But then he realized that the barges were so airtight that they wouldn't let in any light, and so he went and asked the Lord what to do. The Lord basically told him: "What can I do? If you put in windows, they'll be dashed to pieces, and if you use fire. . . well, you simply shall not use fire. Why don't you come up with an idea, and I'll make it happen." And so the Brother of Jared gathered sixteen white stones and told the Lord to touch them with his finger and make them glow, and the Lord complied, and the Brother of

Jared saw his finger and that it was made of flesh and blood. Then we told Ramiz that maybe he should try a new approach to stop smoking. Instead of just asking the Lord for help, maybe he, like the Brother of Jared, should think up creative ideas himself about how to stop smoking, like eating grapefruits or something, and that then he could pray and ask the Lord to help make it happen. This idea really excited Ramiz, and we went home happy that he seemed reinvigorated in his resolve to quit smoking.

While Richardson lay in his bed and studied I went to call the Sisters and give them Zhenya's address. Our apartment was by far the nicest I'd had or seen on my mission – it came furnished with house plants and rugs and walnut bookcases and a TV we couldn't watch. But its nicest feature was the privacy afforded by a small separate room with a desk and a telephone. I went into the room, shut the door so as not to disturb Richardson's studying, sat down at the desk, and looked at my little blue sheet with Zhenya's name and address on it. I thought of her laugh and the way she had looked at me, almost conspiratorially it had seemed to me. I looked until my eyes glazed over. When they refocused I had made the decision not to give the Sisters her address, telling myself that maybe we could get a member from the branch to come visit her with us instead, the procedure for visiting single girls in districts that lacked Sisters. It was a ridiculous idea given that this district had Sisters, but this was my first such district and I could tell myself that I was uninformed as to how things were supposed to work.

I went back into the bedroom, undressed, lay down in bed, put on my headphones and the Beatles' White Album, stared at the wall, and commenced with the ritual drowning out of my thoughts with music until I fell asleep. I was prepared for the usual depressed hazy stupor, but I had to smile when the first song came on:

> Oh, show me round your snow peaked
> mountains way down south
> Take me to your daddy's farm
> Let me hear your balalaika's ringing out
> Come and keep your comrade warm

Thoughts of Zhenya ran through my mind and I didn't even try to suppress them. The jigsaw puzzle pieces were starting to come together in some kind of a picture, a picture which gave me some small measure of joy. It didn't match the picture on the box but I didn't care.

31

Out of My Hands

The next P-Day we took the metro and bus into the office to pick up our mail. The anticipation was building for me, and I knew that any week now I should be getting my parents' response. This was not the week, however, although I did get a package from home, full of gifts for Christmas and my birthday coming up in a couple of weeks: the audio CDs with Truman Madsen's lectures on the prophet Joseph Smith which I'd requested earlier, *Les Misérables*, *War and Peace*, and tastes of America: peanut butter, taco seasoning, beef gravy packets, imitation maple syrup flavoring, pumpkin seeds and Jolly Ranchers.

Before Richardson and I left the office for our weekly McDonalds visit, President Hatcher called me into his office and handed me a printout of an email which he'd received from my parents after they'd called the office to ask for his permission to send it. In the email's short message, my parents told me that they'd written three letters that were on their way, and they urged me not to give up, that the Lord's time frame was not always our own, that it was always darkest right before the dawn, and that if I'd just stick it out marvelous blessings were in store. I was sticking it out at least until I got their letters anyways, and so the email simply heightened my anticipation.

Right away I started in to reading *Les Misérables* in the evenings after work. I also started staying awake reading in the room with the desk long after Richardson had gone to sleep, breaking two rules with one tome by reading unapproved literature and by not going to bed at the same time as my companion. And in the morning I broke even more rules because I kept falling asleep when I should have been doing gospel study or language study. Richardson never said anything, though. He was turning out to be the refreshing Vandeburg sort of companion that let it be as long as we worked hard enough – the don't ask, don't tell policy as it were.

After one such late night of reading, walking into the dark bedroom with my eyes not yet having adjusted, I stubbed my toe hard on the bed post and emitted a sharp yelp of pain. My first thought was one of worry that I'd awoken Richardson. But, to my relief, I heard him breathing the deep, measured breaths of an undisturbed sleep. This simple occurrence was like the flex of the little metal disk in the foot warmers Richardson's mom had sent him to keep his toes warm, the kind where as soon as the disk is flexed it creates a seed crystal in the liquid which spreads until the whole thing turns milky and hard and gives off a surprising amount of heat.

Zhenya. I could feel my thoughts crystallizing and congealing as I lay in bed. Zhenya was the answer. Everything pointed to her, including maybe God, I thought. Out of the hundreds of buildings we could have knocked that day, why hers? What were the chances that she would be home when we knocked? And not just at home, but have her friends there visiting so that we could come inside? And out of the thousands of doors I had knocked, what were the chances that behind hers would be the only cute girl my age with her own apartment that I'd ever met? And what were the chances that she would seem to like me too? And was it just a coincidence that I heard the song *Back in the U.S.S.R.* right after meeting her? And what were the chances of having a three room apartment with a soundly sleeping companion who didn't wake up when I stubbed my toe and who was used to me staying up to read in the other room? And finally, what were the chances that both Zhenya and I would live right next to a major highway so that I could flag down a taxi at any time of the night?

Just what kind of an answer was she? I didn't know. I was becoming delusional; I was trying too hard to see God's hand, someone else's hand, in everything, in something. I knew only that Zhenya *must* be the answer, and that she would somehow tell me something. I also felt that sneaking out to visit her in the middle of the night would be a step further down that path I'd started on when I had bought the Penthouse. A step further away from the muddle and uncertainty of that damned fork. Possibly the step of no return. For if Zhenya led me that way, I was prepared to commit the sin next to murder and seal my fate. For if I fornicated I would go home, no matter what my parents' response in those letters would be. I couldn't decide for myself what to do. God wouldn't tell me. My parents were taking forever in telling me. The *Trichinella* roundworm had refused to make the decision for me. So I would now place my fate in Zhenya's lovely hands.

So, that evening after work, I decided to execute another plot, more conscious and daring than my Penthouse adventure. When we came home, I changed into my robe as I always did, walked into the kitchen, remarked how the garbage needed to be taken out loudly enough for Richardson to hear, and then changed into a pair of jeans and a cotton blue T-shirt in order to go outside and throw out the garbage. I then made us a small supper of oatmeal with apples and cinnamon, wished Richardson a goodnight, and went to the small room with the desk and telephone to read *Les Misérables*, still dressed in my street clothes.

I read until midnight, rereading the same passages over and over again because I was too excited to concentrate. I put the book down, shut off the desk lamp, and walked softly into our bedroom. I stood in the middle of the room holding my breath, waiting for my eyes to adjust to the soft blue moonlight pouring into the room through the gossamer drapes. When my eyes were finally able to make out Richardson's face and verify that he was deeply asleep, I crept back out to the hallway where I carefully put on my boots, coat, hat, gloves, and handbag containing my money, passport, and proselytizing materials. I pulled the door in tight so that I could turn the deadbolt without its scraping against its pit in the door jamb, opened the door, and stepped outside into the stairwell. I slowly closed the door tight, turning the key a degree per second to shut the bolt, all the while sick with nervousness that it would click hard and Richardson would wake up and I would be found out. But the click was soft, and I was free.

I stepped outside, breathed in deep the cold crisp air, and crunched my boots against the hard cold snow. I had never seen Russia like this. It was a different world. There was that same elusive phosphorescence of Russian cities in winter at night as the orange-yellow light from the streetlamps reflected off the snowy ground, the tall tiled buildings, the icicles on tree skeletons, the filmy glass of the cars, the icy sidewalks, and the oily slushy roads, the orange-yellow light reflecting and re-reflecting until it seemed like the whole world was glowing, the whole world was on display late at night, afterhours, in a giant toy store in New York City which sold only orange glow-in-the-dark toys. Only now, instead of just looking wistfully into the store from the street, I was a kid who had magically woken up all alone inside the store at three o'clock in the morning Christmas Day and could play with whatever he wanted until sunrise.

It was strange to be alone. I kept looking over my shoulder for my companion, like the paraplegic who keeps reaching to scratch the itch on his leg. It had been a year since I'd felt that sense of autonomy, that power of self-determination, that independence to do whatever it was my heart desired. It was not exactly pleasant, a bit eerie, and I was anxious to get to Zhenya's as quickly as possible.

I finally flagged down a "taxi," just another dirty white Lada owned by a young engineer who moonlighted as a taxi driver. He had a good face, and I felt the urge to give him the 1st D.

When he let me out in front of Zhenya's building I started to tremble. I felt that nervous feeling I used to get when I was lined up on the track waiting for the pop of the starting gun, and I felt like I needed to urinate. I walked up to a tree in the courtyard, but only a little bit dribbled out.

I entered the stairwell to Zhenya's apartment and started to climb the steps, getting queasier and queasier the higher I climbed. As I got to her door and tried to gather up the courage to ring the doorbell, I was struck by the absurdity of what I was doing. It was 12:30 in the morning, this girl lived alone, and I had only met her once, briefly, a week ago. Maybe she would be frightened and think that I was some kind of stalking creep. So I took out a pen and a piece of paper from my handbag and wrote her a note:

Dear Zhenya,

Writing you this note is Elder Young, the missionary you met last week. I have not stopped thinking about you and I would really like to see you again, but I did not have your telephone number, so I came here last night to give you this note. I came at night while my companion is asleep. If you would like to meet with me (and only me), please call me tomorrow at 9:30 p.m. at 257-58-75.

> *Sincerely,*
> *Jacob Young*

I folded the note and slipped it in the crack between her door and the jamb. I felt relieved. Now my fate was even less in my hands, and I didn't have to do the cold knock in the middle of the night. I took another taxi back to the apartment and slipped into bed without waking Richardson.

All throughout the following day of ice Ds and cement stairwells, I thought of what had been and what was to come. In the stark white of day I was incredulous at my daring in the orange-yellow glow of night. I thought of Zhenya, or, more accurately, I thought of an idea of Zhenya I had created. I thought of the phone call I hoped would come that evening during my *Les Misérables* reading. I could barely wait to get home. I felt almost no guilt for what I'd done or what I might do.

I made sure that we got home early so that I would be sitting at the desk by the telephone in case Zhenya called. Richardson, like all greenies, never answered the phone, never had a reason to, would have been scared witless to, so I was safe there. Right on time the phone rang:

"Hello, can I speak with Jacob please?" I loved that she had called me Jacob. That was a good sign.

"Hi! This is he. I am so glad you called." I was speaking as quietly as I could to avoid Richardson's overhearing the conversation, but I was still choosing my words carefully in case he was listening in.

"I got your note this morning, so I thought I would call."

"Yes, we really were hoping that you would call since we would really like to meet again with you."

"We?"

"No. Just one. But the situation here, you know, cannot arouse suspicion for the other person. Must talk cautiously." I was pretty sure that Richardson wouldn't understand the words "arouse suspicion" and "cautiously" even if he heard them.

"I understand. Would you like to come over tonight?"

"Yes. Very much," I said as calmly as I could.

"What time can you come?"

"Is twelve o'clock too late for you?" Richardson would just think I was setting up an appointment with an investigator.

"No, that's fine."

"Great, we'll see you then. Thank you so much for calling!" I couldn't believe my good fortune.

"Of course. See you tonight."

It was less nerve-wracking to sneak out of the apartment this time, but the outside world was just as magical. I hadn't fantasized, hadn't even thought, about what would happen once I got there. It was out of my hands. What would happen would happen. It would happen *to* me. I would not make it happen.

This time when I got out of the taxi I went right up to her door and rang the bell, with just a bit of nervousness.

"Hi Jacob! Come in please." She put her hand on my shoulder and guided me inside. Even through my thick coat I could feel the heat of her hand, the life force of each dainty finger.

She was dressed in silky pajamas. Loose satiny black pants with an ankle slit at the bottom, and a red top with an Oriental floral print with flowing elbow-length sleeves and a wide V-neck trimmed with black. I could not believe that I was alone with this beautiful woman.

I felt big and clumsy as I bent down to untie my boots. I felt ridiculous for having worn such big boots and wished I had worn my shoes instead. I took off my heavy wool stocking hat and I could feel my hair flat and mussed on my head and wished I hadn't worn a hat and my face started to redden. I took off my coat to reveal my plain old blue cotton T-shirt and scrawny physique and wished that I had some nicer street clothes to wear and I felt ridiculous in my Lee blue jeans.

"Would you like some tea?" she asked. Tea – another good sign. It looked like this was going to be a night of firsts for me.

"Sure," I said, as I followed her into the kitchen.

"Do you want sugar or jam in it?"

"I don't know. I've never drunk tea before. You decide."

"Really? You've never had tea before?" She laughed and shook her head disbelievingly. "Seriously?"

"No," I shook my head sadly.

"Why? Wait, let me guess!" As she said this she put her hand on my shoulder again, as if to stop me from speaking, to give her time to guess. Again the warmth of her touch. "Another rule?"

"Yeah, but this one is more like a commandment than a rule." I wished that I had said something else, taken the conversation someplace different. I hadn't come here to discuss the difference between commandments and rules. Or had I?

"Oh, what's the difference?" She asked, taking two tea cups and saucers out of the cupboard.

"Well, a rule is something that we can't do on our mission, like be apart from our companion, while a commandment is something that we can't do even off our mission, like drink tea or alcohol."

"So would you like something else to drink then?"

"No, tea is good. That's part of the reason I'm here. I'm sick of following all the rules and commandments."

She handed me a small cup of tea on a saucer and looked at me curiously. "Would you like some cookies?"

"Umm, yeah, if you are going to have some. I mean, whatever you do with tea."

She took a package of cookies from the cupboard. "I really like these with tea."

"Looks good."

"Would you like to go into the other room?"

"Yeah, sure. Of course. That is, if you want to."

I followed her into the other room. She moved gracefully and lightly. The couch had one of those hideaway beds which she had pulled out and covered with sheets, blankets, and pillows. In the corner the television flickered and hummed with a replay of a live concert of some Russian band. She sat on the edge of the bed and I sat next to her.

We drank our tea, ate our cookies, and talked, almost exclusively about my situation.

I rambled on for over an hour. I hated that I couldn't stop. I wanted to talk about something else, about something normal. I wanted to ask her about herself, but once I had started talking about my situation I couldn't think about anything else.

"So what are you going to do, then?" she finally asked.

"I don't know," I said.

She had listened sympathetically, attentively. I thought that she must really know what it's all about, living alone and all, studying literature and drinking tea and putting her hand on people's shoulders with such ease and grace.

"What do *you* think I should do?" I asked. I really hoped that she would give me some advice, tell me what I should do. If she had told me to call up President Hatcher that very moment and tell him that I was done being a missionary, I probably would have done it. In fact, I know I would have.

But she said only: "It sounds like you have some really difficult decisions to make. I'm sorry it is so hard for you. But whatever you decide to do I think that you should definitely wait and talk to your family before doing anything drastic like running off."

"Yeah, you're probably right." I felt let down, betrayed almost, as if her loyalty somehow lay with my family, or with the Church, instead of with me.

It was getting really late, nearly two in the morning, and I was feeling tired. I kept expecting the tea to kick in and give me a jolt of something. I knew that it contained caffeine and I had drunk caffeine before, but I also thought that it would have some kind of je ne sais quoi that would make it more, well, more *druggy*. But I'd gotten more kick out of a Coke, and my tea initiation was kind of a let-down. I made a mental note to add tea to my Against list when I got home, and then I thought of a joke one of my college professors had liked to repeat, and I decided to tell it to Zhenya.

"How can you tell a Mormon?"

"I don't know. By their nametags?"

"No, by the temperature of their caffeine."

She didn't get it, of course, so I explained, and she laughed politely.

I was done talking. It had taken me nowhere. Zhenya had been sympathetic but ultimately unhelpful. Maybe talking wasn't the answer.

I lay back on my elbows and looked into her catlike eyes. She smiled and lay back beside me on her side, propped up on her forearm, facing me. I turned to my side and mirrored her pose, legs bent. I was incredibly happy but scared. In a few days I would no longer be an adolescent, but I was still a virgin. Sex was something mysterious and intimidating. I'd pass a teenage couple hanging out on a park bench, draped all over each other, lovesick lust in their eyes, and I'd know that they had been together, that they'd done something that I hadn't, that all I'd done was furtively masturbated. I was starting to fear that it was all that I would ever do, that I was destined to remain a virgin forever, to feel a rush of hormones and heat any time a woman placed her hand upon my shoulder, only to always be followed by a flush of embarrassment and ineptitude and dread. But this could be different. This could be it. This could be what it was all about.

Our heads drew each other in with an imperceptible series of starts, hesitations, and reassurances. Our lips met, hers softly confident, mine assiduously eager. After kissing for a while with nothing but our lips touching she scooted to the back of the bed and lay against the pillows and beckoned me to join her. We continued kissing, still just the lips touching until she moved her hand gently to my face. I stiffly mimicked the motion. My hand felt rough and out of place on her smooth skin.

Our mouths opened to each other and our tongues entwined and the kissing deepened in passion and intensity. She moved her hand to my shoulder and drew us in closer, until I felt her firm breasts, and, suddenly, frightened by what I was doing, I pulled away abruptly. Immediately I felt ashamed and confused as to why I had done this, and I moved closer again and tried to make up for it by kissing her passionately. But, just like that, the magic was gone. My body had turned into a giant overactive brain. What was I doing? Was I doing it right? Was this feeling ok for her? Should I kiss her neck or should I nibble on her ear? Should I touch her breast? I wished that she would take charge and make some kind of move, make something happen. But she no longer seemed to want to take the initiative after I had pulled away so suddenly. It was late and we were tired.

I left the apartment happy. The evening had lacked resoluteness, but it was a good start. I regretted only that once again I had not thought to ask for her phone number.

The next night I sat at the desk reading, hoping that Zhenya would call and invite me over again. I thought of her soft lips, and I missed her. But as midnight came and passed without a phone call, I put away my book and went to bed, where I resolved to visit her again the next night even if she didn't call.

Zhenya opened the door wrapped in a thick blue robe, and it was obvious that I had awoken her. She invited me into the kitchen for tea and inquired about Richardson and whether he had woken up, and then she asked me if I had heard from my family yet. I told her no, explained that we usually only got mail once a week and less than that in Saratov, and then I started blathering on again about how I felt like a hypocrite and was confused and didn't know how much longer I could go on preaching something that I didn't know whether I believed in. I was hoping that she would invite me into the bedroom again, but she yawned and told me she had class early the next morning. I apologized profusely, said that I never should have come, and that I would leave right away. Then I hesitated and asked:

"Should I get your phone number so that I can call before I come again?" I looked at her intently, hopefully.

"I don't know if we should keep seeing each other, Jacob," she said gently, leaning back against the wall.

"Yeah? Why do you think that?" I was not surprised, but I was hurt.

"What kind of future is there for us? You can only come visit me at night while your friend sleeps." She said it so matter-of-factly, as if the idea of there being no future for us was perfectly acceptable to her.

"But maybe that will change, maybe I will quit."

"I don't want you to risk your position for me." Again I felt betrayed. Why was she so loyal to the Church?

"My position? What position?! My position doesn't matter to me!" Couldn't she see that she held all the power? That she could make me do whatever she wanted to?

"I'm sorry, Jacob. But I just don't see how things can continue like this," she looked at me with tenderness, but with finality.

The next evening, still stung by the rejection, I wrote her the following letter, copied it again by hand to fix the mistakes, filed the first copy in my two-ring binder, put the second copy in a pre-stamped envelope, and dropped it in the mailbox when I went to take the garbage out.

Zhenya,

Hi! How are you? I don't know why I'm writing you this letter. I just wanted to explain myself to you, and maybe in the process, I'll find out myself how I feel, and why I acted like I did.

I don't know why I wanted to get acquainted with you. I just felt something between us. I felt some attraction to you. Maybe this attraction came simply from the fact that I wanted "to be free." As part of that freedom, I wanted to rebel against all the limiting church and missionary rules and laws. With you, I saw an opportunity to become free. I wanted to start a new life down a different path. The way I saw it, you could have been the first step along that new path. But, the first step is always the hardest, and it did not work out.

I probably seemed very strange to you, as if I could not solve my own problems and could not make my own decisions. You probably wanted to know why I hesitated so. This hesitation was not because I was afraid or because I was worried about the consequences. I made my decision, I understood all the consequences, I understood all the risks, and I accepted them. I wanted that. I wanted to make that first step. I wanted to start a new life, I wanted to start to live, but it didn't work out with you. I don't know why.

Maybe you just didn't feel any attraction to me. Or perhaps I scared you off by acting so strangely and by hesitating so. Or, as you said, maybe you really did just not want me to "risk my position." Thank you for your unneeded, unwanted protection.

Zhenya, I really like you. You are such a classy, intelligent, unbelievably beautiful woman, perfect really. You said that we had no future together. You said that, not me. I wanted to find out.

Thank you for the first night, it was really nice for me. You are "spectabulous" ☺. I wish you all the best.

With love,
Jacob

The letter is painful for me to read. The transparent way I went about trying to get her back by falsely proclaiming my resoluteness – an attempt to combat what I saw as the reason it hadn't worked between us: my hesitation and doubt. My delusional failure to see the other reasons. The idea that I was speaking of futures together and new lives and things "working out" with a girl I knew nothing about other than that she had had green eyes, liked literature, put her hand on my shoulder and let me kiss her, and listened to me with some sympathy. The longing for contact with someone in a normal, human, non-Elder-White-Bible-proselytizing-Lock-Your-Heart way. The hurt that I had failed in my first attempt to seek such contact. The flailing about for something, anything, that would take away the doubt and confusion, for someone, anyone, to tell me what to do. And the unrequited desire for love.

32

All You Need is Love

The next P-Day we went to the office to pick up our mail, and the three letters from my parents had arrived, along with one from Dave. I told Richardson that I wasn't feeling well and we bypassed the usual P-Day trip to McDonalds and went straight home, where I lay down on my bed on my stomach with my face invisible to Richardson. I put the overture to Wagner's *Tannhäuser* on my headphones and stared at the letters.

The first one I opened, the slenderest one, was from my mom. She started off by saying that she would pretend for a minute that everything was okay and would just write me the usual newsy letter. I glanced over it to ensure that it was indeed strictly newsy, and then I opened the thickest letter, also from my mom.

December 7, 1999 – Tuesday

Dear Jacob,

Your dad and I received your letters yesterday. Certainly when a parent sees a letter in the mail addressed specifically to them, a series of thoughts passes through their mind. I can't say that I was totally surprised by what you had written. For the last few months I have experienced a nagging feeling whenever I would receive one of your letters. You have expressed on several occasions your desires to be filled with more faith like elder-so-and-so, or have a greater testimony like another elder. This concerned me at the time – I wondered why you would say these things. As of late I had also felt that your letters weren't mentioning too many of your spiritual feelings. I brushed that off too — I didn't listen I'm ashamed to say, perhaps because in my heart I felt I couldn't bear it to know that something might be wrong and you're there and I'm here and I couldn't wrap my arms around you and try to make things better as I did when you were a young boy. I would like to, but it just can't be something I can do like that anymore. I just knew that you weren't the same excited Jacob that I put on the plane for Russia last spring.

So here I am sitting in front of the fireplace with your old blue fishing jacket on that you loved so well — you know, the one I claimed wouldn't be here when you got home cuz it's so old and battered. Well, it will still be here and I hope you don't mind sharing it with me for a little while just because I'm your mom and friend and it helps me feel close to you. I'm feeling so full of grief and sorrow. I guess I finally understand the meaning of a broken heart.

Putting all my selfish feelings aside — which really have little to do with the situation anyway, I must tell you now how much I love you Jacob! You will always be my cherished son regardless of any circumstances, I want you to not only know, but to FEEL that at this time. Let that love slowly sink down into your heart and melt away any doubts or insecurities you may be feeling — wondering how your dad and I may be reacting to all of this. Nothing will ever change our devotion to you Jacob. . . .

Before you left on your mission, I prayed that you might learn humility there in Russia. As Job of old IF the Lord allowed the very powers of hell to polish and refine your weaknesses to turn them to strengths — I would accept the Lord's will no matter how hard for me it was to bear as your mom, but I cannot — WILL NOT, give up on you — not now or through eternity. My faith may not be as strong as I wish it was at times, but I have plenty of hope! It is that thin strand of hope that I pray will extend between us. I don't care if you take your end of it and tie it to both your ankles to secure yourself, or hold on to it with all you might, but DON'T let go of it and you can bet that I will do the same! Until the answer or answer you're looking for come, Please, PLEASE hold on for longer than you ever imagined that you had it in you to do. . . ."

Tears were streaming down my face. It was a beautifully written letter, heartfelt, touching, and full of love. She had recognized that what I needed right then, more than anything, was simply to feel love. Her love, my dad's love, Christ's love, and love for myself. And I could feel her motherly love emanating warm and radiant from off the pages, I could feel her sitting in the chair with my old blue fishing jacket, her arms around me, comforting me.

But the sentence that had caused me to start bawling, the sentence that kept echoing painfully through my mind was: *I guess I finally understand the meaning of a broken heart.* I had broken my mother's heart. The heart which had labored so diligently and lovingly to plant in me the good, the godly. The heart that had always been, and always would be, capable of loving me the most, the best.

I buried my face in the pillow and it stayed there until I fell asleep. I woke up and read my dad's letter.

Dear Jacob,

Oh how we feel your pain!! We got the mail yesterday with "the" letter about 1:00 p.m., just as we were heading out the door with Westin and Mandy to go to a concert in Logan. Needless to say it was a very rough, emotional evening for Mom and I. Words can't communicate our deep heartfelt sorrow and grief for you. But our pain isn't what matters here, the sun will shine another day, for us as well as you.

What's really frustrating is the time lapse! Your letter was written on 11/12, and that's been almost a month. Certainly your feelings have changed, one way or another just because of the passage of time. We sure need to get some mode of communication which is faster than the mail, considering the weight of your problem. We did try last night when we returned from Logan to call the mission home. As well as this morning, with no answer.

Jacob, your letter states that you've lost your testimony, and you're clueless as to whether the Church is true or not. Man, how can I as your father respond! I'm sure that being there in Russia, a country which I imagine doesn't have much of the light of Christ, has been pulling you down. The daily grind of missionary work, testifying, proselyting, always being on your best foot in regards to your own testimony, it all takes its toll. Please, don't tempt the Lord or try his patience when your prayers are <u>not</u> answered on <u>your</u> timetable. It might take a week, a month, your whole mission, even your whole life! But you're praying, pleading for a testimony, <u>Or else</u> – I'm going home, calling it quits. You can't do that. The Lord won't honor such a prayer as coming from a sincere heart, and with real intent.

I know you have, or you had, a testimony when you left. You say to spell out all the doubts and concerns, in essence, is unimportant. I really agree with that too, someday when we can really sit and talk we'll have to get into them. Then you say you can't work anything out in your mind, you've pondered and meditated until your head hurts. You'll start to convince yourself, then the other half of your mind will play devil's advocate. Jacob, these kind of statements made me think you're trying too hard with your <u>mind</u> to receive the *answers we all seek in life. You've got what I consider to be one of the "elect" intellects. And as has been prophesied of the very elect being deceived, don't let your deductive, reasoning mind cloud the true warm, emotional, caring heart that you have. The blessing President Hatcher gave you mentions feeling a burning throughout your whole body, especially your heart. Listen with your heart, not your mind. I'm sure you've realized that bit of advice, but, really, it's harder to apply than it might sound. If I think logically of a Christ child conceived by an immortal, born to be a savior of mankind, with wise men seeing a new star, and His life one completely void of sin. Well, it just doesn't fly! As well could be said of the Prophet Joseph Smith's story.*

But, Jacob, please, I __know__ Christ is my savior and the redeemer of mankind because right now my heart is so full, just typing these words, the tears running down my cheeks, and a burning in my heart that tells me it's true. I've struggled personally with the question of feeling the spirit being just my emotions or is it really the spirit. I can't think of it in my mind, only my heart, and my emotions. You know what I mean. Think of the spirit you've felt at home. Only you know what it felt like personally to you. I can try to explain how it is for me, but each one feels it somewhat differently. I can imagine you've had your heart touched in many ways similar to how I have. Of course there's the traditional church meetings, many of which I've been touched by. The eternal truths, taught in such a way as to reach my heart, witnessing to me, truth. I know you haven't seen me stand at the pulpit to bear witness on testimony bearing day very much, if ever. Well if I could only convince you at this crossroads in your life right now, I'd stand every month! I guess I'm bartering with the Lord now, with that remark.

I recognize in my own life many of my early spiritual experiences came as I knelt in prayer in some of my "special" places in the mountains. I've told you before of how many of my days were spent working alone picking rocks and sticks from the land my Dad was breaking out of sage brush up Lundgreen canyon. I've offered many special prayers in the peace and security of those forested mountains which I still so dearly love. I can only hope you've had similar experiences. I remember how much time you spent on the fishing streams. You loved it, and my best guess tells me that it happened to be more than just a passing sport. I believe you recharged your spirit, your batteries, and that you have some of your soul tied to the many hours spent alone with your Maker on the fishing stream.

Jacob, I really feel for you and if I could only make things better you know I would. Your mission is a real growing experience. You might wonder why it's so damn hard! If it was easy, what value would it be of? Those things in life that mean the most are bought and paid for with pain, suffering, tears, doubt, and eventually the rewards do come. Don't be too hard on yourself for feeling that your motives are impure. Man, you accepted a call for two years, have learned a very difficult Russian language, and have spent most of a full year out there. Just hang in there and try your hardest. The Lord is blessing you. Your letters always seem to tell of baptisms pending, it sounds like you're having quite a successful mission. Don't judge your success against your motives. Of course a 100% pure Christlike attitude and testimony would be nice, but you're not perfect, and you never will be in this life. Everyone seems to come home and say at their homecoming of their mission being the best two years of their lives. I said that too, as I'm confident you will – but remember the rest of that little saying – they also were the hardest two years. I can honestly say my two years of my mission have been my hardest times, and I've got quite a few behind me to compare with too. Things will only get better as you grow and mature from serving the Lord. Remember the purpose of this whole gospel plan, why you're teaching people – that man is that he might have joy. Your service and testimony of the truthfulness will bring more joy than all else.

Jacob, with all my heartfelt, sincere prayers I bless you son to have the strength to hang on and be patient in your quest for increased testimony. To be perfectly honest I've felt like your testimony has been stronger than my own. Maybe I was confusing your knowledge with your testimony. I know you have the knowledge of what to do with your life, please, feel the blessings of heaven that I've tried to invoke in your behalf as your father. I love you Jacob and always will. Dad.

Dad's letter, too, was beautiful, and it meant a great deal to me, to have him express himself in so many words, so intimate and unrestrained and full of love. He had never been a man of many words, but he had never been a man who had needed many words to let you know that he loved you unconditionally with the open and deep love of a kind and sensitive father and a very good man. I had always been so proud to be his son, and had looked up to him and respected him enormously. I had also felt a special kinship and bond with him, like we were cut from the same cloth, like he understood at some deep level who I was and what it felt like to be me and to have my personality and to think my thoughts. As I had read his letter, the feeling of being loved and understood by a wiser and better and older version of myself had washed warmly over me. My father had served his mission among the Navajos, and he had never talked about it much, but it now felt as if he understood what I was going through, the toll that serving a mission took. As I read of him alone in the mountains clearing sagebrush up Lundgreen canyon, I

261

felt his experiences as if they were mine, because they had been mine. I *had* felt closest to my Creator on the fishing streams and in the mountains, and a huge part of my soul was and forever would be tied to those places. But as I imagined him sitting in front of the computer in his basement office with the red carpet and the Navajo blanket hanging on the wall with tears running down his cheeks and his heart burning with the knowledge that Christ was his Savior, I felt only an unbearable sadness. I could feel the immense power of this feeling, the strength of his testimony, but it was his and his alone. A few short months ago it would have been mine as well, a wordless and binding level of shared understanding that was a wonderful part of being my father's son. But now it felt like it was no longer me. It was no longer the stuff of a shared and special kinship, it was the stuff of a profound sadness. I worried that things would never now be the same, that *we* would never again be the same. That although my father would love me every bit as much as before, that love would be uncoupled.

I was feeling the wrenching pain of plucking up that which had been planted. I was uprooting myself, tearing myself away from those deep earthy ties that had sustained and nourished me for so long. And for what?

I dried my face on the pillowcase, and rolled over on my back to face Richardson, who was lying in bed with his *Modern Russian Grammar* book. I told him that I still wasn't feeling well and that we wouldn't be working that evening, the first time I had ever pulled the sick card to get out of work.

Dave's letter cheered me up some. He was on his mission back in the Eastern States and I had told him about the problems I was having. He told me to do what I had to do and to take life by the lips and yank. *"'There's a feeling I get, when I look to the west, and my spirit is crying for leaving.' Led Zeppelin."*

The next morning I woke up late. It was my birthday. I'd turned twenty, although I had told no one, not even Richardson. I told him that I was still sick and couldn't work that day. He seemed glad for the extra study time since his Alpha test was coming up in less than a week.

I lay in bed, reading *Les Misérables* and feeling sorry for myself that I had no one to wish me a happy birthday. I then read and reread all the letters.

My parents' letters had helped me to feel that my world would not collapse if I were to come home early for lack of a testimony. That I would still be loved. But they did little to bolster my hope that the search for an answer would be any more fruitful than before.

Nevertheless, I was resolved to keep praying and trying to get an answer, mainly for my parents' sake more than because I thought that it would work. But contrary to what my dad's letter advised, I could not accept the idea that I might have to pray my whole mission, my whole life, to get an answer. In my mind, there had to be some point at which the Lord's failure to answer me meant that either the Lord had answered my prayers by not answering me, or that there was no Lord. I designated that point as January 1st, 2000, the start of a new millennium. If I didn't receive an answer by then, I was going home. Or so I told myself.

A few days later, Richardson and I made phone calls home so that we could set up a time to call for Christmas. This practice was not technically allowed by the rules, but it was not frowned upon too much in the Samara mission. Richardson set up his call for after the New Year since he was convinced that Y2K was going to wreak some kind of apocalyptic havoc, and he wanted to talk to his family to find out what was going on in America. There were all kinds of rumors flying around the mission about how this was really it this time – these were the latter days, the last days, and Christ's Second Coming was nigh. We had been told to stock our shelves with extra food to last for a couple weeks, and we could not leave our apartment from sundown on December 30th to sunrise on January 2nd. I was particularly concerned being in Russia about the nuclear reactors going haywire and melting down, and I wondered if in a couple of weeks this would all be over, the two prophets lying dead in the streets would rise up and start prophesying, and I wouldn't have to worry about a silly little thing like not having a testimony.

My little sister answered the phone, her voice faraway and small. I heard her excitedly announce to my family, "It's Jacob!" and within seconds my mom and dad were on the phone alone with me in their bedroom so that no one could hear.

They asked if I had received their letters and I told them simply that I had. There was silence and I knew they were dying to know what effect the letters had had on me, if they had helped, but I didn't know what I could say that would bring them any comfort.

"How are you feeling about things?" My mom finally asked with concern in her voice.

"Pretty much the same." I wanted to tell them how much I loved them and to thank them for their touching letters and for their love and understanding, but something in me felt that I needed to give them just the cold facts of my situation, the worst case scenario, to test them. "I'm going to give it a couple more weeks, but if I don't get an answer I see no choice but to come home."

"A couple more weeks!" My dad's voice was strained with frustration. It was one of the very few times I had heard him upset. "You went for two years, Jacob. You left knowing that you were serving a mission for two years. You just can't decide to come home because it's getting rough out there."

"It's not about that, Dad. It's not about it getting rough, I can take that. I've taken that for a year." I started to cry hard, and my words began to splatter out wet and desperate. "It's that I don't have a testimony. I'm sick of trying to preach what I don't know. I'm sick of being a hypocrite. I can't go on telling people they need to join this Church unless I have a testimony."

"Well I know you know what you need to do to get one. But you just can't give it two weeks. That's not how the Lord works." He voice was more natural now.

"I'm trying, Dad. I've been trying. I've been trying for the last couple of months. It's not that easy. I wish it was. Believe me, the easiest thing for me to do would be to get my testimony back."

He had needed to let his frustration out, and I could tell he felt badly for reacting the way he did. Before we hung up, he apologized and told me that he knew it must be hard for me, and that I would be loved no matter what I did.

I went to bed and fell asleep, even though it was ten in the morning and Richardson and I were supposed to leave the apartment to start work. I woke up an hour later, put on my gray suit that hadn't been washed or dry-cleaned since I had arrived to Russia, and without saying a word to Richardson I put on my coat, boots, and hat. He got the hint and got dressed as well. We said our going-outside prayer, and went out to street contact at the metro stop. I just stood there. The women in the heavy felt boots at the market called out their greetings, but I ignored them. People walked past and I let them. When I could feel Richardson's eyes upon me, I would approach someone and ask them sadly if I could talk to them about God.

To my surprise, one man actually stopped in response to my halfhearted approach. "Hi. Well, I'm a representative of the Mormon Church and we're out here talking to people about God's plan for us. Do you have about twenty-five minutes so that I can tell you about it?" My voice was flat and monotone, and I avoided eye contact.

"Right now?"

"Yes, you need to hear about this." My voice lacked even a hint of the urgency required to make such a declaration.

"The Mormons, huh? Don't you guys have a bunch of wives?"

Now was the time I'd normally make some joke about how, no, we don't have a bunch of wives, most of us have a hard time keeping one satisfied, etc., but I was too sad to try for humor. "No, the early prophets of the Church had many wives, but we stopped doing that over a hundred years ago."

"Interesting. Why did you stop?"

I just wanted the guy to go away to leave me alone with my depressing thoughts, but my depression-induced candor was having the opposite effect. My heart was not in it. I couldn't do it anymore. So I snuffed out the little bit of normal-human-interactional-and-communicative-spark I had left and spit out, robot-like.

"Most people believe in a Supreme Being, even though they may call him by different names. We know that God lives. We want to share with you our feelings about Him. God is perfect, omniscient, and omnipotent. He is also merciful, kind, and just. We know that we can have faith in Him. We can love Him with all our hearts. . . ."

"Actually, I'm running late. I better get going."

"Okay. Bye."

Two hours went by as we stood in the cold. I gave a dozen or so listless approaches, but for the most part I stood alone with my obsessive thoughts of the hopelessness of my situation. I told Richardson I was feeling faint, and we went home again, where I took another nap.

HARVEST

I woke up hours later, told Richardson that I thought I had the flu or something, and lay in bed listening to classical music and thinking about what life would be like if I came home, if I could live with an uncoupled love.

As the sun went down and the apartment got dark, I flipped on my lamp and pulled out *Les Misérables* again.

I had the Signet Classic paperback edition, 1,463 pages thick. I'm not sure why I had asked that my mom send *Les Misérables* and *War and Peace*. Probably because I didn't dare ask for more than two books and these were the thickest I could think of.

The book was remarkable in its power over me: it plunged through my solipsism until it had grabbed hold of my soul and could do with it what it pleased – lift it gently until it was floating with joy, squeeze it tightly until it released its tears and poison.

Its themes were abstractly universal but emotionally relevant to me at the time. The internal struggle between good and evil, between the demands of justice and the demands of mercy. The story of redemption and how hard it is to forgive oneself. The many stories of love and the poetry of love:

> "Whoever we may be, we all have our living, breathing beings. If they fail us, the air fails us, we stifle, then we die. To die for lack of love is horrible. The asphyxia of the soul." St-Denis, Book 5 Chapter 5, (p. 933).

The asphyxia of the soul. How I longed for love, for my living, breathing beings. And not just the love bestowed from afar on a prodigal son, as great and deep and unconditional and selfless as that love might be, but the love deserved by the good son returning home with honor.

The next morning, Christmas Eve, I told Richardson that we should go do our service for the month. We didn't teach English lessons in that district, and we had no contacts with the schools, hospitals, or orphanages so that we could go chip ice off their sidewalks, so we had to brainstorm up an idea. I can't remember who came up with the idea, and whether it was in jest or seriousness at first, but it was suggested that we play Santa Claus by buying a bunch of metro tokens and standing out in front of the toll gates and handing them out to the metro riders, wishing them a Merry Christmas.

So we bought two hundred tokens for six hundred rubles, or about twenty-five dollars. They were black plastic things the size of a nickel, and we each stuffed a hundred into our pockets and started to hand them out.

"Excuse me babushka, can I talk to you about God, I mean, can I give you a free metro token?"

"What do you mean, *free*?"

"As in I give it to you and you give me nothing. Please, take it." I lifted the token to her eyes for her inspection.

"Well I never… who are you boys? What are you doing?"

"We came all the way from America to Russia to hand out free metro tokens, babushka. Please take it."

"Free, huh?"

"Yeah, absolutely free. Here you go. Merry Christmas!"

"Merry Christmas?"

Russian Orthodox Christmas was not until January 7th.

"Yeah, and a Happy New Year!"

"Yes, yes, Happy New Year to you as well!"

We were having a hard time getting rid of our tokens. People seemed to distrust and avoid us, and they would turn down the offer and go stand in line to buy their own token. It was like giving away free Books of Mormon. People seemed to have the mentality that if it was free it was either worthless or suspicious. I always thought that we would have distributed more books if we'd charged some token amount. But we had two hundred tokens to get rid of. So we began to step up our marketing efforts.

"Free metro tokens! Get your free token here! Why stand in line and pay your hard-earned money when you can get your free token here? Guaranteed quality or your money back! Oh, wait, there's no money to be gotten back – they're free!"

We were having a grand time. We were getting a bit silly, but some people loved our antics, and we even got a bit of applause as we theatrically presented a free token to someone who had taken us up on our offer.

Once we had got the business up off the ground, other people followed suit and we had a steady stream of customers, each of whom we'd wish a Merry Christmas as we handed over the token to their bewilderment and amusement.

We kept at it for an hour until we'd handed out all but about thirty tokens. Then the police showed up and killed the party.

"What are you young people doing?"

"Just giving out free tokens. It's Christmas tomorrow. Would you like a free token?"

"No, we don't want a free token. What Christmas tomorrow? Are you crazy? Where did you get the tokens?"

"We bought them an hour ago. You can ask the lady in the booth."

"Let me see them." I pulled out a handful of tokens and handed them over for their inspection.

"Mmm-hmm. You can't do that here."

"Why?"

"Because people must buy their tokens, and no one will buy them if you give it to them."

"But we already bought them. What's the difference?"

"You can't do that here, we said."

"What is the problem?"

"The problem is that we told you in plain Russian that you can't do that here and you apparently don't understand Russian."

"Whatever. Give me my tokens back and we'll go."

"We better not hear about this happening again."

So we left and went to find white elephant gifts for the Christmas party that we were having with the Samara half of the mission the next day. I bought a cool looking dagger and hoped that my gift wouldn't go to a Sister, for whom it would be even more inappropriate than it already clearly was.

Back at the apartment we warmed up the big pot of borscht I had made earlier in the week, loaded it with sour cream, and took a long lunch/dinner before making the forty-five minute trip out to Ramiz's house. We talked for an hour, came back, and that was our evening.

When we got back, I poured a glass of cherry juice and went to my desk to read *Les Misérables*. By about one in the morning I had finished the book, sobbing quietly. The book had left me emotionally overwhelmed, emotionally fragile. I continued to sit there, just thinking and listening to music.

I thought of the plan of salvation. I thought of the billions of people who would not be able to enter the Celestial Kingdom unless they changed their beliefs and accepted baptism in the LDS Church. I thought of some of the people whose beliefs I had tried unsuccessfully to change. The whole thing did not feel right, and I could not *make* it feel right.

So I stopped thinking about the plan and let myself think of other things. It was early Christmas Day. I was hours away from my phone call with family.

I thought of my parents. My mom sitting in the rocking chair by the fire in my old fishing jacket. Nestling up to her as her warm voice read me stories as a child. The smell of her homemade bread. A certain striped shirt she'd sewn for me. The comforting sound of her piano drifting through the home. Catching stone flies with her in Pebble Creek for my 4-H project. My dad sitting with tears in his eyes in front of the computer monitor. Hiking with him, just me and him, in the hills above his childhood home in the soft pink predawn, looking for deer, learning about Tent Knoll and ponderosa pines. The smell of axle grease, diesel and dirt as we serviced pivots, handing him the quarter inch socket wrench from the toolbox. Conversation in the truck on the way to Pocatello to pick up parts, stopping at Shakey's for pizza and root beer on the way home.

I was close to tears, filled with love and gratitude for the goodness of my parents, for their love.

I then thought of the future, a ribbon of highway fading into the desert horizon, a red gush of thrill, a coyote loneliness, a snarl of black and red figures, a blackness, a blankness, a coldness.

I felt the urge to pray. I shut off my music and got down on my knees, leaned my arms on the chair, buried my head in my arms, and began.

It felt right. I felt comfort, reassurance, familiarity.

I then started to question whether this good feeling was the Spirit telling me I was doing the right thing, or whether it was my own emotions, my own desires to feel something.

But I pushed these thoughts aside and continued to pray, pleading with God to tell me what to do, to tell me what was true, to help me to make sense of it all. But my pleas soon became requests and my requests soon became litanies. My mind drifted back to thinking about the plan of salvation and my parents and the future.

Then I felt some new resolve arise within me and gather strength and momentum until it had filled me with a confidence that wanted to come out. I began again without doubt or skepticism: "My dear Heavenly Father, I admit that I don't understand everything, but I'm willing to accept it all in faith if you'll just give me the assurance that it is right."

As soon as I admitted that I didn't understand everything, and that I didn't *need* to understand everything, and that I was willing to accept it all in faith, something, everything, broke inside me, barriers, dams, resistance, restraints, pride, principles, and in flooded hot joy. I was in ecstasy. Nothing existed but peace and love and happiness, pure and infinite happiness. I had never before experienced anything so powerful.

After some time had passed, a couple of minutes perhaps, the ecstasy dissipated and I returned to consciousness. I became aware that something tremendous had just happened, was still happening. This had to be my answer. The Church must be true! It all must be true!

This realization was quickly followed by fear. I was invaded by an evil horror, a cold dread. I was so unclean, such a revolting junkie of filth, so polluted and wicked.

The evil feeling didn't last long. I simply told myself that I did not want to feel that way anymore and the horror vanished. A great and gentle peace filled my mind, and I felt like my sins had been forgiven, that I was clean.

I became filled with an immense gratitude. Gratitude for the gift of life, gratitude for my family, gratitude for President Hatcher, gratitude for all the chances God had given me, for all the times He'd saved me from serious error.

As I poured out my gratitude to my Heavenly Father, I was engulfed by love, an unconditional, kind, and tender love. A love that made me feel like I was being cradled in the hands of God.

33

Epilogue of Sorts

"[P]rinciples are the only thing that adolescents, unlike adults, really own."
Zadie Smith

I had received my answer from God, my telegram, and I was staying.

The relief of my parents was palpably sweet when I presented them with the news on Christmas Day. I was happy.

The next zone conference I stood and bore my testimony about how the Lord answers prayers. I saw the pride in President Hatcher's face, and I cried. The next transfer I was made zone leader of the Togliatti zone. Two months later I was made branch president back in Novokuibyshevsk, where I stayed for nine months, until I was made AP for the final month of my mission. I baptized dozens more people.

But the doubts and questions never really went away. I stood in front of stalls of cabbage and dried fish for hundreds and hundreds more hours and talked philosophy and religion with hard-line atheists, nostalgic Stalinists, and old-school communists. With thoughtful humanists, could-care-less-about-religion secularists, America-loving consumerists, and pleasure-seeking hedonists. With Russian Orthodox, Muslims, Jehovah's Witnesses, Seventh Day Adventists, Jews, Catholics, Armenian Gregorians, Pentecostals, Baptists, and Old Believers. With freethinking skeptics who had Internet access, good English skills, and curiosity about Mormonism and its history.

HARVEST

Taking a clue from Enders and learning to creatively count the Ds for statistical purposes, I stopped pushing so hard to get in the rote recitation, and I just talked to these people, actually engaged in mutual communication, gave and took, listened and pondered. I tried to keep an open mind and thoughtfully consider the things people had to say instead of just trying to convince them of my putative beliefs. And I learned things, not just about other systems of belief, but about my own. Like the time one of those freethinking skeptics asked me for my response to the fact that Joseph Smith had secretly wed and bedded numerous teenage wives behind his wife's back and that he had given wildly diverging accounts of the First Vision at different points in his life. Instead of reflexively denying this or shying away from such a topic like we had been taught to do, I listened to him, asked him questions, tried to check his sources as best I could with my limited resources. I was embarrassed that this investigator, thanks to a couple of hours on the Internet, knew more about Joseph Smith and his First Vision than I, who was supposed to be teaching *him*, did after years and years of lessons in Church, Seminary, and Family Home Evenings. I resolved that I would better study the Church and its history when I got back home and could freely research the topic.

But home was a long ways away, and so, in the meantime, I tried hard to shelve the doubts, shelve the hard questions, and shelve the discomfort that inevitably came from trying to push my beliefs on others whose beliefs I was trying to understand and respect.

President Hatcher, in my mind, deserves credit for recognizing that I struggled with this discomfort and putting me in positions which minimized it. As zone leader I had lots of administrative and leadership responsibilities that cut into my proselytizing time. And as AP I barely had any time for proselytizing: I accompanied Hatcher as a translator to a church discipline court, zone conferences, and other events; I planned out transfers, bought all the train tickets, and coordinated with the zone leaders to make sure that they went smoothly; I spent ten days touring the mission with my fellow AP to train other missionaries. And the nine months I spent as branch president were the best of my mission, without a doubt. I worked closely with the members and developed enduring friendships. I arranged the purchase of a branch dacha, and labored there once a week planting potatoes and picking cherries with the members. I was busy with some kind of branch business or activity nearly every day: Seminary and Institute classes, picnics, English lessons, conferences in Samara, baptisms, bowling, Mutual, ping pong, home teaching, visits to members, church welfare disbursements, trainings, Relief Society events, Sunday meetings.

For better or worse, whatever it was inside of me that had always made me be so focused on my *self*, so painfully aware of my self, so prone to constantly evaluate my self against my internal standards, that thing had given up, exhausted, broken. As a result, I spent less time worrying about myself.

I wrote sloppy letters home, emotionally detached.

I made superficial entries in my journal.

I read lots of books, both in Russian and in English, in order to occupy my mind.

And there were other diversions. A companion who spied on me through the small high window of our bathroom with the use of a handheld mirror to ensure that I was not masturbating, the theft of my camera and passport, excommunications, a companion who only wanted to eat raw eggs and nuts and was obsessed with bodybuilding, trips to Moscow and Finland, frequent visits to the banya, cultural nights, a companion who was a great chess player and cook, a newspaper article by a reporter who attended a Sunday meeting of the Novokuibyshevsk branch and ridiculed my performance in his article ("He was trying to appear serious, and with a wise look he addressed the congregation as 'Brothers and Sisters,' most of whom could have been his parents or grandparents. All of this was close to a farce. I could barely sit to the end. . . ."), an accordion I bought on the street and tried to learn how to play in the mornings, Slava, a sixteen-year old member of the Novokuibyshevsk branch and my best friend in Russia, who would "run into" me while I was street contacting and play little word games we invented for hours, a break-in of our apartment by axe to wooden door, an assignment by President Hatcher to use the power of the priesthood to cast the demons out of the apartment of one Elder Jones who claimed that the demons would levitate his body during the night, but who, in hindsight, was probably just looking for a way home.

HARVEST

All the diversions and leadership responsibilities helped to minimize the incidence of the discomfort but they could not eliminate it. There was always proselytizing to be done, and I was never able to overcome my distaste for our proselytizing tactics.

My distaste for how our relentless pressure forced polite people to be impolite. To someone conditioned to the slammed door response, a woman's polite "Sorry, I'm kinda busy right now," meant Eureka!, a foot in the door, a wedge to use to pry into her future time, to leverage our position – just talk to us now for fifteen minutes or we'll keep coming back. Some companions even tried to keep a Book-of-Mormon-wielding hand in between the door jamb and the open door so that it couldn't be closed. It was all a part of being bold, of being confident, of contacting with the faith that you had the most important message in the world to share. About a month into it with Goddard I had abandoned the high pressure approaches for the most part, and unless I was feeling the pressure myself from a highly-strung companion or from a recent zone conference that had emphasized boldness I tried to respect boundaries. But I had to stand by uncomfortably through countless such approaches from zealous companions who thought that being a bold missionary meant never taking no for an answer.

My distaste for pressuring people so hard into getting baptized. We pestered our wishy-washy indecisive investigators incessantly about baptism, emphasizing the need for it over and over and over until they either relented or quit meeting with us. We baptized lonely or emotionally fragile people when they were most vulnerable. And despite the Church's emphasis on families, we very rarely baptized complete families, sowing dissent in families by baptizing young people without their parents' permission or knowledge and by baptizing women despite their husbands' opposition. We baptized quickly, often within a week after first introducing people to the Church. In fact, halfway through my mission President Hatcher came out with a policy that required us to ask for a commitment to baptism within the first fifteen minutes of meeting an investigator. I found it so absurd, so farcical, to be asking about baptism so early on, that, on days when I was feeling particularly subversive, I would lead with this question in my street contacting approach, but only with girls around our age. "Excuse me there girl. My name is Elder Young. I am from America.

How would you like to get baptized by an American in the Mormon Church?" If they said no I would follow up with, "Ok. Well, would you like to marry me then?"

My distaste for the equation that getting people to feel the Spirit = baptism, and that our job was thus to manufacture the Spirit, Bonneville Communications Heartsell® style, to be an actor, an infomercial pitchman, a testimonial giver, an unpaid performer in "strategic emotional advertising that stimulates a response."

There were other things besides my distaste for the soul-sucking day-to-day core of proselytizing that I never really could get over, like the feeling of guilt that came from living so relatively affluently in the midst of such extreme poverty. We ate at McDonalds, bought our Cokes and Snickers bars, mailed home CDs, and rented private rooms at the banya while a homeless man froze to death during the night right outside our apartment building, while Sergei sold his blood for vodka, while old babushkas lived on fifteen dollars a month, while members walked miles to Sacrament meeting in the cold winter because they couldn't afford the ten cent bus fare, while little children with big eyes knocked on our apartment door to beg for food. I never stopped resenting the fact that we were limited to four hours of service a week and barred from doing service in the evenings, on weekends, and during holidays. I never lost that feeling I had first experienced with Natasha and the steel door where I wished that I was doing something more helpful to serve people than simply trying to convert them. I couldn't help but think about the good that a church-like organization that's spending untold billions on a luxury shopping mall and condominium complex in downtown Salt Lake City and deploying a 50,000 plus strong force of energetic young volunteers could do if we weren't so exclusively focused on bringing in new converts.

I lost most of my idealism and never got it back.

I never got to feel the inspired feeling of having the Lord speak to me like I had been so eagerly anticipating when I gave my first priesthood blessing to the polysyllabic Yekaterina Vyacheslavovicha Preobrazhensky. As branch president, I knew I was supposed to receive inspiration regarding the callings which I gave to members, but I could not say that I felt any kind of heavenly communication prompting me to call Sister Ivanova as Second Counselor in the Relief Society.

I never got comfortable asking teenage girls about their compliance with the law of chastity in the priesthood interviews I conducted with them. I never got comfortable interviewing women for baptism, asking them the abortion question, and then telling them that they had to speak with President Hatcher for approval to get baptized if they had committed one.

And despite living in Russia for two years, I never got over the feeling of being an unwanted outsider – a pest – an oddity – a curio. People accused us all the time of being agents of the CIA; there were several local newspaper articles to that effect. I often felt like one. Like I was there to subvert Russian culture and traditions, to undermine Russian institutions, to carry off Russian women to a Utah Zion, to Westernize, to Mormonize, to sanitize. I wanted to really experience their culture, on their terms, but that was impossible to do as a missionary.

I never bought a briefcase, but I did find myself, as AP on my second-to-last day in Russia, whizzing through Samara in a taxi in hot pursuit of a Russian kid from Samara who had just been officially "set apart" as a missionary. His flight to the MTC in Provo had been delayed for two days and he was trying to visit his girlfriend one final time before he left for two years. Since he had already been set apart this was, of course, strictly, scandalously, against the rules, but President Hatcher and the missionaries at the office had failed to stop him from leaving the office. They had succeeded, however, in sending one of the office missionaries to tail him. My companion and I had been urgently dispatched to meet up with these two and try to avert the disaster. We were waiting for him when he got out of the taxi in front of the apartment building where his girlfriend lived. So it went that I found myself looking into the eyes of this nineteen year old kid who was excited to serve the Lord but a little daunted by the thought of not seeing his girlfriend for two long years. His eyes were brimmed with stubborn determination about to come out in tears, and I pitied him. I knew what lay in store for him – the drudgery, the loneliness, the homesickness, the guilt, the blame, the rejection, the boredom of street contacting, the monotony of knocking, the struggle to lock your heart and to shut down your little factory. If anyone had ever deserved to spend a few hours with his girlfriend, it was this kid. And if there was anyone who knew this, it was me. But so it went that I found myself drawing myself up to my full AP stature and persuading this kid that God would be disappointed in him and that the Church would cancel his plane ticket to America if he chose to visit his girlfriend. I hated myself. Hated myself but did it anyway. My only consolation was that the next day I would be done forever with that sort of thing.

Men are that they might have joy. At times, despite the doubts and discomfort, I thought that I might be productively engaged in a good work that brought joy to people.

I felt that way every time I saw Ramiz. He quit smoking, got married, and got baptized. Every Sunday he was the first one at Sacrament meeting, his face lit up with the biggest smile I've ever seen. He was so grateful to us for bringing him to baptism, and he told me every time I saw him what his smile made clear without the words: "The Gospel has changed my life, and I have never been happier."

I felt that way every time I met Nina, the first babushka whom Quamme and I had baptized, out at the branch dacha, where she would feed us with the soup, dumplings, chicken, fresh vegetables, and compote that she had lovingly made the night before and then lugged the two miles out to the dacha on her little dolly. She was so happy to have little grandsons to feed before she died.

I felt that way every time I witnessed the transformation in someone, like that of Lilya and Rita, the mother and daughter whom I baptized as branch president. They found in the Gospel precious eternal truths, a purpose in life, friends, comfort, and joy, and their lives would never be the same. Case in point: Rita just finished serving a mission in Salt Lake City.

I felt that way the time when I went back to Togliatti at the end of my mission as AP to translate for President Hatcher, and two of the babushkas I had baptized there during the height of my doubt and depression were still active and proudly stood up to bear their tearful testimonies about how grateful they were for the knock of Elder Young and the joy that the Gospel had brought into their lives.

And as for me and my joy?

All these kinds of experiences certainly made me feel good for a while, and those few minutes of ecstatic religious joy remain something very special.

And learning a new language and living in a different culture was an incredible experience, one which I thoroughly enjoyed, despite the occasional difficulties.

And it was no small thing to be able to cast off the materialism, selfishness, and egoism of the world to serve a cause greater than oneself for two years. In fact, there are times that I miss that. A lot.

And I learned about myself and life. I matured emotionally and was weathered spiritually.

But, upon returning home, when confronted with that implicit question in the eyes of my family at the airport, "Was it the best two years of your life?" the best that I could answer them was: "*Wouldn't it be pretty to think so.*"

Made in the USA
San Bernardino, CA
16 February 2013